Continuities in Highland Maya Social Organization

Continuities in Highland Maya Social

Organization:

Ethnohistory in Sacapulas, Guatemala

Robert M. Hill II and John Monaghan

With a Foreword by Victoria R. Bricker

uµµ University of Pennsylvania Press   Philadelphia   1987

The University of Pennsylvania Press

ETHNOHISTORY   SERIES

Edited by Anthony F. C. Wallace and Lee V. Cassanelli

A complete listing of the books in this series appears
at the back of this volume

Library of Congress Cataloging-in-Publication Data

Hill, Robert M., 1952–
   Continuities in highland Maya social organization.

   (Ethnohistory series)
   Bibliography: p.
   Includes index.
   1. Quichés—Social life and customs.   2. Sacapulas
(Guatemala)—History.   3. Quichés—History.   4. Indians
of Central America—Guatemala—Sacapulas—Social life
and customs.   5. Indians of Central America—Guatemala—
Sacapulas—History.   I. Monaghan, John.   II. Title.
III. Series: Ethnohistory series (Philadelphia, Pa.)
F1465.2.Q5H55   1987   972.81'72   87-15856
ISBN 0-8122-8070-9

To Ruben E. Reina
Scholar,
Teacher,
and Friend

Contents

Illustrations   ix

Tables   xi

Foreword by Victoria R. Bricker   xiii

Preface and Acknowledgments   xv

1   Sacapulas Today: An Ethnographic Summary of Its *Cantón* Organization   1

2   *Chinamit* and *Molab:* Precursors of the *Cantón*   24

3   *Parcialidades,* Population, and Processes in Sacapulas: A Historical Overview   43

4   Preconquest Political Geography   63

5   Initial Contacts and Formation of the *Pueblo: Congregación* in Sacapulas   76

6   Boundary Disputes: "Range Wars"   90

7   *Ejido* and *Pueblo* versus *Parcialidad:* An Attempt at Directed Change   102

8   An *Amaq'* Breaks Down   115

9   Continuity in Change   133

10   Conclusions and Implications   147

Notes   157

Glossary   161

Bibliography   165

Index   173

Illustrations

Frontispiece: *Cofradía* members of San Francisco in procession.

FIGURES

1-1. Panoramic view of Sacapulas from the road to Cunén. 3
1-2a. Sacapulas *salinas*. 6
1-2b. *Salinas,* viewed from Chutinamit. 7
1-3. Sacapultecos, Chiquimulas, and *ladinos* in the plaza on market day. 8
1-4. *Aldea* of Tzununul, viewed from the north. 10
1-5. *Cofradía* procession returning to church. 17

4-1. Reconstruction drawing of Xolchun, Department of El Quiché. 66
4-2. Xoltinamit, viewed from the south. 67
4-3. Reconstruction drawing of Chutixtiox. 69
4-4. Patzagel, viewed from Chutixtiox. 70
4-5. Xetzagel, viewed from Chutixtiox. 71
4-6. Ixpapal, viewed from Chutixtiox. 72

6-1. Plain of Mixcolajá. 91
6-2. Valley of Pichiquil, viewed from the north. 93

9-1. *Aldea* of Parraxtut, viewed from the south. 93

MAPS

1-1. Guatemala, showing Sacapulas and other important towns. 2
1-2. Sacapulas area, showing local places, archaeological sites, and *parcialidad* boundaries. 4

7-1. Facsimile of Barroeta survey map. 105

8-1. Facsimile of Hidalgo 1794 survey map. 121
8-2. Facsimile of Hidalgo 1798 survey map. 124

Tables

3-1. *Caciques* of Sacapulas area *parcialidades*, c. 1573   48
3-2. *Parcialidad* populations   53
3-3. Sacapulas population   54

Foreword

There has been a major change in the thrust of ethnohistorical research in Mesoamerica during the past twenty years. Beginning with Charles Gibson's monumental works on the Valley of Mexico and Tlaxcala, the emphasis has shifted in two directions: among anthropologists, from the Late Postclassic to the Colonial period, and, among historians, from the Spanish overlords to their Indian subjects. The result is a better understanding of the impact of Spanish colonial policies on the Indian community, including, but not limited to, an appreciation of the diversity of responses to Spanish rule in different parts of the area.

A quiet and almost unnoticed development during this period has been the growing interest in the application of ethnographic analytical techniques to historical data. The questions asked are different from those posed by traditional ethnohistorians, and so are the answers obtained. Scholars with this bent look for information concerning the social organization of individual Indian communities, rather than linguistically defined ethnic groups or whole regions. They are part of a revolution similar to that introduced by Robert Redfield in ethnographic research half a century ago.

Ethnohistorians work under certain constraints not usually encountered by ethnographers. Their "informants" are long dead and cannot be interviewed to clarify obscure points in the historical record. Ethnohistorians are also limited to the kinds of documents that happen to have survived in town, regional, or national archives. If those documents are primarily concerned with disputes over land, then they will provide excellent information on principles of land tenure, inheritance, and territorial organization, but not, perhaps, on political succession, social stratification, or religion. If, on the other hand, only the records of municipal organization survive, then it may be possible to reconstruct the principles of political succession, town finance, and social stratification, but not of land tenure, inheritance, or religion. Only rarely are the records of a community complete enough to provide comparable information in all areas of social life.

It is in this context that the present work can best be understood. It is not an ethnohistory of a "tribe" or a region, but a "documentary ethnography" of a single Quichean community in highland Guatemala. The authors, Robert Hill and John Monaghan, mine a series of documents from Sacapulas concerned with disputes over land, extracting from them the data necessary to reconstruct the town's principles of territorial organization during the colonial period. From this they infer that the traditional basis of land tenure in Sacapulas was not, as commonly believed, the patrilineal kin group, but a territorial unit similar to the Aztec *calpulli*, known as the *chinamit* or *molab*. Furthermore, they show through ethnographic research that this system of territorial organization survived the vicissitudes of the Spanish Conquest and the colonial period into modern times. The patterns are subtle and have been partially disguised by Spanish terminology. Their microscopic examination of the documents permits them to peel away the colonial accretions to reveal structures of pre-Columbian origin.

The methodology employed in this work is of special interest for the ethnohistory of highland Guatemala. The documents in question have as a common theme jurisdictional disputes over land that took place at irregular intervals over a period of four centuries. The continuing concern over how the lands of one community should be apportioned among several competing *parcialidades* provides a uniform context for identifying and comparing Indian and Spanish views of territorial organization and land ownership over a broad sweep of time. The authors skillfully comb the documents for clues to the underlying cultural principles and world view at each point in time, in the process demonstrating that the deep structure persisted even when the surface structure seemed to have changed. Their sensitive, fine-grained analysis of the historical record, combined with focused, ethnographic investigations in Sacapulas, will serve as a model for extending such research to other communities in highland Guatemala.

In the 1930s, Redfield believed that it was premature to expend effort in defining an entity called "Quiché culture" before baseline studies of Quichean communities had been carried out. Thanks to his influence, we now have a wealth of social and cultural data from a number of modern communities in the Quiché region, and it is now possible to assess their differences as well as their similarities in a systematic way. This volume represents such an in-depth community study for an earlier period. We need comparable "documentary ethnographies" for other towns in the Quiché region in order to understand how their societies and cultures functioned during the period of Spanish rule.

Victoria R. Bricker

Preface and Acknowledgments

The authors' interest in Sacapulas began when one of us (Hill) and Ruben E. Reina visited there briefly in the summer of 1974 while studying traditional pottery making (Reina and Hill 1978). We returned again in 1976 and spent several days inspecting the numerous archaeological sites in the *municipio*. The size and density of sites, particularly from the immediate preconquest period, struck us as unusual and worthy of further investigation. At the same time, we were aware of some documents pertaining to Sacapulas in the Archivo General de Centro America (AGCA) in Guatemala that had been cited in R. M. Carmack's survey (1973) of ethnohistorical sources for the Quiché Maya. A brief search of the archive's files in 1976 turned up many more documents. Accordingly, we arranged for typed transcripts of all the Sacapulas documents with Horacio Cabezas. Over the next several years ethnohistorical work on Sacapulas stopped while Hill was engaged in archaeological investigations with the Misión Científica Franco-Guatemalteca, downstream from Sacapulas on the Río Negro, which contributed to his doctoral dissertation. However, ethnohistorical research connected with the thesis did produce the model of the *chinamit* that is one of the keys to understanding Sacapulas' organization.

In 1979 Reina introduced Monaghan to Sacapulas. He and Reina spent three weeks there making general ethnographic observations and documenting the ancient salt-making process (Reina and Monaghan 1981). Monaghan returned in the summer of 1980 for three months of intensive ethnographic fieldwork focusing on *cantón* and *municipio* organization. The results of that work appear in this volume in Chapters 1 and 9. Meanwhile, from 1979 through 1983, Hill worked with the transcripts of the documents from the AGCA. In the summer of 1983 Hill spent a month in Sacapulas checking, on the ground, information about boundaries and archaeological sites contained in the documents, as well as examining the parochial archive. During this visit he learned that the municipal archives had been burned by terrorists during the unsettled months of 1981–82. Thus, our plans to supplement the study with information from this local source were laid to rest, and an unknown amount of Sacapulas' past was lost.

While our initial interest with Sacapulas was basically archaeological, we soon became intrigued with theoretical and methodological concerns.

Hill's experience in researching traditional highland pottery making impressed on him the extent of continuity in this aspect of Maya culture. Apparently crucial to the survival of the craft is the community culture, or *costumbre,* of the closed corporate community in which it was embedded. Following *costumbre,* being a potter and using techniques and clays passed down from the ancestors to produce vessels whose forms are also inherited are moral obligations. Other characteristics of the closed corporate community are related to its very closedness and corporateness. The community is closed in a social sense: It is largely endogamous and outsiders find full acceptance into the community practically impossible. The community is corporate in that key natural resources and technologies belong (or at least are believed to belong) to the group rather than to individuals. Supporting and maintaining the community and its culture is a combined civil and religious organization composed of a hierarchy of offices through which, ideally, an individual passes in his career of service to the community (Wolf 1955). What were the origins of this type of community?

Eric Wolf, who developed the concept of the closed corporate community, seems to have had ambivalent feelings on the topic of its origins. In his original formulation he suggested that the closed corporate community in Mesoamerica was a survival from pre-Columbian times, yet he chose to focus on the structural features of such communities for comparative purposes rather than on their origins and possible continuity (Wolf 1955, 456). In a second article Wolf, regarding origins, concluded that,

> historically, the closed corporate peasant configuration in Mesoamerica is a creature of the Spanish Conquest. Authorities differ as to the characteristics of the pre-Hispanic community in the area, but there is general recognition that thoroughgoing changes divide the post-Hispanic community from its preconquest predecessor. (Wolf 1957, 7)

Ultimately, for Wolf, the origins of the closed corporate community were economic, resulting from a "dualization of society into a dominant entrepreneurial sector and a dominated sector of native peasants" (ibid., 8).

The lack of evidence to support Wolf's assertions suggests that the economic theory of the origins of closed corporate communities in Mesoamerica, and by extension elsewhere, was more a matter of faith than of proven facts. Indeed, given the state of our knowledge at that time concerning Mesoamerican ethnohistory, and preconquest social organization in particular, one cannot blame Wolf too much for arriving at the conclusions he did. Wolf wrote during a period when the idea that preconquest Mesoamerican societies (especially Aztec) were kin- or descent-based still dominated ethnohistorical interpretation. In particular, it was widely felt that the fundamental unit of society, the Aztec *calpulli,* was some sort of clan or at least the remnant of a clan. Replacement of social units based on descent by others based only on territoriality could indeed be considered a thoroughgoing change. If true for the Aztecs, could the preconquest Maya have been different? In Chapter 2, the current thinking on the nature of the preconquest *calpulli* will be briefly reviewed. Suffice it to say here that, while *calpulli* may have been several different things, it was not a clan. (See Offner 1983 for an extended discussion of the history of anthropological interpretation of the *calpulli.*)

Thus, Wolf's thesis concerning the origins of the closed corporate community appeared to fit the facts as they were then known, but he undertook no investigations to demonstrate his theory's validity, or to determine if the same economic conditions occurred throughout the region, or just how, in specific instances, the transformation he proposed occurred. Yet despite the lack of a demonstration, Wolf's formulation has become axiomatic in Mesoamerican studies for both anthropologists and historians, the major debate centering on the timing of the transformation in different subareas (most recently see Farriss 1984, 382; Chance and Taylor 1985).

Wolf himself recently reevaluated his original formulation, after twenty-five years of additional research by other scholars, and noted some of the limitations of his earlier papers (Wolf 1986). Specifically:

> The history of the 1950's was still largely centered on the Aztecs and Incas, and too little concerned with the other ethnikons of the Andes and Mesoamerica. It was still a history that relied primarily on Spanish sources—written from the top down, as it were—and not enough on accounts representing the point of view of the conquered or written in the native languages. This led to a disregard of territorial entities and kinship structures intermediate between household and community. . . . (ibid., 326–27)

We hope that the present study contributes to the growing literature that attempts to advance our knowledge by focusing precisely on the limitations noted above by Wolf in one community.

In spite of subsequent elaboration, two nagging questions remained with regard to the origins of the closed corporate community in Mesoamerica. First, were there in fact preconquest social units similar to closed corporate communities and if so how similar were they? Second, on the assumption that such preconquest units existed, how were they transformed? With these questions in mind Hill began to examine the major Spanish-Maya dictionaries of the colonial period in search of information on native social units. The results appear in Chapter 2, where it is argued that the Quiché-Cakchiquel *chinamit* and the Pokomám-Pokomchí-Kekchí *molab* were closed corporate social units embodying the basic principles of preconquest highland Maya social organization.

The concept of cultural principles is taken from a concept of culture developed by Ruben E. Reina. For him, as for us, a culture may be usefully conceived of as

> the accumulation of human events through *time,* directly *experienced* by members of a specific social group, from which the living members derive *assumptions* and create *principles* to guide their thinking and behavior. (Reina 1973, xviii)

Principles may be thought of as ways of organizing other shared elements of behavior. Accordingly, individual elements may be substituted for, or new elements introduced, without necessarily affecting the underlying principles. When individual elements are substituted for others, but incorporated into the culture according to its principles, a change may have occurred. This is not cultural change, however, since the principles remain unchanged (see also Wallace's [1970] concept of moving equilibrium process). The same may be said for new, introduced elements. These may be directly incorporated according to the particular cultural principles. In some cases the new elements are altered so as to comply with the principles and then incorporated, but, again, cultural changes cannot be said to have occurred. Using the concept of culture presented here, cultural change occurs only when the underlying principles change (see also Wallace's [1972] concept of paradigmatic processes of culture change). Thus, an individual culture can be resilient and flexible when confronted with both everyday stresses and unexpected crises. Adopting this view, some degree of cultural continuity is inevitable. Indeed, how can it be otherwise? How else can people confront and interpret new situations except in terms of the range of alternatives provided by their culture? As long as cultural principles work, as long as they successfully explain experience and organize behavior, they will continue to have value for the people who hold them and they will thus endure.

As stated above, however, we wished to do more than simply reconstruct an aspect of preconquest organization. We also wanted to understand how the *chinamitales* were transformed into closed corporate communities. Sacapulas immediately suggested itself as an example, since we already knew, from published sources, of the existence there of *parcialidades*.

As we began the ethnographic and ethnohistorical study of Sacapulas, however, our investigations became a kind of classic misadventure and our objectives changed considerably. From the documents, Hill discovered that the *chinamitales-parcialidades* retained most of their characteristic functions down through the late nineteenth century, while Monaghan learned that the same units have continued to function in an only slightly attenuated form until very recently. We were no longer dealing with a prototypic closed corporate community but with a number of already closed corporate social groups accidently brought together by the Spaniards in the sixteenth century. Our objective then became understanding what happened to these groups over time and why they did *not* become merged in a single, homogeneous community.

Documenting the fact of continuity in the *chinamit-parcialidad* principle was fairly straightforward. Tribute lists and records of legal disputes over land provided clear and unequivocal evidence. Explaining continuity was a different matter. Personalities do not emerge in any detail from the documents, aside from those of a few Spanish officials in their reports. The Sacapultecos themselves, despite lists of their names in censuses and petitions, can be perceived only dimly in the documents, mostly in the results of their actions. Individuals whose leadership at particular moments may have been crucial to the *parcialidades'* continuation—despite pointed attempts by the Spaniards to eliminate such units—remain unknown. Thus, in explaining continuity as a dynamic process we are unable to make much direct use of psychologically oriented theories of culture change, such as those of Hallowell (1945), Barnett (1953), or Wallace (1970). Instead, we have been forced to rely on the structure of the acculturative situation itself: the number and kinds of people in contact, the nature of those contacts, the Spanish policies of directed change, the ways in which those policies were implemented, and the alternative responses available to the Sacapultecos.

This book was written with a diverse audience in mind. Anthropologists generally and Mesoamerican specialists in particular were our main concern. For them, this work represents the first community study in the area in which the entire historical continuum is dealt with. As such, it may be a useful supplementary text in courses on Maya or Mesoamerican ethnology. Since the time factor is controlled to an extent, we also feel the work has value as an acculturation study in which the native people were not—to use anthropologist Alfred Kroeber's (1957) phrase and criticism—

"bulldozed." Archaeologists may find the section on preconquest political geography of particular interest. Not only have two forms of preconquest sociopolitical organization been reconstructed, but examples of their appearance on the ground are presented, which may be of use in interpreting remains in other archaeological zones of the Maya highlands. Historians may be interested in a community-level view of the colonial period as experienced by highland Maya people, especially since we now have several regional treatments (MacLeod 1973; Sherman 1981). Finally, given the political situation in Central America, other social scientists as well as general readers may find that this study provides some historical insights into Guatemala's current problems.

Since we have not attempted to write a history of Sacapulas, the chapters are not organized in strict chronological sequence and a few words of explanation may be in order:

Chapter 1 serves to introduce Sacapulas briefly to the reader, focusing on its internal organization, which seems anomalous when compared with much of the extant literature on closed corporate communities in the Maya area.

In Chapter 2 we suggest that the contemporary Sacapulas *cantones* are nothing less than the direct descendants of preconquest units of social organization, and we present a reconstruction of such units based on a variety of colonial-period documents.

Chapter 3 demonstrates the continuity of preconquest principles of social organization in Sacapulas. It also reviews the fortunes of the groups that formed Sacapulas. Most importantly, the fluctuations in Sacapulas' population over time are sketched, population being part of the dynamics that both threatened and preserved the traditional social organization.

Chapter 4 briefly summarizes our knowledge of the area's archaeology. More important, it shows how the groups that would later compose Sacapulas occupied the land, and the kinds of concerns the patterns of their occupation seem to reflect.

Chapters 5 through 8 examine factors determining the course of continuity and change in Sacapulas' social organization. Much of these chapters consists of fairly detailed reviews of litigation records pertaining to disputes brought before the Spanish authorities. These records are the prime source of information about Sacapulas during the colonial period. We have tried to summarize where possible, skipping over many boring procedural matters; still, there is some danger that the reader may perceive these litigation proceedings as tedious. In many ways, however, the litigation proceedings and their outcomes are crucial to an understanding of the continuity in Sacapulas' social organization. They represent both the symptoms of difficult problems confronting the Sacapultecos and the means of their solution. The extent to which the Sacapultecos mastered the Spanish legal system directly affected the degree to which they could, or would have to, retain their preconquest social units. It is useful, therefore, to think of the litigation proceedings as dramas in which the dynamics of human population, strictly limited natural resources, continuity in principles of social organization, and Spanish demands were played out.

In Chapter 9, the lack of post-colonial, nineteenth-century documentation pertinent to the topic of Sacapulas' social organization forces us to pick up the trail of continuity late in the period. By relying on statements of informants it is possible to trace some significant courses of change early in the twentieth century and to suggest some trends for the future.

Chapter 10 analyzes the factors that appear to have contributed most to continuity in Sacapulas and stresses the importance of the historical perspective in understanding the community today. Comparisons with the limited numer of other extant studies suggest key variables in the historical experience of highland Maya peoples that may help account for the diversity in their social organization as it has been recorded ethnographically.

Monaghan was responsible for the ethnographic study of Sacapulas. His 1980 material forms the bulk of Chapters 3 and 10, supplemented by the observations made in 1983 by Hill. The rest of the book is the work of Hill. The authors take full responsibility for their respective contributions.

It is a pleasure to acknowledge the many people whose assistance made this work possible. First and foremost, we wish to thank Ruben E. Reina who, in addition to being our teacher, introduced both of us to Sacapulas and encouraged us in our investigations. Through the Hispanic American Research Fund controlled by Reina at the University of Pennsylvania, the generous contributions of Robert F. Maxwell, Edwin C. Bauxbaum, and Mr. and Mrs. Robert M. Hill were used to defray the costs of transcribing the Sacapulas documents. The Anthropology Department of the University of Pennsylvania provided funds for Hill's trip to Sacapulas in 1976 and for Monaghan's trips. The University Museum also provided funds for Reina and Monaghan in 1979. At the University of Texas at San Antonio, Dean Dwight F. Henderson made funds available to assist with the artwork. Woodruff D. Smith and Charlotte W. Hill read the manuscript and gave us a number of very helpful suggestions. The staff of the Office of Media Resources at the University of Texas at

San Antonio produced both the photographic prints from negatives supplied by Hill and the facsimiles of the colonial survey maps. Kenneth Brown produced the contemporary maps. Elisa Jimenez, Elaine Miller, and Martha La Roque assisted with the typing of various portions and revisions of the manuscript.

In Guatemala, the Instituto Nacional de Antropología e Historia and its former directors, Francís Polo Sifontes and René Humberto Gordillo Miranda, provided liberal assistance at every stage of the research. The civil and military authorities of the Department of El Quiché and the *Municipio* of Sacapulas all extended every effort to ensure the success of our investigations. Finally, our friends in Sacapulas, through their interest, companionship, and good humor, made our investigations there successful.

To all the individuals and institutions mentioned, our sincerest thanks.

Sacapulas Today: An Ethnographic Summary

of Its *Cantón* Organization

Today, Sacapulas is a *municipio* (township) approximately two hundred square kilometers in extent in the western highlands of Guatemala. It is located in the present-day Department of El Quiché, forty-eight kilometers north of Santa Cruz, the departmental capital (see Map 1-1). The *municipio* lies astride the major river variously called the Río Negro, Chixoy, Sacapulas, or Cauinal, and its main tributary, the Río Blanco (see Figure 1-1 and Map 1-2). Sacapulas lies in the middle of a region that is diverse both linguistically and ecologically. To the north, across an extension of the rugged Cuchumatanes Mountains, the three Ixil-Maya-speaking communities of Nebaj, Cotzal, and Chajul occupy a high, luxuriant tropical environment that makes the Sacapulas valley bottoms seem dry by comparison. Centered in a well-watered valley to the west is the *municipio* of Aguacatán with its own distinct dialect. Northeast of Sacapulas are Cunén, near the top of the Cuchumatanes extension, and Uspantán, which lies in the valley of another tributary of the Río Negro. Both are Quiché-speaking communities. Today, dirt roads and buses connect all these communities, with Sacapulas occupying a central position for east-west and north-south traffic. However, intense interaction among them is by no means a recent phenomenon. The only road leading south bypasses Sacapulas' nearest neighbor in that direction, San Bartolomé Jocotenango, and no road leads from Sacapulas to San Andrés Sajcabajá, which lies in a wide and fertile highland valley to the southeast. Yet good trails do exist to both of these Quiché-speaking communities and travel distances are not great; thus any isolation is more one of appearance than reality.[1]

Sacapulas contains three different ethnic groups. The largest group is made up of Sacapultec Maya Indians, hereafter called Sacapultecos. These Indians are set apart from the other ethnic groups by their language, the distinctive dress of their women, and because they are the descendants of the original inhabitants of the area. The second largest ethnic group is also composed of Maya Indians, but they speak a different language and dress differently from the Sacapultecos. This group is made up of the descendants of Quiché sheepherders from the Santa María Chiquimula area, who

I

L. Petén

R. Negro

● JACALTENANGO

NEBAJ
CHIANTLA ● ●
AGUACATÁN
● USPANTÁN
● COBÁN
SACAPULAS
SANTA CRUZ ●
SAJCABAJÁ ● RABINAL
TOTONICAPÁN ●
TECPÁN
GUATEMALA *Río Motagua*
L. Atitlán
● ANTIGUA

O   IOO km

Map 1-1. Guatemala, showing site of Sacapulas and other important towns.

began to settle in Sacapulas about a century ago. They were given the use of some unoccupied land in return for which they continue to pay a nominal annual rent to the *municipio*. They are also required to provide various supplies, such as a quantity of candles, incense, and rockets, as well as marimba bands and a number of dancers for the *fiesta* of Santo Domingo in August. Each adult male also owes one day of work service per year in the *pueblo*, or town center. This service usually consists of sweeping the plaza, repairing public buildings, painting, and other odd jobs.

The third ethnic group in the municipality consists of *ladinos*, Guatemalans who identify with the dominant national culture. Although they are small in number compared with the other two groups, *ladinos* wield a great deal of power in Sacapulas. They have complete control of the offices

Figure 1-1. Panoramic view of Sacapulas and the Río Negro Valley, viewed from the northeast on the road to Cunen.

of the municipal government, and have been quick to seize any posts created within Sacapulas by the national government. The *ladinos* of Sacapulas are concentrated in the town center and in a small settlement in the western part of the municipality.

According to the most recent reliable census (1950), the *municipio* has a total population of 10,897, of which 10,182 are Maya Indians (*Diccionario Geográfico de Guatemala*, 2:102). The remainder of the population is *ladino*. While traditionally grouped as Quiché speakers, John DuBois recently suggested that the Sacapulteco dialect is sufficiently distinct to deserve classification as a separate language (Dubois 1981, 55–56). DuBois estimates that in 1977 there were roughly 7,500 Sacapultec speakers and a similar number of Chiquimulas, and about a thousand *ladinos* (ibid., 9–11).

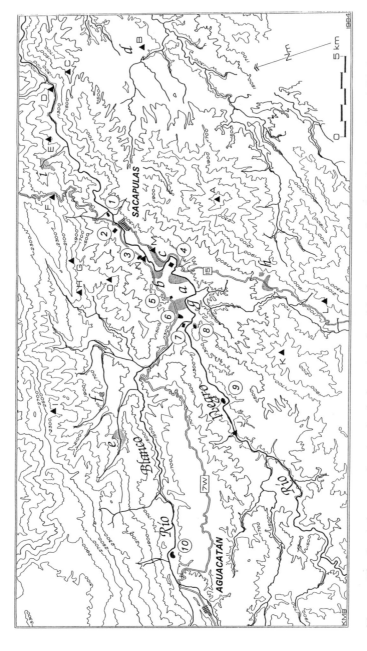

Map 1-2. The Sacapulas area, showing local places (mentioned in the text), archaeological sites, and *parcialidad* boundary markers. *Places mentioned in the text*: a, Patzagel; b, Xetzagel; c, Ixpapal; d, Mixcolaja; e, Pichiquil; f, Parraxtut; g, Río Blanco; h, Rancho de Teja; i, Turbalyá. *Archaeological sites*: 1, Xecatloj; 2, Chutinamit; 3, Papsacá (Chuchun); 4, Chutixtiox; 5, Xolpacol; 6, Xolcoxoy (Río Blanco); 7, Xolchun; 8, Pacot; 9, Xoltinamit; 10, Xolchun-Tenam. *Boundary markers (mojones)*: A, Chupacbalam; B, Momosijuyu; C, Ixcolpulil; D, Peña Negra; E, Sanaca uleu; F, Cerro Chibuc; G, Xajouabal; H, Ximalcajol; I, Chinamitan juyab; J, Río Negro; K, Chui Cahbab; L, Xechiley; M, Ixpapal; N, Piedra Canoa; O, Chu Ixil Abaj.

4

Human occupation is centered in the river valleys, which generally are narrow and steep-sided. Despite a valley-floor altitude of 1196.16 meters above sea level, the climate is warm, especially during the dry season from January through June. The valley, like most of the region's interior drainages, is subject to a rain-shadow effect: the mountains on each side, and especially the north, block the prevailing rain-carrying air currents. As a result, the rainy season begins much later here and dry-climate plants, such as various cacti, are prominent in the landscape. The total effect is that of a distinct ecological zone, quite at variance with the popular concept of highland Guatemala as a high tropical region enjoying an eternal spring.

There is little arable land generally in the *municipio* and most of it is concentrated along the two major rivers and their tributaries. Irrigation is practiced in the relatively wide alluvial deposits at the confluence of the Río Blanco and the Río Negro. Most other workable land occurs in small plots, while pine and oak, used for building and firewood, grow on the mountain slopes. Limited agricultural resources aside, the salt flats constitute the economic resource that has made occupation of the area viable for a considerable portion of the population. The flats are located just east (downstream) of the *pueblo,* adjacent to the Río Negro. Catastrophic flooding of the Río Negro covered most of the flats with several meters of silt and cobbles in the 1940s (see Figure 1-2a and 2b). Despite the disaster, exploitation of the salt flats continues on a reduced scale with a technology essentially unchanged since before the Spanish conquest (Reina and Monaghan 1981).

The limited agricultural resources and the salt flats are two enduring features of the local environment that have long forced Sacapultecos to augment their livelihoods through extracommunity enterprises and arrangements. These, in turn, constitute the main mechanisms by which Sacapulas has historically been integrated in the region. Salt making is a dry-season activity and therefore does not interfere with the agricultural cycle. It does require considerable labor, however, since both water and firewood are used in large quantities. Historically, this labor has not always come exclusively from Sacapulas itself. For example, three Dominican friars, while reporting on conditions between 1544 and 1574, stated that men regularly traveled west to Sacapulas from the Verapaz region to work at salt making. The workers received payment for their labor in salt, which they took back home with them to sell, presumably at a handsome profit (Viana, Gallegos, and Cadena 1955, 22).

Sacapultecos have traditionally traded their salt to the Ixil-speaking Maya communities to the north, from which corn was obtained in return.

Figure 1-2a. The Sacapulas *salinas*. Note the area where several meters of cobbles and silt had to be removed in order to reexpose the working surface after floods in the 1940s.

Sacapulas traders also traveled south through the Department of El Quiché and as far as the major Cakchiquel market town of Sololá on the north side of Lake Atitlán. Since the introduction of motor transport in the 1930s, many Sacapulas women have been successful produce merchants, traveling without their men to markets in surrounding communities and beyond (see Figure 1-3).

Beginning more recently, many Sacapultecos have left the community to find jobs in Guatemala City; DuBois estimates that as many as 2,500 people left in 1977 (DuBois 1981, 10). Women typically find employment as domestics, while men's fields are more diverse. Since the 1950s, however, Sacapulas has enjoyed a certain notoriety for the disproportionate number

Figure 1-2b. The Sacapulas *salinas* viewed from the archaeological site of Chutin-amit on the north side of the Río Negro.

of its sons who have followed careers in the National Police. While quantitative data are lacking, the preferred pattern in all these arrangements seems to be to return home as soon as economically feasible or upon retirement.

Because of these outside contacts and experiences with diverse peoples, many Sacapultecos have an excellent knowledge of Spanish; the many retired policemen, with their training, are literate. Subjectively, Sacapultecos in general also seem quite cosmopolitan, especially when compared with the Chiquimulas and other Maya speakers in neighboring communities. They are also much more open and direct in their dealings with strangers, with whom even women (normally the most reticent people in Maya communities) may engage in lively casual conversation.

Figure 1-3. Sacapultecos, Chiquimulas, and *ladinos* in the plaza on market day.

Like many highland Maya *municipios,* only a portion of the population resides in the *pueblo,* or town center. Again according to the 1950
census, 2,218 people, or some 20 percent of the total *municipio* population,
reside in the *pueblo,* with the remaining 80 percent, or 8,679 people, living
in small rural settlements called *aldeas,* and even smaller *caseríos.* Officially
there are nine *aldeas* and thirty-two *caseríos* in Sacapulas. In addition to
these units, we also note that the *pueblo* is divided into five *barrios* (neighborhoods), and the *municipio* is divided into five territorial subdivisions
called *cantones.*

If we were to attempt to fit Sacapulas into the cultural typologies
devised by anthropologists for Mesoamerican peoples generally, and Maya
peoples in particular, we would first have to classify it as a traditional
closed corporate community (Wolf 1955). In conformity with Wolf's original definition, Sacapulas exhibits (a) a predominantly Indian population,

(b) a bounded social system corresponding to the physical limits of the community (that is to say, the community is strongly endogamous), (c) membership in the community based on birth in it, (d) community control (until fairly recently) over a significant portion of the total land in the *municipio,* and finally (e) a hierarchically organized political-religious system. Further, we note that the *municipio* boasts salt making as an *oficio,* a specialized, institutionalized economic activity, in conformity with the general pattern of community economic specialization among the highland Maya (MacBryde 1947; Reina and Hill 1978).

Similarly, Sacapulas may be identified with the intermediate type of *municipio* as defined by Tax (1937). This type of *municipio* falls between Tax's more polar types of "vacant town" and "town nucleus" *municipios.* In the former, only a few families live permanently in the *pueblo.* The vast majority live in *aldeas,* from which they travel periodically to the *pueblo,* the focus of formal, civil, and religious, as well as market, activities. The opposite of the vacant town is the town nucleus *municipio,* in which the population is centered in the *pueblo,* with few or no *aldeas.* Although the proportion of people residing in the *pueblo* of Sacapulas is small relative to the total population, it is certainly a significant enough number that the *pueblo* never seems vacant to an observer. We must therefore assign Sacapulas to the residual category of intermediate-type *municipios.*

Tax's and Wolf's typologies have both been useful in focusing attention on the *municipio* as the basic unit of ethnographic study. The idea of "tribes" as known among North American Indians is inappropriate here. However, as we proceed ethnographically beyond the attempt to fit Sacapulas superficially into this or that classificatory scheme, we are struck by the presence of other kinds of units within the *municipio,* units whose nature and functions are neither predicted nor discussed in terms of *municipio* or community type.

We have already noted in passing the presence of several subunits of the Sacapulas *municipio:* the *pueblo, aldeas, caseríos, barrios,* and *cantones.* How, ethnographically, can we understand the interrelated presence and functioning of these units? How does such understanding further our knowledge of the Maya or Mesoamerican peoples in general? An attempt to deal, at least descriptively, with these units in Mesoamerica generally has been made by Hunt and Nash (1967) in a review of the literature. They note that the term *cantón* (or its Mexican equivalent, *paraje*) "has been applied to three functionally distinct territorial units: (1) a named geographical unit, (2) a group of agricultural plots, and (3) a small settlement of households . . . which control the agricultural plots and have primary

Figure 1-4. The *aldea* of Tzununul on the south side of the Río Negro, viewed from the north.

rights of usufruct . . ." (ibid., 256). It is the third use of the term that will concern us here, though, as we shall see, the *cantón* is more complex both ethnographically and historically than the brief characterization would indicate.

An *aldea* is defined as "a population aggregate within the *municipio* limits which is dependent on the political administration of the center" (ibid., 258) (see Figure 1-4). Yet, to a certain degree, *aldea* and *cantón* are parallel since "within the *aldea* as within the *paraje* [*cantón*] all life-cycle ceremonies are held, in addition to those rituals connected with the agricultural cycle" (ibid., 259). Both units may have their own officers or representatives to the *municipio*-wide political and religious administrations (ibid., 257, 259). Another unit, the *barrio,* may also have similar functions. The number of *barrios* can also be used to characterize the *municipio* as a whole (ibid., 262–64). Dual *barrio* systems have either two *barrios* or two groups of *barrios* and tend to be associated with Indian-dominated, traditional communities. An imaginary line across the central plaza divides the two; respective memberships are based on descent within the endogamous group. While each group sees to its own internal affairs, formal political responsibility is divided between them. There is, supposedly, no economic specialization among the component *barrios*. The contrasting multiple *barrio* system is associated with more acculturated communities where non-Indian *ladinos* are in control politically. In such a system the *pueblo* plaza center forms a nucleus, with the separate *barrios* arranged around it. The *barrio* endogamy rule is lacking. Political power may become centralized in one *barrio*, while economic specializations are distributed along *barrio* lines.

Unfortunately, the above characterizations begin to break down when we attempt to apply them to Sacapulas. A cause of persistent difficulty in the study of local, social, and territorial subdivisions has been the use of Spanish as opposed to native terminology. While the latter has a distribution restricted to the linguistic area, Spanish has regional variants and its use may obscure qualitatively different kinds of indigenous units. An additional problem has been the failure to distinguish between units that perform different functions. Some units are recognized administrative subdivisions of the national government. Others are types of settlements, social units, or, finally, cultural units. Thus, as far as the national government is concerned, there are four types of administrative subdivisions in Sacapulas. The most inclusive is the *municipio* itself, the unit just below the level of department in the official hierarchy. The *pueblo* is recognized as the seat of the *municipio* government, and the place where national and local administrative functions meet. In addition, there are also officially recognized small rural settlements, *aldeas* and even smaller *caseríos*. The most basic unit of settlement, the household, occasionally occurs by itself within the *municipio*, but is most commonly associated with others in an *aldea* or *caserío*. Even when physically isolated, the household is assigned to an *aldea* or *caserío* for administrative purposes.

The units recognized by the government closely parallel the types of settlements that occur. Again we have the *pueblo* as a nucleated settlement with a *plaza*, church, government buildings, market, and generally substantial houses. In contrast, *aldeas* tend to be less nucleated and lack the ecclesiastical and public services available in the *pueblo*. The *caserío* is simply an extreme of the *aldea* trends, smaller and more isolated.

The inventory changes, however, when we examine social and cultural units recognized by the Sacapultecos. As noted earlier, we have tradition-ally looked at the *municipio* itself as the basic social and cultural unit for the highland Maya. In Sacapulas, however, we notice the presence of *cantones* as distinct sociocultural groupings within the *municipio*. In fact, the role of the *cantones* in the social, political, economic, and religious orga-nization of Sacapulas rivals that of the *municipio* itself. It is to a description of the *cantón* functions that we now turn.

The *Cantones* of Sacapulas

If a Sacapulteco is asked to describe the *municipio,* he will invariably divide it into five bounded territorial units that he calls *cantones:* San Sebastián, Santiago, San Pedro, Santo Tomás, and San Francisco. Such *cantón* units are not unique to Sacapulas; their occurrence in other highland Maya communities is attested to in the literature (Bunzel, 1952; Nash 1958; Reina 1966; Tedlock 1982).

CANTÓN MEMBERSHIP

Of the three ethnic groups, only the Sacapultecos and the Chiquimulas can have membership in a *cantón*. The criterion for determining *cantón* membership is birth in its territory. Every Sacapulteco is thus a lifelong member of the *cantón* in which he or she is born. Membership in the *cantón* of birth is retained despite changes in residence. However, if some-one moves to another *cantón,* and his or her children are born there, the children become members of the *cantón* in which they were born, not that of their father or mother. Although *cantón* membership is, in most cases, coincident with place of residence and patrilineal descent, it is place of birth that is most important for determining membership.

That place of birth is the most important criterion for determining *cantón* membership is illustrated in the case of the Chiquimulas. The first Chiquimulas to move into Sacapulas were not considered to be members of any of the *cantones*. However, as children were born to the new immi-grants, these children became members of the *cantón* in which they were born, at least from the Sacapultecos' viewpoint. Today, most Chiquimulas are considered by the Sacapultecos to be members of one of the five *cantones*. This is true even though the Chiquimulas have maintained their distinctive language and dress, and members of the two Maya groups, Chiquimula and Sacapulteco, rarely intermarry. However, *cantón* member-ship is not a significant distinction to the Chiquimulas themselves. This has created problems of community integration, which are discussed in Chapter 9.

Before examining the role of the *cantones* in the organization of Sacapulas, several confusing points about the way in which the *cantones* divide the municipality should be clarified. First, the town center (*tinimit* or *chihay*) is located in the *cantón* of San Sebastián and Santiago. The proper Maya name for the town center is Tuhal, although when speaking Spanish people refer to it as Sacapulas. Second, it is impossible to distinguish ethnographically between the land of the *cantón* San Sebastián and the land of *cantón* Santiago. Traditionally, the people of the two *cantones* have been salt makers, they live in the same section of the town center, and the two *cantones* share the same ruling council (see below). Despite this they are not considered to be the same *cantón*. They are, rather, two *cantones* that always "go together, like brothers." The reason they do so is explained by reference to a myth, the following version of which was recorded by Monaghan:

> Santiago and San Sebastián came from a mountain in the direction of San Andrés (Sajcabajá). They were on their way to the salt fields. Santiago was faster than San Sebastián, because he was on his horse. But, as they were nearing Tuhal, the wind blew Santiago's hat into a barranca. Well, Santiago went down to get his hat, so San Sebastián arrived before Santiago. They always go together, but Santiago always arrives behind San Sebastián.

The informant went on to say that this is the reason why San Sebastián obtained a larger portion of the salt fields than Santiago.

From this point on, the *cantón* San Sebastián and the *cantón* Santiago will be referred to collectively as the *cantón* San Sebastián and Santiago. This phraseology is meant to express the unique relationship that exists between the two, and the fact that in many contexts they function as if they were one, even though they are discrete entities in the minds of Sacapultecos.

THE *CANTÓN* AND LAND TENURE

Within each *cantón* there are two types of properties: those that are privately owned by individual families within the *cantón,* and those that are collectively owned by the members of the *cantón*. Use of the latter properties is restricted to the members of the *cantón*. If an outsider wishes to use these properties, he must ask permission of the *ax waab'*, the *cantón's* twelve-man council of elders, and, if permission is granted, he must pay the *cantón* for this privilege. For the most part, the collectively owned properties are confined to the *monte* or wooded areas of the *cantón*. The most productive agricultural land belongs to individual families, or is fast on its way to falling into private hands. However, the *monte* represents a valuable resource since it can be used for grazing and, more important, for the gathering of firewood. Traditionally, there were many families in Sacapulas who derived a substantial part of their yearly income from the gathering and sale of firewood, much of which is used in salt production.

The only restriction on the complete capitalization of *cantón* land that belongs to individual families is that the land can be sold only to other members of the *cantón*. In other words, one cannot be a member of one *cantón* and own land in another.

CANTONES AND THE MUNICIPAL GOVERNMENT

There are two types of positions within the municipal government: those that are filled through an election carried out among the municipality's inhabitants, and those filled through appointment by the municipality's elected officials. An election is held every four years, and several parties may put forward a slate. The winning party appoints the top three posts in the municipality administration (*alcalde, síndico,* and first *regidor*), with the rest divided among the losing parties according to the proportion of votes received. Until recently, almost all municipal positions, whether their incumbents were elected or appointed, were held by *ladinos*.

The Indians' participation in the municipal government in modern times has been restricted to a few subordinate posts and to the one *regidor* and six *auxiliares* that are appointed to serve from each of the *cantones* (*cantón* San Sebastián and Santiago share the same *regidor* and *auxiliares*). The *regidor* is normally a mature man, while the *auxiliares* are younger. The people appointed to serve as *regidores* and *auxiliares* alternate with one another by *cantón* on a weekly basis. Thus, one week the *regidor* and *auxiliares* from San Pedro will serve, while the next week it will be the turn of those from Santo Tomás. This rotation continues for an entire year, after which new *regidores* and *auxiliares* are chosen.

The work required from the *regidores* and *auxiliares* is not demanding. They spend most of their week of service lounging on the steps of the municipal building, only occasionally running messages for the *juez de paz* or doing odd jobs such as sweeping and painting. If an *auxiliar* lives too far away from the town center to travel back and forth during his week of service, he will sleep overnight in the municipal building. The *regidor* acts as night watchman and must sleep in the municipal building.

While the posts usually occupied by *ladinos* are salaried, neither the *regidor* nor the *auxiliares* receive any pay. Although the work required of the *regidores* and *auxiliares* is limited, it does require a substantial amount of time that could otherwise be spent pursuing more remunerative undertakings. This service becomes especially burdensome during critical periods in the agricultural cycle, when the time required in the town center takes the *regidor* and *auxiliares* away from planting and harvesting.

It is only by placing the positions of *regidor* and *auxiliar* within the context of the Maya concept of service, or *patan,* that it can be understood why, of all the positions in the municipal government, these two are unsalaried. The Maya notion of *patan* encompasses not only tribute, but also ideas of obligation, and calling, and fulfilling one's proper role in the universe. *Patan* is a burden, but a burden whose performance is a virtue. The idea of *patan* thus confounds economic transactions with moral commitment, and taxation and tribute with vocation. Serving as a *regidor* and *auxiliar* is part of the *patan* of every Sacapulteco. Remuneration is not expected, nor would it be moral to accept it.

The service owed the municipality by the *regidores* and the *auxiliares* has two features that are of interest. The first is that the service is mediated by the *cantón.* In other words, the *regidores* and *auxiliares* participate in the municipal government as *cantón* members, not as members of the municipality. The service they perform is service that is owed by their *cantón* to the municipality, not service that they owe as individual members of the municipality. The second feature of interest, related to the first, is that although the *cantones* are not officially recognized as administrative units, they nevertheless structure the way that the municipal government recruits its Indian personnel.

THE *CANTONES* AND THE *ALCALDÍA INDÍGENA*

Located in the same building as the municipality offices are the offices of the *Alcaldía Indígena.* This organization, combined with the *cofradías* (see below) makes up the Sacapulteco civil-religious hierarchy. The civil-religious hierarchy is an institution found throughout Mesoamerica in which "adult males serve in a series of hierarchically arranged offices devoted to both political and ceremonial aspects of community life" (Cancian 1967, 283). People alternate between the *cofradías* and the *Alcaldía,* slowly advancing up the ladder of offices, all the while gaining in prestige and authority. Ultimate authority in the institution is concentrated in the hands of those who have passed through all its offices. This group of men is called an *ax waab'.*[2] In Sacapulas, there are four *ax waab',* corresponding to the four *cantones,* each with twelve members (Santiago and San Sebastián share the same *ax waab'*).

In Sacapulas, personnel are recruited to the offices of the *Alcaldía Indígena* based on their ability to afford the expenses of office and on their membership in a *cantón.* In this discussion, it is the latter requirement that is of most interest.

Every level of office in the *Alcaldía Indígena* is distributed evenly among the *cantones* (San Sebastián and Santiago are treated as one *cantón*). Some offices are circulated among the *cantones* from year to year until each *cantón* has filled the office. Other offices are composed of four positions, each of them filled by a representative from each of the *cantones.* The way in which offices circulate is illustrated by the rotation of the positions of first *alcalde* and second *alcalde.* These two positions are always filled by the members of paired *cantones.* The two pairs are San Sebastián/Santiago and San Francisco, on the one hand, and San Pedro and Santo Tomás on the other. It takes four years for a cycle to be completed. In year one the first *alcalde* will be from San Sebastián/Santiago, and the second *alcalde* will be from San Francisco. In year two the first *alcalde* will be from San Pedro, and the second *alcalde* from Santo Tomás. In year three, the two offices return to the first pair, but this time the first *alcalde* is from San Francisco, while the second *alcalde* is from San Sebastián/Santiago. Finally, the cycle is completed in year four when a man from Santo Tomás becomes the first *alcalde,* and one from San Pedro becomes the second *alcalde.*

The *regidor* level is filled by a representative of each of the *cantones.* Thus there will always be one *regidor* from San Francisco, one from San Pedro, and so on. Each one of the positions allotted to a *cantón* is filled by the decision of the *ax waab'* of the *cantón.*

The most important task that confronts the *Alcaldía Indígena* is the coordination of ritual activities within the town center. The Catholic priest must arrange with the *Alcaldía* for the use of the church on Sunday, the *cofradías* must clear their schedule for processions with it, and the *Alcaldía* must make sure that everything runs smoothly during the four days of the patronal fiesta in August. The *Alcaldía Indígena* is also in charge of the church, which must be kept in good repair, and is responsible for the safekeeping of church valuables. Every member of the *Alcaldía Indígena* must report to the town center on Sundays and religious holidays. In addition, each member must serve a two-day stint every twelve days or so in the town center, guarding the church and manning the *Alcaldía* offices.

In Sacapulas, service in the *Alcaldía Indígena,* like the service owed the municipality by the *regidor* and *auxiliar,* is *patan.* However, the *Alcal-*

Figure 1-5. A *cofradía* procession returning to the church. (Photograph by Ruben E. Reina.)

día Indígena organizes Indian service in a way that is much more complex than in the municipality. Through a series of interdependent and annually circulating service obligations, the *Alcaldía Indígena* has the effect of integrating the various *cantones* into one organization. This integration should not be overemphasized, however. One still serves in the *Alcaldía Indígena* because one is a member of a *cantón* and not because one is an inhabitant of Sacapulas. A man becomes first *alcalde* because it is his *cantón's* turn to provide someone for the post. Obligation to serve in this institution, even though it does integrate the *cantones* on a higher level, is still an obligation owed by the individual to his *cantón*.

CANTONES AND *COFRADÍAS*

Associated with each *cantón* is a *cofradía*, or *patanibal* (see Figure 1-5). The Sacapulas *cofradías* are much like those found elsewhere in Mesoamerica (see Reina 1966, 97–165, for a discussion of *cofradías*). The core of the Sacapulteco *cofradía* is made up of five graded positions that are occupied in succession by those passing through it. Some *cofradías* have five women's positions paralleling those of the men that are usually, but not always, occupied by the wives of the men serving in the *cofradía*. Men reach the top positions in the *cofradía—Kajawixel*—when they are in their late forties or early fifties. As its Maya name *patanibal* suggests, service in the *cofradía* is considered to be *patan* by Sacapultecos.

The expenses of climbing the steps in the *cofradía* organization are enormous. The *Kajawixel* of the Santo Domingo *cofradía* in 1980 estimated that the five men serving that year would spend 1,500 to 2,000 *quetzales* (the *quetzal* was valued on par with the U.S. dollar). The *Kajawixel* of the *cofradía* of San Francisco estimated an expenditure of 350 *quetzales* for each of the men in his *cofradía*. This was at a time when the average daily wage for an agricultural worker was two *quetzales*. It should come as no surprise then, that a man is given at least three years of "rest" between positions.

The *ax waab'* of a *cantón* choose the *Kajawixel* for the *cofradía* associated with their *cantón*. Several members of the *ax waab'* go to the candidate's house, invite him to partake of the liquor and cigarettes they have brought with them, and then make their request. Then they leave, to give the prospective *Kajawixel* time to think it over. When they return after a week or so he gives them his answer. The position is usually accepted. Around the same time the *ax waab'* appoint a man to act as adviser.

After he has accepted the position, the *Kajawixel* must go and look for his "sons," that is, four other men who will join him as *cofrades*. He petitions them in the same way the *ax waab'* petitioned him—first going to each candidate's house with liquor and cigarettes, making his request, leaving, and then returning a week or two later for the answer.

The adviser, a man experienced in *cofradía* matters, is appointed by the *ax waab'* of a *cantón* to guide the *Kajawixel*. He instructs the *Kajawixel* on the rituals to be performed, and advises him on matters pertaining to the more mundane affairs of the *cofradía* (where to rent a marimba, how many candles to buy, and so on). The adviser is normally a member of the *ax waab'*, and has gained his experience through once being *Kajawixel* himself. He also reports to the *ax waab'* on how the *Kajawixel* is performing his duties. In this sense the adviser is as much a watchdog for the *ax waab'* as he is a counselor to the *Kajawixel*.

CANTONES AND THE TOWN CENTER

The *pueblo* of Sacapulas is divided into four neighborhoods, or *barrios*, each corresponding to one of the *cantones* (San Sebastián and Santiago share the same *barrio*). Traditionally, the houses in these *barrios* belonged to people who, for the most part, lived on their plots of land in the *cantones*. They came in to occupy their houses in the town center only during market days, for religious celebrations and weddings, and on the occasions when the men had service obligations to perform. However, one portion of the town was occupied on a year-round basis by two distinct groups of people. The smallest group was made up of *ladinos*, who lived around the main plaza and who formed no definite *barrio*. The *ladinos*, with a few exceptions, owned none of the land outside the town center. They made their living either by working for the *municipio* or by operating small stores. Some also lived on government pensions. The larger group was made up of the members of the *cantón* San Sebastián and Santiago. Almost the entire population of this *cantón* was (and still is) concentrated in the town center. There are very few members of the *cantón* San Sebastián and Santiago who own houses further out on the *cantón* land. This concentration of population is one of the keys to understanding settlement patterns in Sacapulas.

It will be recalled that the town center of Sacapulas is situated on land belonging to the *cantón* San Sebastián and Santiago. Thus a distinction is made between the houses in the town center and the land on which the houses rest. While the houses of any particular *barrio* belong to the members of the *cantón* to which that *barrio* corresponds, the land belongs only to the *cantón* of San Sebastián and Santiago. Informants pointed out many times that while people from other *cantones* owned houses in the town center, none of them owned any of the farmland or salt fields in San Sebastián and Santiago. *Cantón* San Sebastián and Santiago is thus unique in Sacapulas because the members own both the houses in the town center and the land on which the houses rest.

While their ownership of the land explains the interest of the members of the *cantón* of San Sebastián and Santiago in the center (see below), and why they may choose to settle there, it does not in itself explain why they are able to nucleate while the other *cantones* maintain a more dispersed settlement pattern. Important in this context is the nature of the agricultural land owned by the *cantón,* and the specialization in salt making.

Most of the land owned by the *cantón* of San Sebastián and Santiago is mountainous and poorly watered, used mostly for the gathering of firewood. The suitable agricultural land that does exist is located in alluvial fans along the river a short walk from the town center. The land close to the river is the most fertile, but it is frequently flooded during the rainy season and the crops planted there are lost. The land that slopes up from the river at the base of the mountains is safe from floods, but much less fertile. Almost everyone in the *cantón* San Sebastián and Santiago agrees that there is a chronic shortage of good farmland.

This lack of suitable farmland means that few people in the *cantón* are self-sufficient in either of the staple foods, corn and beans. Most families raise enough corn to meet their needs for nine to ten months out of the year, but they must purchase the rest. This is not a recent phenomenon. Older informants say it was as much a problem when they were young as it is now.

In the past, people in San Sebastián and Santiago have been able to make up the deficit through their specialization in salt making. The salt fields are exclusively owned by members of the *cantón* San Sebastián and Santiago. Before a disastrous series of floods in the mid-1940s, which buried about four-fifths of the salt fields under tons of silt and rock, nearly everyone in the *cantón* was employed in making salt (Reina and Monaghan 1981). Salt was traded for corn both in the Sacapulas market and in the Ixil-speaking *municipios* to the north. Apparently salt making was a lucrative enterprise (as it is today for those who pursue it), making San Sebastián and Santiago the most prosperous of all the *cantones* in the municipality.

Thus, the concentration of the population of the *cantón* San Sebastián and Santiago in the town center can be attributed to the interplay of three factors. First, the land on which the town center is located is owned by the *cantón*. Second, the *cantón* lacks sufficient agricultural land and what it does possess is concentrated around the town center. Finally, the nature of their economic specialization, salt making, allows *cantón* members to concentrate on a resource that is limited to a small area (about the size of a football field) but that can also sustain a large number of people.

The *Barrios* and the *Cofradías*

Housed with each *cantón*'s *barrio* is the saint's image associated with the *cantón*'s *cofradía*. The saint is said to "live" with the people of a *barrio*, and a *barrio* derives its name directly from the saint who lives in it. Thus, in the minds of many Sacapultecos there is no longer a Santo Tomás *barrio* in the town center, since the members of this *cantón* removed their saint in the early 1960s (see Chapter 9).

The most important *cofradía* celebrations take place in the town center. Fireworks are set off and candles and incense burned at these noisy celebrations that consist of long speeches, processions, and ritual drinking. An invariable element in the *cofradía* celebrations is the procession of the saint's image around the four chapels in town. Each of these chapels is dedicated to one of the *cantón/cofradía* saints, with the exception of San Francisco and Santo Tomás, which share a single chapel. The arrangement of these chapels around the church parallels the arrangement of the *cantones* around the *pueblo*. During the feast of Corpus Christi each of the chapels is decorated, and the images of their respective saints are placed inside. The images of Santo Domingo and the *Pan Divina Sacramenta,* the church's monstrance, then are carried by procession to each of the chapels by the *Alcaldía Indígena* and the *cofradía* of Santo Domingo, respectively. Santo Domingo *cofradía* draws members from all the *cantones* and thus provides a measure of ritual integration for the community. When they arrive at one of the chapels, the *cofradía* members inside invite the *alcaldía* officers and members of the *cofradía* of Santo Domingo to drink and smoke cigarettes. The latter reciprocate, and then move on to repeat this performance at the next chapel. After stopping at each of the four chapels, the procession returns to the church.

One interpretation of these processions has to do with their function in promoting and expressing the unity of the five *cantones*. The processions on Corpus Christi and the feast day of Santo Domingo involve the people of Sacapulas in rituals that transcend *cantón* boundaries. Each *cantón's cofradía* is dependent on the goodwill and cooperation of the others (that is, their performance of *patan*) for the successful completion of the rituals. A procession such as the one held on Santo Domingo's feast day involves hundreds of people who must somehow coordinate their activities so that each element in the celebration is enacted in the proper sequence. It is no coincidence that the *Alcaldía Indígena,* which was defined as a series of interdependent and annually circulating service obligations uniting the various *cantones* in one organization, has a central role in these rituals. Its members are in charge of coordinating the activities of the groups involved, and are also in the procession itself, either carrying *Pan Divina Sacramenta,* as at Corpus, or walking alongside the saint's image, as in the procession on Santo Domingo's feast day. The similarity in the integrative functions of the *Alcaldía Indígena* and the saint's processions is further indicated by elements of the saint's dress and the formal titles given the saints. Each of the *cofradía* saints, with the exception of Santo Domingo, carries a staff office (*vara*) that is a duplicate of the ones carried by the *regidores*. Not only that, but the *cofradía* saints—San Sebastián, Santiago, San Francisco, San Pedro, and Santo Tomás—are sometimes referred to as *"regidores."* Santo Domingo also carries a *vara,* but it is the *vara* of the first *alcalde.* He is, not surprisingly, referred to as "first *alcalde."*

It can be concluded that the same principle of *cantón* integration underlies both the *Alcaldía Indígena* and the ritual organization of the town center. Both unite the *cantones* through a series of interlocking service obligations. The focus of these is the town center, to which the members of the municipal *Alcaldía Indígena* and *cofradías* must travel to perform their service. The arrangement of the ritual buildings and the *barrios* in the town center reflect the arrangement of the *cantones* in Sacapulas, making the town center a microcosm of the service obligations that define the relationship of the *cantones* to one another.

Discussion

This brief description of the primacy of the *cantones* in the social, economic, and civil-religious structure of Sacapulas stands in sharp contrast to the accepted picture of highland Maya community organization. As Tax originally noted, even in communities where *cantón*-like units exist, their roles are not nearly as prominent (Tax 1937, 443). Compared with its apparently predominant role in many other communities, the *municipio* in Sacapulas seems a tenuous and even artificial collection of *cantones.* Integration within the *municipio* is only periodically achieved and demonstrated in the context of *cantón* cooperation for major *fiestas.* Otherwise, individual participation in *municipio* administration is structured by primary obligations to one's *cantón.* In fact, it is the *cantón* that appears to be the controlling social unit in Sacapulas, traditionally performing several functions normally associated with the *municipio. Cantones* are landholding units whose members occupy a delimited territory. They have their own civil-religious administration, including the *ax waab'* and *cofradía* personnel. Representatives to the *Alcaldía Indígena* are not selected at random from among the different *aldeas* and *caseríos,* but are instead chosen by the individual *cantones* to fulfill the groups' obligations at the *municipio* level. *Cantones* even define *oficios* in Sacapulas, only members of Santiago and San Sebastián being salt makers.

What accounts for the importance of *cantones* in Sacapulas? Is there some ecological factor that forces the permanent dispersal of a large portion of the population so that subunits within the *municipio* take on important functions? Are these perhaps recent trends as new economic possibilities and transportation facilities allow for changes in traditional allegiances of the *cantones* to the *municipio*? Are we simply seeing a variant on known ethnographic patterns for the area?

None of these possibilities appears to answer the basic question. Dispersion of the population is not at all unusual among the Maya; in fact, except for the towns around Lake Atitlan, dispersion seems to be the rule. Far from being a recent innovation, *cantón* primacy in the local organization is, according to older informants, the traditional pattern. If we are simply dealing with a variant of known ethnographic patterns, Sacapulas seems an extreme case. Even if so, this is not an explanation of *why* such variation occurs.

As we hope to demonstrate in the succeeding chapters, the traditional organization of Sacapulas—variant or not—can be understood only in historical terms. The seeming artificiality of the *municipio* and the attendant independence of the *cantones* can be accounted for only to a slight degree in functional, ecological, or economic terms in the present. Rather, Sacapulas is best explained and understood in terms of a long historical process that began before the Spanish conquest and extended through the people's experience in the succeeding colonial, republic, and modern periods. The proper questions to be asked are: What were *cantones* in earlier periods? Have they always had the same characteristics? Did they exist in pre-conquest times? How have they changed? Why have they continued down to the present? When the historical experience of the Sacapultecos is examined, we see that the foremost reason for their present organization has, through time, been a conscious effort to maintain continuity in those cultural principles that organize group formation, interaction, and utilization of the local environment. Or, put another way, to understand the contemporary organization of the Sacapultecos, we must first understand the pre-conquest Maya social units and the 450 years of adjustment to changing conditions they have achieved by maintaining continuity with their past.

Chinamit and *Molab*:

Precursors of the *Cantón*

This chapter explores the extent to which documentary evidence from the colonial period in Guatemala can be used to identify and characterize preconquest social units similar to the ethnographically described *cantones*.[1] Analysis focuses on a type of social unit called *chinamit* by the Quiché and Cakchiquel and *molab* by the Pokom.[2] Though differing in name, the documentary descriptions point to similar organization and functions of this unit for both linguistic groups, and further indicate the similarity of *chinamit* and *molab* to contemporary *cantones*. The emphasis here is on the reconstruction of aspects of preconquest social organization from postconquest sources.

The problem to be faced in this undertaking is familiar to many ethnohistorians studying non-Western and non- or semiliterate societies through documents produced by and for members of another society: that of extracting ethnographic information from documents not produced for that purpose, composed by individuals without anthropological training. In other words, we are attempting to reconstruct an aspect of one culture (the highland Maya) primarily through documents produced by members of another culture (Spanish). If that were not enough, in this chapter we are also faced with another problem: by definition, none of the Spaniards writing the documents were observers during the preconquest period for which the reconstruction is intended. In part, the problem of reconstruction is solved by historical and antiquarian interests on the part of some Spanish clerics and officials. The rest of the solution is provided by the fact that several of the important sources were composed in the early postconquest period, which gives us confidence that the behaviors and institutions reported on are still primarily indigenous.

For the purposes of this study it is useful to divide the documentary sources into the categories of general and specific, to reflect the significant differences in the referents of documents and their implications for the ethnohistorian. Documents in the general category typically refer to large geographical or administrative areas and the people who occupy them. In the case of highland Guatemala, such areas typically included many different communities, often with different linguistic affiliations. In cases where references to specific localities are not made, it is often difficult to establish which group or community an author based his descriptions on, even when details of the author's career and movements are known. In the specific category are documents that pertain to a particular community. In this case, the specific documents pertain to Sacapulas itself and these are discussed in Chapter 3. The distinction between general and specific sources in highland Maya ethnohistory is significant since the former have been known to scholars for years (though probably not to others, hence this discussion) and have been the basis for several attempts at preconquest cultural reconstruction and colonial history. Assuming most such general sources are indeed known to us, it becomes evident that the only way to refine our knowledge is through the investigation of local conditions at the community level through specific sources.[3]

The general sources themselves focus on Quiché-Cakchiquel and Pokom Maya linguistic groups. The latter includes both Pokomám and Pokomchí speakers (Miles, 1957, 736–38). The effort expended by the Spaniards in amassing the material reflects the political and territorial dominance of these linguistic groups at the time of the Spanish conquest, and their continuing preeminence in terms of population, tribute, and labor during succeeding periods. Therefore, institutions or cultural principles shared by the Quiché-Cakchiquel and Pokomám-Pokomchí may with some justification be said to have been general for the Late Postclassic highland Maya.

Dictionaries were the most numerous of the documents used. Invariably they were compiled by Spanish missionaries who had spent considerable time learning Maya languages. The dictionaries were in turn used to teach new missionary personnel on their arrival in the *Audiencia*. However, O'Flaherty has pointed out that the majority of the Spanish religious personnel never did master the Maya languages, despite the efforts of compilers and copyists (O'Flaherty 1979, 172). Dictionaries were subsequently copied and added to by later missionaries, sometimes giving credit to the original author. Thus, while the original may have been lost, in some cases a seventeenth- or eighteenth-century copy has survived. However, the usefulness of dictionaries for ethnohistorical research can be highly variable, depending, it would seem, mostly on the effort of the compiler or copyist to include descriptive definitions of the Maya terms as opposed to merely the approximate equivalents in Spanish.

The originals of the earliest dictionaries, compiled by Parra and Betanzos in the first half of the sixteenth century are lost to us (Carmack

1973, 116). Carmack, who has attempted to trace the history of the various highland Maya dictionaries, believes most of these two lost works are contained in the Varea dictionary (ibid., 116). Francisco Varea's *Calepino en lengua Cakchiquel* was probably composed early in the seventeenth century since he arrived in Guatemala in 1596 and remained until 1630 (ibid., 116). The copy used in the present research was made by Francisco Zeron in 1699 and is in the collection of the American Philosophical Society. It was donated along with other documents (including the Coto dictionary, see below) in 1836 by Guatemalan President Mariano Galvez, who received membership in the society in gratitude for his donation.

Also in the American Philosophical Society is Tomás Coto's *Vocabulario de la lengua Cakchiquel y Guatemalteca.* This work was compiled near the end of the seventeenth century, but drew upon fifty years of Coto's personal experiences and a sixteenth-century dictionary by Juan de Alonso (Coto, 120).

The *Calepino Grande Castellano y Quiché* is attributed to Juan de Alonso by Carmack (ibid., 119). Another candidate for authorship is Felix Solano. In either case the document in question would have been written in the second half of the sixteenth century (ibid., 119). The copy used in this research was made in the seventeenth or eighteenth century and is today part of the collections of the Newberry Library, from which a microfilm copy was obtained. Another presumed copy of the Alonso dictionary was made in Sacapulas in 1787 by Fermín José Tirado (ibid., 118). In the latter case the original entries were much shortened by the copyist. The copy of Tirado's *Vocabulario de la lengua Kiché* used in this research is a photocopy in the collection of the Museum Library of the University of Pennsylvania.

Perhaps the earliest of the dictionaries for the highland Maya area is Domingo de Vico's *Vocabulario de la lengua Cakchiquel y Quiché.* This work had to have been completed before 1555, the year of Vico's death (ibid., 114). The copy used in the present research was made in the seventeenth century and is part of the collections of the Newberry Library in Chicago, from which a photocopy was obtained.

Not mentioned by Carmack is Benito de Villacañas' *Arte y Vocabulario de la lengua Cakchiquel.* The exact date of its compilation is not known, though Villacañas himself died in 1610 at the age of seventy-three (Remesal 1966, 2:483). Villacañas arrived in the *Audiencia* shortly after taking his vows in Mexico in 1573. His first assignment was to the town of Sacapulas where, among other duties, he oversaw the construction of a masonry bridge over the Río Negro. This assignment in Sacapulas appears to have been short, however, as he is credited with spending most of his time with the Cakchiquel Maya of the Sacatepéquez area. The history of Villacañas' dictionary is confused. The original is apparently lost, but a copy of it was made in 1692. The linguist Karl H. Berendt copied this volume in New York in 1871 and the copy became part of the Brinton Collection in the University Museum at the University of Pennsylvania. A microfilm copy of Berendt's manuscript exists, but the original has been lost.

The final dictionary deals with the Pokom branch of the Maya languages as opposed to the very closely related Quiché and Cakchiquel. It was supposedly based on a now lost sixteenth-century dictionary compiled by Francisco de Viana who arrived in the Verapaz in 1556 shortly after its pacification (Carmack 1973, 120). The dictionary was compiled by Dionysius Zuñiga, a student of Viana, who arrived in the Verapaz in 1597 and began copying his master's work after the latter's death in 1608 (ibid., 120–21). Berendt obtained the remaining parts of Zuñiga's *Diccionario Pocomchí-Castellano y Castellano Pocomchí de San Cristóbal Cahcoh* at San Cristobal in 1875 and this subsequently became part of the holdings of the University of Pennsylvania, where a photocopy was studied for this research. Much of the ethnographic data in this dictionary was assembled by Miles for her innovative study of Pokom-Maya in the sixteenth century (Miles, 1957).

A final linguistic document is Francisco Maldonado's seventeenth-century *Ramillete manual para los indios sobre la doctrina cristiana* (Carrasco 1963). This guide to Catholic doctrine was written in Cakchiquel for the use of priests in explaining the complexities of the Spaniards' religion to the Indians in their own tongue. It is valuable in that native practices are sometimes described in order to compare them with usages permitted by the church.

Relaciones are descriptions written by Spanish officials and, on occasion, by friars. They usually describe a specific area in some detail. Some mention was usually made of the Indian population, and, depending on the interests and intellectual curiosity of the reporter, much valuable information on native culture may be presented. Captain Martín Alfonso Tovilla's *Relación histórica descriptiva de las provincias de la Verapaz y de la del Manché,* written in 1635, is based primarily on information gathered during the five years he spent touring the area in his capacity as *Alcalde Mayor.* The manuscript was apparently used by Fuentes y Guzmán (see below) for parts of his history before it finally came to rest in the public library of Toledo, Spain (Carmack 1973, 182). The version used in this research was prepared by Scholes and Adams and published in Guatemala (Tovilla [1635] 1960). Although written considerably after the conquest, it must be remembered that the Verapaz did not come completely under Spanish rule until 1547 and even then the inhabitants were not subdued by force as in the case of most other highland Maya, but were peacefully subdued by Spanish missionaries, notably Bartolomé de Las Casas (King 1974, 21). In exchange for pacifying the Verapaz, the Dominicans were given control over the area and Spanish colonists were kept out. In this way the disruptive influences of the *encomienda* system and slavery were avoided, and the potential existed for native culture to continue with fewer changes than in other areas.

Five colonial histories contain evidence pertaining to the present research. Fr. Bartolomé de Las Casas' *Apologética Historia de las Indias* is a monumental work dealing with the entire then-known New World (Las Casas [c. 1550] 1909). Thirteen chapters are given over to a description of the highland Maya based largely on Las Casas' own experience among them from 1539 to 1544. His work is important as he was familiar with both major highland linguistic groups, the Quiché-Cakchiquel and the Pokom (Carmack 1973, 101–2).

Another colonial history containing both general and specific references was written by a noncleric, Guatemalan-born Francisco Antonio de Fuentes y Guzmán. His *Recordación Flórida* was finished in 1690, more than 150 years after the conquest. However, Fuentes y Guzmán, as an official of the *Audiencia,* had access to its archives. He was thus in a unique position to chronicle the history of the *Audiencia* as seen and reported by secular officials. Dominican Fr. Francisco Ximenez, writing only a few years later in his *Historia de la Provincia de San Vincente de Chiapa y Guatemala,* takes considerable trouble to point out many inaccuracies of Fuentes y Guzmán's account. Ximenez does not, however, take issue with statements on the condition of the Maya in preconquest times, a subject with which Ximenez may be said to have been familiar.

Ximenez' *Historia* was written some time before his death in 1729–30 (Ximenez [c. 1729] 1929–31; Carmack 1973, 189). Arriving in Guatemala in 1688, his experience included ten years in Rabinal, four years in Sacapulas, and three years in Chichicastenango where he rediscovered, copied, and translated the *Popol Vuh* (Carmack 1973, 189; Recinos 1953, 37–55). Most of the first volume of Ximenez' history is given over to a description of the preconquest highland Maya and their history, and the subsequent Spanish conquest. Although writing nearly two hundred years after the events, Ximenez did have most of the earlier works to refer to and many other documents (Carmack 1973, 190). More important, Ximenez spoke Quiché fluently for the purposes of preaching. He was thus able to penetrate the native culture to some extent, something only he appears to have done during the colonial period.

A century earlier another Dominican, Fr. Antonio de Remesal, wrote a history of his order's activities entitled *Historia General de las Indias Occidentales y Particular de la Gobernación de Chiapa y Guatemala* (Remesal [1615–17] 1964–66). Based on documentary records rather than firsthand experience, Remesal's work includes the now-famous account of Bartolomé de Las Casas' peaceful conquest of the Verapaz, in which a Sacapulas *cacique* (native political leader) figured prominently. In his preliminary study of Remesal's work, Saenz noted a number of discrepancies in this account, particularly the important place given to Sacapulas, where the source used by Remesal was supposedly written (Saenz 1964, 33–34, 50–54). Carmack has proposed that Don Juan, the *cacique's* name after baptism, was not from Sacapulas at all but rather from the area of Rabinal farther to the east (Carmack 1973, 179).

A history of Franciscan missionary activities in Guatemala was written by Francisco Vázquez. His *Crónica de la Provincia del Santísimo Nombre de Jesus de Guatemala* was the product of work beginning in 1683 and continuing until his death in 1713–14 (Lamadrid in Vázquez [1714–17] 1937, 1:x-xiv). Like Remesal's, Vázquez' work is based on documentary sources. He does, however, recount the early missionary work by Méndez and Betanzos in the Sacapulas area.

Finally, there is Thomas Gage's ([1648] 1929) unique *A New Survey of the West Indies, 1648: The English American.* Gage was one of very few non-Spaniards to penetrate the interior of New Spain during the earlier part of the colonial period. He wrote his survey on his return to England, for English readers. It is thus not properly a *relación,* but more of a personal, polemical kind of memoir with political and religious overtones. The document does, however, contain some useful references to the condition of the highland Maya during the 1630s.

The Evidence

Even the most cursory examination of the major native chronicles, such as the *Popol Vuh* and the *Annals of the Cakchiquels,* cannot fail to demonstrate the importance, if not primacy, of a unit called *chinamit* in the social and political organization of the Late Postclassic highland Maya (Edmonson 1971, Villacorta 1934). Since these chronicles were concerned with dynastic fortunes, however, the reader gains only glimpses of the organization and function of this unit, and only at the highest political level.

The importance of the *chinamit* was realized by the Spanish friars, particularly by those involved in compiling Quiché and Cakchiquel-Spanish dictionaries. Relatively large amounts of space were devoted to describing and presenting analogies and, in this way, to understanding the *chinamit*. As will be demonstrated, however, the individual Spanish friars never managed to grasp the principles behind the *chinamit* or its role in the organization of highland Maya society. The dictionary data are the basic source of information about the *chinamit*, though, and do allow interpretation as to its function and organization. Analysis must, therefore, begin with examination of this material. Definitions and descriptions from the Maya-Spanish dictionaries are presented below.[4]

CHINAMIT. Linage, apellido, o tribu (Vico, 64)

NU CHINAMITAL, a chinamital. Apellidos de linage, tienen infinitos, y son nombres de ríos, de signos en que nascero; suele ser comunes; de mi parcialidad (Coto [c. 1690], 32) [Surnames of lineage, of which they have an infinity, and these are names of rivers, of signs under which one was born; they are common, of my group]

NU CHINAMITAL. Casta, linage (ibid., 77)

CHINAMITAL. Generación, linage, familia (ibid., 201)

CHINAMITAL. Linage; parcialidad, o los que son de un mismo apellido y así para deslindar entre ellos sus parentescos, y linages es menester mucho y saver mucha lengua, por la equivocación que tienen en tratarse como parientes, o, con los nombres de que usan en sus parentescos (ibid., 258) ["Lineage"; "group," or those of the same surname; and thus in order to delineate among the Indians their relatives and "lineages" it is necessary to know much about their language, due to the mistakes they make in treating each other as relatives or in using kinship terms]

   También usan del nombre chinamit por las parcialidades calpules, que ellos tienen entre si . . . cada parcialidad esta de por si junta y distinta de las otras . . . (ibid., 324, under entry for parcialidad) [They also use the term *chinamit* for their *parcialidades, calpules* which they have among themselves . . . each group by itself and distinct from the others]

CHINAMITAL. Linage (*Calepino Grande Castellano-Quiché,* 294)

CHINAMITAL. Generación como linage (ibid., 246)

CHINAMIT. Casta, linage (ibid., 94)

CHINAMITAL. Abolorio (ibid., 3)

CHINAMITAL. Apellido de linage (ibid., 33)

CHINAMITAL BI. Renombre de linage (ibid., 391)

The references to "calpules" (Nahuatl *calpulli*) and *parcialidad* in defining *chinamit* are significant as the same analogies are made for the neighboring Pokom-Maya (Pokomám, Pokomchí).

QUIAB. Es apellido de linage y calpul en San Cristóbal (Cahcoh) (Zuñiga [c. 1610], 467) [A "lineage" surname and *calpul* in San Cristóbal Cahcoh]

BACAH. Es nombre do un sitio antiguo donde estuvieron los de una parcialidad de pueblo de San Filipe que está poblado en San Cristóbal y de allí tienen el apellido fulano bacah. Ah bacah los del barrio de bacah, los de bacah (ibid., 27) [The name of an ancient place where the San Filipe *parcialidad* of this town of San Cristóbal used to live. And from that place they have their surname, someone Bacah, the ah Bacah, those of the *barrio* de Bacah, those of Bacah]

The Pokom term for this *"linage"* was *molab*.

LINAGE, PARENTELA PROPIA. Molab, mobabil (ibid., 290)

Mi venerable padre fray Francisco de Viana lo dige con Molab (que dice tribu, parentela) . . . (ibid., 229) [My venerable Father Fray Francisco de Viana used *Molab* for "tribe," "kindred"]

IGLESIA, CONGREGACIÓN. Molab (ibid., 272)

Descent: A Non-Principle

The Spaniards apparently believed the *chinamit-molab* unit to be a kin group based on a descent principle. Their use of terms such as *linage, casta, parentela,* and *abolorio* indicate this. By the late sixteenth to early seventeenth centuries these terms were bound up in the idea of descent, especially as it applied to the great families of Spain.

LINAGE. La decendencia de las casas y familias. Díxose a linea porque van decendiendo de padres, hijos y nietos, etc. como por linea rect. (Cobarruvias [1610] 1977, 768) [The descent of houses and families. One says line (of descent) because they descend from fathers to sons to grandsons, as in a straight line]

CASTA. Vale linage noble y castizo, el que es de buena linea y decendencia, no embargante que dezimos es buena casta y mala casta. Castizos llamamos a los que son de buen linage y casta (ibid., 316) [Means a noble line of descent and *castizo* means one who is of a good line and descent]

PARENTELA. Los parientes de un linage (ibid., 854) [The relatives within a line of descent]

ABOLENGO Y ABOLORIO. La ascendencia de aguelos y bisaguelos, etc. (ibid., 29) [The ancestry of grandfathers and great grandfathers, and so on]

Perhaps the misunderstanding of descent as the principle behind the *chinamit-molab* was engendered by the use of the same surname, or *apellido,* by members of the group. For the Spaniards the idea of *apellido* was

associated with the concepts of great families and descent. Under the entry
for *apellidor:*

> Y assi los del apellido se juntan y llegan a su parcialidad y de aqui los nombres
> de las casas principales se llamavan apellidos, porque los demas se allegavan a
> ellas, . . . (ibid., 130) [And thus those of the same surname come together and
> become a *parcialidad* and from this the names of the principle houses are called
> surnames, because the rest collected themselves together to them]

Evidence suggests that agnatic descent may have been of some importance at the highest level of Maya society with regard to succession of
power and inheritance (see below). Other data, however, suggest that
principles other than descent or kinship were at work. Under the entry for
hani:

> Es de mi chinamital aunque no somos parientes (Calepino *Grande Castellano-
> Quiché,* 94) [He is of my *chinamital* although we are not relatives]

Under the entry for *chinamit:*

> linage y gente debajo un apellido y de un casique: aunque recogen a cualquier
> se quiera llegar a este linage y hermandad de hente (ibid., 77) [Line of descent
> and people beneath one surname and one ruler; although they collect anyone
> who wants to become part of this line of descent and brotherhood of people]

Several interpretations of this evidence are possible. The last quotation,
however, suggests a particular kind of organization. It seems likely that
the significant criterion of *chinamit* membership was to be subject to and
take the surname of a leader called *cacique* by the Spaniards. A core family
or lineage (in the anthropological sense) of higher status is suggested, out
of whose number came the *cacique.*

> ATZ CH'AME. Este es el nombre de cabeza de *chinamital* como atz pop, atz qalel
> y otros, . . . (Coto [c. 1690], 30) [This is the name of a head of a *chinamital,*
> as are atz pop, atz qalel and others]
>
> ATZ K'AHOL. Los que son cabezas de *chinamitales* o calpules (ibid., 132) [Those
> who are heads of *chinamitales* or *calpules*]
>
> AH CHINAMITAL. Señor de vasallos (ibid., 433) [A lord over vassals]
>
> ATZ OHINAK. Cargo de cacique de cierto *chinamital* (Calepino *Grande Caste-
> llano-Quiché,* 18) [The position of *cacique* of a *chinamital*]
>
> MAMA. Los casiques y cabezas de los calpules (ibid., 173) [The *caciques* and heads
> of *calpules*] (Also the word for grandfather, perhaps a term of address rather
> than a title)

NIMA VINAK. Cazique, cabeza de qualquier chinam[ital] (ibid., 217) [*Cacique,* head of whatever *chinamital*]

A similar internal organization is suggested by Pokom terms for the head of the *molab.*

MOLABIL. La cabeza de tal calpul o tribu (molab) (Zuñiga [c. 1610], 4) [The head of a *calpul* or "tribe"]

POP CAM HA. Dize hombre constituido e dignidad, cabeza de calpul, principal y en éste sentido nunca dizen solo el pop in pop sino como otro cam ha, in pop cam ha. 'soy principal, soy hidalgo, soy cabeza de calpul, de molab' (ibid., 457) [Means an established and dignified man, head of a *calpul*, a leading man and in this sense they never say only *pop*—I am *pop*—but only with *cam ha*, I am *pop cam ha* "I am a leading man, a noble, the head of a *calpul*, of a *molab*"]

The other members of the *chinamit-molab* would have been of lesser status and not necessarily related to the core family. Membership at this level was evidently expressed by adopting the surname of the *cacique,* acknowledging his authority, and by residence in the area under his control. The status of *cacique* endured as an officially recognized institution well into the colonial period. *Caciques* were distinguished by the addition of the Spanish honorific *don* to their names. As we shall see, *caciques* were present among Sacapulas *chinamitales* through the 1570s, and the presence of a *cacique* may have been important in defining a group as a *chinamit.* In Sacapulas and elsewhere *caciques* continued to play a significant role in local politics by taking over the offices of *alcalde* and *regidor* introduced by the Spaniards (Collins 1980, 224, 235).

Political Hierarchy

Some evidence of internal *chinamit* political hierarchy is offered by the Quiché term for *principales, ru camahay (Calepino Grande Castellano-Quiché,* 359). Not all the functions of these individuals are known. However, they appear to have acted as a body and elected or selected other minor officials of the *chinamit,* such as messengers:

TAKOM CAMAHEL, YA OL TZITZ, NU K'ULTZITZ NAOVINAK ACHI. Mandadero, mensajero, recaudero lo eligen los principales cada año, cada chinamital lo suyo; para que lleven los recaudos, ordenes a los otros chinamitales . . . (Coto [c. 1690], 273) [Errand runner, messenger, tax collector. He is elected by the *principales* each year, each *chinamital* its own: in order that they carry the taxes and orders to the other *chinamitales*]

There is no suggestion of the *"principales"* having a ceremonial as well as political rule. Today the two are intimately associated (Tax and Hinshaw 1969, 89).

The core family or lineage may well have been the group on which the Spaniards focused their observations, given their predilection for using elite sources and informants elsewhere in Mesoamerica. When Las Casas and others discuss *chinamit* exogamy, they are probably basing their statements on the actions of this leading family and assuming the rest of the group acted similarly. It will be argued later that such was not the case and that perhaps, aside from the leading family, the *chinamit* was an endogamous unit.

The *chinamit* and *molab,* then, appear to share the same basic characteristics. Affiliation was recognized through the use of a common surname by members of the group. The group was localized in terms of settlement. Both groups were led or governed by a single individual who had a body of assistants at his disposal.

Ceremonial Unit

The extent to which the *chinamit-molab* was a ceremonial unit, in addition to its functions as a political and territorial unit, is difficult to assess. This should not be surprising, however, as the major interest the Spanish friars had in native Maya religion was in its eradication. Nevertheless, a few Maya-Spanish dictionary entries are suggestive:

> MOC. Parcialidad, junta, congregación, cofradía (Coto, 324)
> MOC. La parcialidad de cualquier casique (Varea [1699], 187)
> MOLAB. Inglesia, congregación (Zuñiga [c. 1610], 272)

The apparent equivalence of *parcialidad* with *cofradía* (a type of religious sodality supposedly introduced in the colonial period; see Reina 1966, 97–165), and of *molab* as *iglesia* and *congregación* in addition to its other meanings is the only specific evidence of ceremonial functions for the *chinamit-molab.*

Corporateness: Social Responsibility

In terms of corporate responsibility for members' actions we find descriptions of the Quiché-Cakchiquel and Pokom term *nut*. According to the *Calepino en lengua Cakchiquel* (Varea [1699]), this was the cacao asked for from each house or family of a *chinamit*. Each family gave ten or twenty cacao beans upon the marriage of one of their number, or for the costs of litigation, or for one who was in jail.

> NUT. El cacao que se pide en cada casa de un chinamital, dan diez o viente cada casa cuando se casa uno de ellos o para su pleyto o está uno en cárcel (Varea [1699], 223)

Coto agrees, saying it consisted of collecting cacao from house to house among the *chinamitales*. Ten or twenty cacao seeds were collected from each house to help with someone's marriage, or to get him out of jail.

> NUT. recoger de casa en casa los chinamitales cacao. Diez o veinte cacaos de cada casa para ayudar a casar alguno, sacando de la carcel . . . este nombre *nut* significa esta junta asi, recogimiento de cacao (Coto [c. 1690], 390)

The same term and behavior were found among the Pokom. According to Zuñiga it consisted of the contribution for that which was necessary. Usually or properly it was the contribution made by the relatives and the *molab* to one of their number who married. This was to defray the cost of the celebration, and each person gave a small amount in coin or cacao. In a wider sense *nut* was used to denote the contribution for another purpose such as each family contributing a *real* (a Spanish coin) for some work for the whole group.

> NUT. La contribución para aquello que es menester para lo que se pide y se da . . . comunmente o propiamente se dize de la contribución que dan los parientes y el molab del que se casa de los suyos para festejar el casamiento, que cada uno da un tanto, o tomín, o cacao y largo modo se dize por la derrama o contribución para otra cosa diferente como si por el pueblo se echase un real cada casa para tal o tal obra común (Zuñiga [c. 1610], 438)

An additional point of considerable importance is Zuñiga's distinction between the relatives (*parientes*) and fellow *molab* members. This distinction reinforces the earlier assertion that the *molab* (and by extension the *chinamit*) was not based on kinship or descent.

Further evidence of corporate responsibility for fellow members' actions in *chinamit-molab* groups comes from Fuentes y Guzmán. Writing about the preconquest laws of the Quiché in the *Recordación Flórida,* he discussed the penalties for various crimes (Fuentes y Guzmán [1690]1932–33, 1:12–13). The punishment for an individual caught stealing three times was death. However, if he was of a rich family and the *calpul* (*chinamit*) to which he belonged "bought" him, and also paid for all the things he had stolen and gave another amount for the treasury of the king, he would remain free.

> pasando a tercer latrocinio, recaía en pena de muerte. Pero si era de familia rica y le compraba el calpul a donde pertenecía, pagando por el todos los hurtos que le probaban y en otra cantidad para el Erario y desposito del Rey, quedaba libre . . . (ibid., 1:12).

This responsibility extended to undesirable actions in the field of religion. Fuentes y Guzmán writes that the stealing of sacred articles, the profanation of temples, or disrespect shown to a native priest were severely punished. The perpetrator and his family were thrown into infamy and perpetual slavery. In case of another such infraction, the entire *calpul* (*chinamit*) passed into slavery. A third offense resulted in the individual's death.

> Y así, el hurto de las casas sagradas, profanción de los ministros o *Papaces* de los ídolos, se castigaba con dura mano, despeñando al reo, y todos los de su familia quedaban en linea de infames y en esclavitud perpetua . . . y por la reincidencia pasaba la esclavitud a comprehender a toto el calpul que es un linaje, y a la tercera vez moría despeñado. (ibid., 1:13)

Finally, Fuentes y Guzmán tells us that members of the *chinamit* were responsible for their fellows' actions with regard to the relationship with the rulers. He states that in the case of an individual absenting himself from the domain of his lord, his *calpul* (*chinamit*) paid to the lord a quantity of cotton cloth. A second occurrence carried the death penalty for the individual. He goes on to say this law provided that everyone was always subservient and obedient.

> El que se huía, y ausentaba del dominio o señorío de su dueño, pagaba su calpul por el, cierta cantidad de mantas, y reincidiendo en la culpa era condenado a muerte de horca, procurando siempre que todos estuviesen sujetos y obedientes. (ibid., 1:13)

Evidence of corporate responsibility for social control by the Pokom *molab* comes from Gage who was the priest of Mixco in the 1630s. Although a century had elapsed since the conquest, the Pokomám Indians had retained most of their native ways, including their religion, which Gage was continually at pains to eliminate. This endurance must be ascribed to the fact that very few Spaniards lived in the Valley of Guatemala at this time. The capital of the *Audiencia* and only major center of Spanish colonists was at Santiago de los Caballeros de Guatemala, present-day Antigua, some twenty miles away in the Almolonga Valley. As Gage states:

> Among themselves, if any Complaint be made against any Indian, they dare not meddle with him till they call all his kindred, and especially the head of the Tribe (*molabil*) to which he belongs; who if he and the rest (of the molab) together find him to deserve imprisonment, or whipping, or any other Punishment, then the Officers of Justice, the *Alcaldes* or *Mayores,* and their brethren the jurates inflict upon him the punishment which all agree upon. (Gage, [1648] 1929, 246)

Community Specialization

The practice of a common specialization (*oficio*) is an important aspect of contemporary highland Maya closed corporate communities. Although limited to two references, evidence for such *oficios* in preconquest times is firm and specific. For the Pokom we find a statement by Zuñiga concerning the meaning of the word *xoy.*

According to Zuñiga, *xoy* meant to polish. In the form *xoyemah* it meant to polish stones, or lapidary work. By placing the prefix *ah* the term for lapidary was formed. The plural form *ahxoyib* was the name of those belonging to the *calpul* and *parcialidad* (*molab*) of a place called *Xoy* on the Río Chixoy. Before the conquest these people had the *oficio* of lapidaries. Zuñiga goes on to say that he did not deduce this on his own but that he found it out from old and learned Indians of San Cristóbal where members of the *xoyib* still lived. His use of *calpul* and *parcialidad* indicate Zuñiga was referring to a *molab.*

> XOYEMAH. Significa el verbo esmaltar de diversas colores como el lapidario jaspea y esmalta una piedra y el escultor la escultura de diversas colores, xoy que dize esmalta o jaspa y anteponiéndose ah, ahxoy, dize el esmaltador el oficial de esmaltar, y ahxoyib el plural y así se llaman los del calpul y parcialidad de aquel sitio del río dicho Zacapula [the Río Chixoy] que en su antiguedad tenían éste oficio de esmaltar, no es pensamiento mío a que ésto sino sabido de los indios viejos y ladinos de este pueblo de San Cristóbal donde hay y está calpul y parcialidad de los xoyib (Zuñiga, [c. 1610], 502)

> XOYABAH. Y pienso que por la misma razón [the presence of polished stones probably serpentine or jade] llaman xoy al sitio del paso del río grande que viene de Zacapula [Sacapulas] que oiras muchas veces decir chixoy en el río xoy. y no es nombre de río que Tuhalha [Sacapulas] le llaman al río de

> Zacapula. y a los de tal sitio llaman ahxoyib. devían de esmaltar piedras los
> de aquel lugar (ibid., 502)

Evidence for a common specialization among members of a given
chinamit comes from Sacapulas itself. Tovilla, the *Alcalde Mayor* of the
Verapaz in the 1630s, described the process of salt making in the town.
This was something in which he had both interest and experience, having
been administrator of saltworks in Murcia in his native Spain (Tovilla
[1635] 1960, 218). He went on to report on the organization of the town
and its salt industry. He said that the town of Sacapulas was divided into
six *parcialidades,* and that in each there was a head called *calpul.* The presence of the six groups resulted from the friars bringing together a like
number of small settlements to make a larger one (*congregación*). Each
parcialidad (*chinamit*) retained the name of the settlement from which it
came. It also retained the land in which it made its *milpas.* The *parcialidad*
of Sacapulas was the foremost of the town, its members being indigenous
to the place and at one time masters of it. This *parcialidad* had the salt flats
and exploited them without allowing any of the others to do so.

> Está éste pueblo de Sacapulas dividido en seis parcialidades, y en cada una de
> ellas hay una cabeza a que llaman calpul, porque cuando los padres [friars] los
> juntaron, como ellos tenían pequeñas poblaciones, traían cuatro o cinco a cada
> pueblo que hacían para que fuese grande, y así cada parcialidad se quedo con el
> nombre del pueblo de donde vinieron. Y las tierras que tenían por suyas las
> gozan hoy y las gozaran para hacer sus milpas y demas menesteres. La parciali-
> dad de Sacapulas como la mas principal de éste pueblo, que son naturales y
> señores de el, tiene éstas salinas y las goza sin que los demás vecinos pueden
> labrar sal. (Tovilla [1635] 1960, 18)

This important passage tells us several things. Each *chinamit* was a
residential unit (which has already been demonstrated). It held land as a
unit. It held specific natural resources as a unit (salt flats). Its members
had exclusive rights to exploit these resources which they all seem to have
done.

Chinamit–Molab Endogamy

The question of endogamy versus exogamy among *chinamit-molab* groups
is perhaps the most difficult to resolve, for a number of reasons. Principal
among these is the Spaniards' failure to fully understand the *chinamit-
molab* in the first place. Other important problems include demographic

changes and the level of society that chroniclers studied in order to learn marriage customs.

Starting again from the dictionaries, the evidence is consistently for an interpretation of *chinamit* exogamy:

> No acostumbran casarse los de un mismo *chinamital* sino raras veces; . . . (Coto [c. 1690], 201) [Those of the same *chinamital* do not customarily marry each other, except on rare occasions]
>
> Dicen a los que se quieren casar 'sois de diversos linages' y esto se pide por que se conserve su orden de vivir (Varea [1699], 77) [They say to those who want to marry "you are of different lineages" and this they do in order to pre-serve their way of life]

Las Casas discusses marriage customs for the highland Maya gener-ally and states that they have the following customs. The first is that on no account would they intermarry with those of their "tribe," "family," or "kin" in the way they undertsood these relationships. They did not count as members of their family or their kin the children of the "adjacent tribe" or *linage,* even if the mother originally came from their own group. Las Casas goes on to say that kinship was attributed to or traced only through men. In this way, if a *señor* gave his daughter in marriage to a *señor* or individual of another town, the children of that daughter, by being in another *pueblo* and being children of it, would have no part in his inheri-tance, even though the *señor* may have no one else to inherit from him. In a subsequent passage, Las Casas confuses the issue by stating that if a *señor* or the son of a *señor* was to marry, he usually looked for a woman from another town. In this way, he says, they established kinship between the towns, and this was a cause of their living in peace.

> Cuanto a los casamientos y matrimonios tenían los usos y costumbres sig-uientes; la primera es que por ningún caso ni necesidad se casaban con los de su tribu, o familia, o parentesco, a su parecer contado, porque no contaban por de su familia, o parentesco los hijos que nacían en el tribu o linage ageno, aunque la muger fuese de su linage o tribu . . . aquel tal parentesco se atribuía a solo hombres, por manera que si algun señor daba su hija casándola con el señor o persona de otro pueblo, aunque no tuviese otro heredero alguno, sino los hijos de aquella hija, por estar en otro pueblo y ser hijos de aquel no tenían parte alguna en tal herencia.
>
> Si era señor o hijo de senor el que se casaba, comunmente le buscaban muger de otro pueblo y asi se contraría parentesco entre los pueblos y era causa de vivir siempre muy pacíficos. (Las Casas [c. 1550], 1909, 624)

Although Las Casas described preconquest marriage customs gener-ally, his constant use of the term *señor* (in the sense of ruler) versus *persona* (a commoner), leads one to believe that he based his description on marriages practiced by the *señores* or rulers. He apparently accepted this as being the case for commoners as well. Las Casas would appear to have been following the common practice of early Spanish students of Mesoamerican Indian culture, that of using nobles and other elite-status individuals as informants.[5] While there is little doubt this was the case for the ruling class (the *Popul Vuh* contains many examples), it need not follow that the same applied to commoners.

The crucial reference with regard to preconquest marriage customs is in the seventeenth-century *Ramillete manual para los indios sobre la doctrina cristiana* by Fr. Francisco Maldonado (Carrasco 1963). In it, among other things, Maldonado discusses the marriages permitted by the Church, usages of the Cakchiquel Indians in the seventeenth century, and customs they practiced "anciently" (in preconquest times). The key passage exhorts that it is proper that people marry within their *chinamit*. It is not a sin and there is no clerical impediment against it. Maldonado goes so far as to say that it is good that one marries a girl or boy from one's *chinamit*. There evidently was a previous church ban on marriage within the *chinamit*, probably based on the Spaniards' misunderstanding of it. This is suggested by Maldonado's statement that it is no longer a sin but that the Indians were deceived before this latest word of God came. His final phrase seems an exhortation to return to the preconquest custom of marrying within the *chinamit*.

> Es justo que os caséis dentro de vuestro clan [chinamit]. No es pecado, no hay impedimento para que os caséis dentro. Bién te casas con la hija de tus parientes clanicos o el hijo de tus parientes clanicos. Ya no es pecado ésto porque estabáis engañados antes que viniera la palabra de Diós. *Como entonces haciáis antiguamente cada uno de su clan eran vuestros casados.* (Carrasco 1963, 194) [Carrasco's translation from Cakchiquel to Spanish; emphasis added]

Here then is the evidence for *chinamit* endogamy. Maldonado's use of the perfect tense, and specific mention of what the custom was "*antiguamente*," stand in marked contrast to all the dictionary entries made in the present tense. Las Casas was probably correct about the customs of the elite members of society, but Maldonado was writing for a general audience and used the example of preconquest customs to make his point.

Summary

The data collected from the various ethnohistorical documents point to the *chinamit-molab* unit as a Late Postclassic Maya counterpart of the ethnographically known *cantones.*[6] It has been demonstrated that the *chinamit-molab* was a social unit, the members of which lived together in a settlement or defined area *vis à vis* other such groups. Members of the *chinamit-molab* had a corporate or group identity expressed through common ownership of land and other resources, and the recognition of group responsibility for individual members' actions. Responsibility extended from helping to defray the cost of marriage festivities, through secular crimes (thievery, desertion of one's lord), to religious offenses. Most members of the *chinamit-molab* practiced a common specialization or *oficio.* The existence of such a common specialization indicates the existence of community culture. Except perhaps for its core family, the *chinamit-molab* was an endogamous unit. Finally, there is evidence of an internal political hierarchy centered on an aristocratic core family, and of the *chinamit-molab* as a religious or ceremonial unit. However, it is not possible at this time to demonstrate the interrelationship between political and religious organization.

Students of ancient Mesoamerican cultures will by now have recognized similarities between the characterization of the *chinamit-molab* presented here and the current interpretations of the Aztec *calpulli* (most recently summarized by Carrasco 1971, and Berdan 1982). In fact, the term *chinamit* is itself a Mayanized Nahuatl term—*chinamitl*—which was used interchangeably with *calpulli* in some parts of central Mexico (Carrasco 1971, 364). Therefore, the resemblances between Maya *chinamit-molab* and Aztec *calpulli* are probably not just superficial, but reflect a widespread principle of preconquest Mesoamerican organization with some local and regional variations.

Both Berdan and Carrasco agree that the *calpulli* was basically a territorial unit and not kin-based. At the same time, Berdan feels that the *calpulli* "tended toward endogamy" (Berdan 1982, 68). There may also have been some relationship between *calpulli* and craft specialization, and each *calpulli* maintained its own temple. The *calpulli* also functioned as a unit for the purposes of regional political administration, with tribute as well as labor and military drafts organized according to these units.

One of the *calpulli's* primary functions was to act as a landholding unit, through which members acquired rights to agricultural land. These rights could be inherited, but a failure to cultivate the land or an absence of heirs resulted in the land reverting back to the *calpulli* for reassignment by its leadership. In areas away from the urban centers of the Valley of Mexico, the redistribution of land may have been a regular event (ibid., 57–58). In any case, an individual "would not customarily sell or otherwise alienate the plot he worked" (ibid., 56). However, land could be "rented" to members of other groups, with the proceeds being used to meet *calpulli* expenditures. It seems possible that similar practices of land distribution existed among the highland Maya (see Chapter 8).

Keeping track of land allocation was the primary responsibility of the *calpulli* leadership. The headman or *calpullec* was selected to his post, though "it was considered preferable for the position to stay in the same family over generations" (ibid., 57). Although commoners might hold the post, it was probably more common for a member of the nobility (*tecutli*) to lead the *calpulli* with the aid of a group of elders.

These similarities between the Aztec *calpulli* and their Maya counterparts were not lost on the Spaniards who frequently used the term *calpules* (along with *parcialidades*) to refer to the *chinamit-molab* groups. By the early nineteenth century, *calpul* was even used interchangeably with *chinamit* in at least one of the Quiché chronicles, the Título Tamub (Recinos 1957, 54–60). As we shall see in Chapter 9, the term *calpul* was still used by *ladino* officials in the 1880s to refer to the groups of the Sacapulas area.

The characterizations of *chinamit* and *molab* as preconquest precursors of *cantones* has been made through the use of a wide variety of sources. This has been necessary since it was only by marshaling all available data that an accurate composite description could be compiled. Assuming the interpretation of *chinamit* and *molab* is essentially correct, a number of questions immediately arise. What happened to such groups as a result of the Spanish conquest and subsequent centuries of colonial administration? Are these groups demonstrably precursors of *cantones*? If so, how is it that in some places *chinamitales* appear to have endured down to the present? To answer these questions we must look initially at a specific case and try to trace developments through time. In the process, it will also be possible to determine why the *chinamit-cantón* principle has continued to such an extent in Sacapulas.

Parcialidades, Population, and Processes in

Sacapulas: A Historical Overview

This chapter provides an overview of the careers of the *chinamitales,* or *parcialidades* as they were most commonly called during the colonial period, in Sacapulas as a background for more detailed treatment in succeeding chapters.

For the study of Sacapulas itself, the major sources fall in the specific category and consist of litigation records preserved in the Archivo General de Centro America (AGCA) in Guatemala City. On a volume basis, the litigation records make up more than one-half the total corpus of documents relating to Sacapulas. The litigation proceedings were disputes between component *parcialidades* of Sacapulas, or between a Sacapulas *parcialidad* and an adjacent community. The arguments were always over land; other complaints were sometimes included.

Since many of us are ignorant of legal procedures even in our own society, it may be useful to sketch here the typical steps followed in land dispute cases of the colonial era. Litigation started with a complaint presented by the local community, or one of its component groups, to the *Alcalde Mayor.* This official was responsible for the administration of a province (provinces were rather larger than present-day departments). In the earlier part of the colonial period the *Alcalde Mayor* often responded to complaints on his own initiative, naming *procuradores* (legal counselors) for the Indians, and referring his decision to the *Audiencia* only for confirmation. Later, especially in disputes over land, he would send the complaint on to the *Audiencia* in the capital. As a land dispute, the complaint would fall under the jurisdiction of the *Juez Privativo del Real Derecho de Tierras.* Since this judge usually lacked any information at this point, aside from the complaint itself, a request would be made for an investigation into the particulars of the case at the local level as the basis for a decision. Orders would accordingly be drawn up to that effect and sent to the *Alcalde Mayor.* He might conduct the inquiry himself or delegate the task to others, the *Subdelegado* or *Comisionado.*

The local investigation usually included complaints and counter-denunciations by the parties involved. Mutual intelligibility was ensured through the use of interpreters throughout the colonial period. A record of statements made was kept by a secretary. In addition to the complaints, testimony could be solicited and documents presented in an attempt to support the claims of one side or the other. Land disputes usually involved a *vista de ojos,* or personal inspection, by the presiding official. Sometimes formal surveys were also carried out. Based on his visit, the *Alcalde Mayor* or his assistant would write a summary report of the situation and give his assessment. The report and all other documents would then be sent back to the *Audiencia.*

If the information thus provided was sufficient, the *Juez Privativo* might make his decision. In this case, the matter was referred to the *Fiscal* (roughly equivalent to an attorney general). A positive statement by this official usually resulted in confirmation by the *Audiencia.* However, sometimes the information provided by the *Alcalde Mayor* was not sufficient and a new, more precise set of orders would be issued and another visit to the community made. In the event that a decision was made, the *Audiencia* informed the *Alcalde Mayor* who in turn was ordered to notify the parties concerned.

Based on the cases used in the present study it is evident that the course of litigation was rarely so simple. The main complicating factor seems to have been the appeals process, to which every decision was subject. The Sacapulas people and their neighbors were not slow in appreciating the practical applications of the process. As noted by Woodrow Borah for New Spain generally:

> From the beginning of orderly royal administration . . . the Indians . . . found that they could haul any official into court and challenge his decisions, that any grant of land could be disputed, that boundaries and political arrangements could be challenged, and that any private person or corporate entity could be held to redress for damage done or be forestalled through petition for an order of *ámparo.* They found very quickly, furthermore, that any decision once rendered could be appealed up the long line of reviews provided by Castilian law. (Borah 1982, 272)

Once an appeal was made, the *Audiencia* was obliged to assign an official to review the case record. *Procuradores* (legal counselors) might be named for the litigious parties, if not already so represented, in order to organize the array of claims, counterclaims, arguments, and evidence. The reviewer might decide additional information was still necessary and recommend another local inquiry. Whatever the outcome, there does not seem to have been any end to the process; appeals could be pursued by all parties involved in a dispute until each one was satisfied with a decision. The unending appeals process is a major reason that litigation could drag on for many years.

Thus, in addition to the proceedings themselves, the records contain several other significant kinds of information. Surveys were conducted and maps made in order to locate and fix *mojones* (boundary markers), and thereby establish boundaries between groups. Spanish authorities used the Maya names of the *mojones,* some of which appear to have figured largely in the local cosmology and religion. Some of the *parcialidades* presented all or part of their traditional histories which, to the Maya's thinking, gave them rights to the land they occupied. These histories were called *títulos* (titles) by both the Maya and the Spaniards, and appear to have been written sometime after the conquest in a written form of Maya using Spanish characters. When presented in a litigation, the contents of the *título* were normally translated (rather unevenly) into Spanish for the convenience of the monolingual officials, thus losing much of their meaning and value. In some cases, the record of a particular dispute contains copies of still earlier litigation proceedings and conditional Spanish land titles not otherwise preserved in the record. Such information was presented to establish a prior claim or a legal precedent in what were sometimes recurring or ongoing disputes. Finally, some form of census record may have been created by the Spaniards for a particular case. This resulted from the need to establish the proportion of a *parcialidad's* population to the area of land its members occupied. The Spaniards' objective here was to equalize the man/land ratio among the different *parcialidades*. In one case, the information included a detailed map and analysis of the land actually suitable for *milpa,* the "owners" (users) of the plots, and a fairly detailed census of two *parcialidades'* populations. Better information could hardly be obtained by an ethnographer.

Because these are litigation records, and because people have been known to bend the truth in order to present their case in the best possible light, some evaluation of the documents' reliability is appropriate. Between *parcialidades,* many tactics were employed to try to win the dispute. In one example this even included collusion with one side (significantly, the side with the least justification in the case) on the part of the presiding Spanish official. Thus, false claims were sometimes made, especially by the weaker side. The Sacapultecos never seem to have fully understood the Spanish legal procedures, let alone their legal concepts. Therefore, Spanish *procuradores* were often used. On the positive side, these Spanish professionals were often able to reduce their clients' claims and counterclaims to some order, and present evidence in a logical manner relative to the proceedings. However, it is difficult to assess the extent to which *procuradores* redirected or prolonged disputes, or even fomented new ones. Despite these potentially confusing factors, the majority of Spanish officials involved in the disputes do seem to have been dedicated to establishing the truth and just precedents. Furthermore, it seems that sooner or later, the truth was usually established, though the same officials did not necessarily act according to its implications. In some cases, the litigation records do present problems of interpretation. However, because they are legal documents, and because most officials involved were conscientious, the documents as a whole are reliable and inconsistencies can be identified.

Parcialidades

Since this work focuses on a number of named social units over a period of some four hundred years, the key to establishing continuity from *chinamit* to *parcialidad* and finally to *cantón* is to identify and trace the various groups through time. Critical periods were those when some reorganization along traditional lines apparently occurred. To the extent possible, this section traces the history of the names, status, and fortunes of the groups associated at one time or another with Sacapulas. However, before examining the course of continuity in the organization of the Sacapulas people in detail, some idea of their numbers and of population trends through time must also be formed. At the outset it must be stated that precise population information is lacking until relatively late in the colonial period. Therefore, population estimates are largely a matter of informed reconstruction. At the same time, however, population loss early in the colonial period has long been assumed to have been an important factor affecting Maya culture. The man/land ratio was probably also a significant factor in determining the kind and intensity of interaction among the Sacapulas *parcialidades* themselves, and between them and their neighbors. Other factors certainly played a part in conditioning social relationships. The organization of production, extractive technology, crops and domesticated animals, trade and tribute all come immediately to mind in this regard. Unfortunately, these factors are at least as difficult to document as population, if not more so. Especially as a starting point, it is necessary to reconstruct Sacapulas' population through time. Finally, the apparent processes or regularities in the ways in which the Sacapultecos dealt with the changing numbers and composition of their member groups should be pointed out. While both population decline and growth occurred at different moments in time, their effects on the *chinamit-parcialidad* principle are unexpected.

The earliest mention of distinct, named *parcialidades* in the Sacapulas documents occurs in 1572 in connection with a legal case described in Chapter 4. At that time the six major groups still retained their pre-conquest appellations. In the case, the six *parcialidades* were divided in two opposing groups of three each, the "native" and "foreign" *parcialidades,* respectively. A seventh group of "Iztapanecas" is also mentioned by the Spaniards as residing with the three native *parcialidades,* though they were never mentioned by the latter and seem to represent a remnant group in the process of incorporation. The two groups of three *parcialidades* represent continuity of a level of preconquest political association above that of the individual *chinamit.* The term *amaq'* appears to have been used to denote such a unit.

The major native chronicles are of some help in attempting to project from the situation in 1572 back to before the conquest. Among other *amaq'* listed in the *Popol Vuh* are the Tuhal Ha, Uchabajá, and Lamakib (Edmonson 1971, 156). The same three are mentioned in the *Anales de los Cakchiqueles* (Villacorta 1934, 189). Therefore, at some point before the conquest there seem to have been three *amaq'* in the immediate Sacapulas area. The Tuhalha *amaq'* was probably composed of the Ah Canil and Ah Toltecat, since Tuhal was the ancient name for Sacapulas (based on *tuh,* the Quiché word for sweat bath and also for the ovens used in salt production) and since the town was formed in their territory. The Lamakib *amaq'* would have included the Coatecas, Sitaltecas, and Zacualpanecas, precisely the three groups that formed the block of foreign *parcialidades* in 1572. The Uchabajá may at one time have been more important, but by the late preconquest period they appear to have been a small *amaq',* dependent on and perhaps in the process of incorporation into the Tuhalha. Thus, several contiguous *chinamitales* would together form an *amaq'.* To a limited extent, therefore, an *amaq'* was a territorial unit, though in colonial times the component *chinamitales* jealously guarded their lands. Some degree of political association is also indicated.

During the course of the 1572 litigation we learn that the heads of the *chinamitales* still existed and were recognized as *caciques* (a general term used by the Spaniards to identify native rulers) and nobles; the honorific term *don* being applied to their names. The information is summarized in Table 3-1. Two *caciques* were listed for the Sacapultecos (meaning the Ah Canil and Toltecas), Don Francisco Marroquín and Don Martín Pérez. The references do not specify the *chinamit* affiliations of the two men,

TABLE 3-1 *Caciques* of Sacapulas area *parcialidades,* c. 1573

Sacapultecos (Ah Canil and Ah Toltecat)
 Don Francisco Marroquín
 Don Martín Perez (*alcalde*)
Iztapanecas
 Don Francisco Azeytuno (Uchabajá)
 Don Francisco Mendóza
Sitaltecas
 Don Diego Hah (*alcalde*)
Zacualpanecas
 Don Juan Calel
Coatecas
 Don Alonso de Paz (*gobernador*)

though Don Martín was serving as *alcalde* (one of three in 1573) at the time. Don Francisco Mendoza was stated to be a *cacique* of the Iztapanecas as was Don Francisco Azeytuno. Based on later statements it would seem that this second Don Francisco was not an Iztapaneca but *cacique* of the Uchabajá. Don Diego Hah was *cacique* of the Sitaltecas and *alcalde* at this time. Don Juan Calel was *cacique* of the Zacualpanecas. The *cacique* of the Coatecas, Don Alonso de Paz, was also the Spanish-appointed *Gobernador* (responsible for tribute collection) of Sacapulas (AI Leg. 5942 Exp. 51995:32v–41v). One can note the continuing importance of the *caciques* as a group by the fact that they occupied two of the three *alcalde* positions as well as that of *Gobernador.* Unfortunately, the documents do not allow us to trace the history of the *caciques* in Sacapulas, though elsewhere this has been done (Collins 1980, 235–39).

In 1645, when problems again arose between the "native" and "foreign" *parcialidades,* the preconquest names were still in use, though the Sitaltecas did not mention their associates when pressing their demands. The Iztapanecas had disappeared from the record. Containing only twenty-one *vecinos* in 1572, it is doubtful that the group could maintain itself as a socially autonomous unit. Both groups were probably incorporated into the Coatecas, since their former lands are part of *parcialidad* San Francisco by the eighteenth century at the latest. Such absorption of remnant *chinamitales* is repeated and more fully documented in the eighteenth century when the *parcialidad* of Santa María Magdalena was nearly wiped out by disease (see below).

By 1684 most of the *parcialidades* incorporated the name of a patron saint with their preconquest titles (A3.2 Leg. 825 Exp. 15207). The names

San Francisco Coatlán and San Sebastián Tulteca facilitate the correlation of preconquest *chinamitales* and colonial-modern *parcialidad-cantón* groups. The Ah Canil still retained that name only. Two new groups are mentioned for the first time: San Pedro Beabac and Santa María Magdalena. The former do not appear to have occupied the Sacapulas area in preconquest times (as is illustrated by the dispute described in Chapter 7). Rather, they seem to have been brought to Sacapulas by the Spaniards. The Santa María Magdalena people inhabited a small valley containing a salt spring and a tributary stream of the Río Blanco. The Uchabajá, Sital-tecas, and Zacualpanecas are not mentioned during this period.

In 1692 only four *parcialidades* were mentioned: San Francisco Guat-lán (Coatlán), the Tultecas (minus their patron saint's name), Santa María Magdalena, and the Uchabajá (A 3.16 Leg. 1601 Exp. 26391). From 1724 to 1729 the list of *parcialidades* is the same as in 1684 (for 1724, A 3.16 Leg. 2074 Exp. 31570; for 1725, A 3.16 Leg. 2505 Exp. 36584; for 1727–28, A 3.16 Leg. 2075 Exp. 31588; for 1728–29, A 3.16 Leg. 2504 Exp. 36576; for 1729, A 3.16 Leg. 502 Exp. 10284). In 1725, however, the patron saint Santiago is first applied to the *parcialidad* Ah Canil (A 3.2 Leg. 707 Exp. 13120). *Parcialidades* are not listed by name in the extant tribute records from 1735 to 1742. However, names are given in a litigation of 1739 (AI Leg. 5978 Exp. 52517). At that time they were San Sebastián, Santiago, San Pedro, Santo Tomás, and San Francisco. From 1757 to 1764 San Francisco, Santiago, San Pedro, San Sebastián, and Santa María Magdelena are listed, but Santo Tomás is not mentioned.

By 1788, at the latest, the list of *parcialidades* had assumed the form it maintains to the present in which Sacapulas contains Santiago, San Sebastián, San Pedro, San Francisco, and Santo Tomás. Sometime prior to 1788 the Santa María Magdalena people suffered a severe population loss as the result of an epidemic. Some of the survivors were taken in by the other five *parcialidades,* with the majority going to San Sebastián. Others went to the neighboring town of Cunén (see below).

Population

Drastic population decline, due primarily to Old World diseases unintentionally introduced by the Spaniards, has long been thought to have been a major factor in culture loss and a precondition for the acculturation of the Maya and native Mesoamerican peoples in general. Before Spaniards ever set foot in the Guatemala highlands, messengers and traders from Mexico had brought European diseases to the highland Maya. This area, like much of the Americas, is one where, as MacLeod points out, "many of the major scourges known in the Old World since ancient times were not present . . . before the arrival of Europeans at the end of the fifteenth century" (MacLeod 1973, 16). He goes on to list some of the new diseases introduced at this time. They include plague (both bubonic and pneumonic), smallpox, measles, cholera, yellow fever, typhoid, typhus, tuberculosis, and malaria (ibid., 16). The first of three major Central American pandemics struck the Maya highlands in 1519 and 1520, four years before Pedro de Alvarado's conquest of the area. The effects of this unintentional germ warfare were catastrophic.

> Given present day knowledge of the impact of smallpox and plague on a people without previous immunities, it is safe, indeed conservative, to say that a third of the Guatemalan highland population died during the holocaust. Knowledge of past epidemics in Europe and of the aftermath of smallpox and plague can also lead us to assert that those who survived were left at least for a year or so in a weakened condition, with greatly lowered resistance to the minor ills, colds, bronchitis, pneumonia, and influenza which carry off so many invalids. It was then in large part the sickly survivors of a disaster whom Alvarado and his men encountered on the Pacific Coast of Central America. (ibid., 41)

The protracted and bloody conquest of the highlands only added to the disaster. In addition to losses of men in battle, deaths of women and children must also be assumed to have been great as a result of a presumed reduction of farming activity on the part of the debilitated population (and the consequent food shortages). Periodic uprisings by the Cakchiquels (disaffected Spanish allies early in the conquest) and other, only partially subjugated, groups added to the toll.

Even before Spanish domination was everywhere firmly established, another drain was made on the native population: slave labor for gold washing in Honduras and for trans-isthmian portage work in Panama during the 1530s (ibid., 46–57). During the same period (1532–34) another pandemic, evidently measles, struck (ibid., 98). From 1545 to 1548 pneumonic plague ravaged the highland peoples (ibid., 98): "The number of the inhabitants cannot have been more than half of what it was in 1520" (ibid., 110). It struck again barely a generation later from 1576 to 1577 (ibid., 98): "The severe epidemics of the 1570's, second in intensity only to those of the 1540's, had drastically and suddenly dropped some Indian populations by as much as 40 percent" (ibid., 185). Using MacLeod's figures we arrive at a total population loss of somewhere near 70 percent within the span of only fifty years. The Indian population would not stabilize and begin to recover until the beginning of the eighteenth century (ibid., 343–44).

Sacapulas Population: Methodology

Prior to the mid-eighteenth century the Spaniards do not appear to have been interested in the number of people under their control, nor with demographics. The only figure of importance was the number of *tributarios enteros* (entire or full tributaries), which was used to determine the civil tribute obligations of a particular community or group. Married couples, called *casados,* counted as full tributaries, while single people of either sex over the age of eighteen counted as *medios* or half tributaries. People over age fifty-five (fifty after 1754) and Indian officers of the municipal government were *reservados* or exempt from tribute (Villacorta 1942, 144). The number of *tributarios enteros* was obtained by adding the number of *casados* and one-half the number of *medios*. From about 1600 on, each *entero* was subject to the *servicio del tostón* assessed at one *tostón* per year. Payment of a community's total yearly tribute was made by *tercios* or on a six-month basis. To arrive at population estimates for the sixteenth and seventeenth centuries a formula must be developed to convert *tributarios enteros* (all adults over eighteen and younger than fifty-five not otherwise exempted) to a total population figure. To an extent, this can be accomplished through analysis of later eighteenth-century census material.

More or less detailed population figures for the whole of Sacapulas were given only once during the colonial period, in 1769. Another set of detailed data is available in the form of censuses made of Santo Tomás and San Francisco *parcialidades* in 1797. These two sets of information agree in general terms as to relative proportions of people by broad categories. They thus form a basic population profile that can be projected back through time as a constant in population calculations.

In 1769, Don Joséph Manuel Corzo de Rivera, the priest for Uspantán, Cunén, and Sacapulas, responded to an official questionnaire regarding the towns in his care (AGI Guatemala 948). Included in his answers are some comparatively detailed population figures. At that time there were 410 *hómbres* (adult males), 468 *mujeres* (adult females), 104 *solteros* (male adolescents), 353 *solteras* (female adolescents), and 288 *niños* (children) (ibid.). The total population was thus 1,623. The figures are significant since they give some idea of the relative proportions of children, adolescents, and adults (about 46 percent of the total population were children and adolescents).

In 1797, as part of an epic legal battle between Santo Tomás and San Francisco *parcialidades,* a fairly detailed census was made of the two groups in order to assess their respective needs for land (AI 80 Leg. 6042 Exp. 53327). At that time, *hijos* (children living with their parents) made up 202 of 455 people, or 44.8 percent, for San Francisco, and 107 of 255, or 42 percent, for Santo Tomás (ibid., 54–57). These percentages agree with the 46 percent of the population that children and adolescents composed in 1769. An additional piece of information from the 1797 censuses concerns the proportion of *reservados* (individuals exempted from tribute obligations). There were fifty-eight *reservados* for San Francisco, or 12.8 percent of the total, and twenty-six *reservados* for Santo Tomás, or 10 percent of the total.

For the later eighteenth century then, the approximate proportions of the broad categories of the population were as follows: Adult men and women made up 45 percent. Children and adolescents accounted for another 45 percent. *Reservados,* including men over fifty and individuals serving in some official capacity in the municipal government composed 10 percent. Members of *parcialidades* living in the town itself evidently had a larger number of *reservados,* which was presumably related to their proportionately greater participation in duties that qualified them for that status. The 10 percent figure should thus be taken as a minimum, but it is utilized in all the estimates presented here. As noted above, these proportions are important for estimating populations in the past because prior to the mid-eighteenth century there is no similar information, only tribute lists. Significantly, for our purposes, the number of *enteros* multiplied by two equals the total number of tribute-paying adults in a group. As stated, this group composed 45 percent of the population in the late eighteenth century, so a simple calculation is all that is required to convert the number of *tributarios* to a population estimate.

A word of caution is in order with regard to the figures derived from the use of this method. First, the formula used to convert tributaries to total populations is derived from figures pertaining to the later eighteenth century, especially the 45 percent children/adolescents and 10 percent *reservados.* The proportion of children in particular may have varied greatly, decreasing dramatically because of epidemics and increasing during periods of population growth. The 45 percent figure is used simply because it is attested to at some point in the record. Second, as will be noted again, there is evidence that local Maya officials intentionally gave low tributary figures, despite Spanish efforts to ensure full and accurate counts (Collins 1980, 45–48). Collins is of the opinion that such practices were more wide-

TABLE 3-2 *Parcialidad* populations

1573	Ah Canil or Ah Toltecat	47 *vecinos,* approx. 208 people
	Ah Canil or Ah Toltecat plus Uchabajá	75 *vecinos,* approx. 333 people
	Iztapanecas	21 *vecinos,* approx. 93 people
	Sitaltecas	31 *vecinos,* approx. 138 people
	Zacualpanecas	19 *vecinos,* approx. 84 people
	Coatecas	7 *vecinos,* approx. 31 people
1692	Toltecas	45 *tributarios enteros,* approx. 200 people
	Uchabajá	46 *tributarios enteros,* approx. 204 people
	San Francisco Coatlán (Sitaltecas, Zacualpanecas, and Coatecas combined? including Santo Tomás?)	92 *tributarios enteros,* approx. 409 people
	Santa María Magdalena	12 *enteros,* approx. 53 people
1795	San Sebastián	25 *reservados,* 123 *tributarios,* approx. 546 people
	Santiago	10 *reservados,* 18 *tributarios,* approx. 80 people
	San Pedro	9 *reservados,* 67 *tributarios,* approx. 298 people
	Santo Tomás	15 *reservados,* 60 *tributarios,* approx. 267 people
	San Francisco	28 *reservados,* 98 *tributarios,* approx. 436 people

spread during the later colonial period, though their effects would in any case even out in the long run because of losses through disease (ibid., 47–48). Third, the *parcialidades* demonstrably varied greatly in population (see Table 3-2). In 1573, for example, the *parcialidades* that would become Santiago and San Sebastián numbered 122 *vecinos* (citizens, similar to *tributarios*), while three other *parcialidades* that later became Santo Tomás and San Francisco included only 31, 19, and 7 *vecinos,* respectively (AI Leg. 5942 Exp. 51995:37v–38v). Similarly, in the 1690s, the Santa María Magdalena *parcialidad* contained only twelve *tributarios enteros,* while San Francisco (combined with Santo Tomás?) boasted ninety-two *enteros* and the Tultecas (later San Sebastián) forty-five *enteros* (A3.16 Leg. 1601 Exp. 26391). Thus, the population estimates are at best approximations, though one

TABLE 3-3 Sacapulas population

Year	Total population	Notes
1500	Approx. 1,800	See text
1548	Approx. 1,400	160 *tributarios* from Cerrato census, representing "native" *parcialidades*
1572	Approx. 890	6 *parcialidades*, 200 *tributarios*
1664	Approx. 1,200	Approx. 984 for 4 or 5 *parcialidades* subject to tribute
1692	Approx. 1,300	Approx. 1,080 for 4 or 5 *parcialidades* subject to tribute
1741	Approx. 1,300	596 *partidas* (see text)
1769	1,623	Cortés y Larraz ([1770] 1958, 40) cites 1,608 in 1768–70
1779	1,941	Zenith of colonial population
1782	942	Reflects loss of 300 people in smallpox epidemic of 1780, and presumably deaths due to secondary infections, as well as an exodus from town
1783	1,732	
1792	1,366	
1795	Approx. 1,600	366 *tributarios*
1808	1,792	Figure cited by Juarros (Solano 1974, 179)
1812	2,408	Official parochial figures (including 85 non-Indians)
1821	1,920	Census of 1821
1880	3,314	Figure does not differentiate Sacapultecos from migrating Chiquimulas (Imp. 1933:435)
1893	5,511	Same problem as with 1880 figure; community still 93.6 percent Indian (1921 census; Wauchope 1948, 51)

suspects the several variables involved cancel each other out to some extent.

Sacapulas Population: Sources and Estimates

Population estimates are summarized in Table 3-3. The earliest figures for Sacapulas are contained in the Cerrato census of 1548–50 (Solano 1974, 80). Sacapulas is entered twice, each figure of 80 *tributarios* representing a *mitad,* or half of the tributary population. This interpretation is confirmed since in 1549 the two halves of the tributary population were assigned as separate *encomiendas* with identical tribute obligations (AGI Guatemala 128). The 160 *tributarios* multiplied by two yields 320 tribute-paying adults, forming 45 percent of the population. The total population referred to, then, was a little over 700.

However, it is quite likely that the 1548–50 figures represent only half the *parcialidades;* those living in or near what would become the town of Sacapulas, that is, the "native" Ah Canil, Ah Toltecat, and perhaps the Uchabajá. Two different pieces of evidence support this interpretation. First, it is known from the 1572 litigation pertaining to the formation of Sacapulas that the process had begun only about 1564. Before that time, the three "foreign" *parcialidades* were not part of Sacapulas and would thus not have been assessed for tribute as part of it. This is supported by the Cerrato census, which contains an entry of forty *tributarios* for a place called Citalá, most likely the Sitaltecas of the Sacapulas area (ibid., 82). Also named is a place called Coatlán, again, probably the Coatecas, though no figure was recorded for the group. Second, part of the tribute owed by the two "halves" of Sacapulas to their *encomenderos* consisted of four *hanegas* (or *fanega,* one of which equals approximately one and one-half bushels) of salt per half per year (AGI Guatemala 128). As traditional, and during the colonial period exclusive, exploiters of the salt flats, the Ah Canil and Ah Toltecat would logically have been assessed some part of their tribute payment in salt, while the other *parcialidades* would have been unable to easily supply it. With the figure cited in the Cerrato census only representing about half the tributary population of the Sacapulas area, the population estimate should be approximately doubled to about 1,400 people.

We cannot know with any certainty the extent of population loss among the Sacapultecos in the early sixteenth century since we lack a baseline population figure. The 1548–50 estimate of about 1,400 people pertains to a period in which decline had already occurred and was continuing. Attempting to extrapolate from this figure to back before population loss began is, therefore, highly problematical, all the more so since we lack any documentation as to the sequence and severity of epidemics in Sacapulas itself. Assuming the 50 percent reduction proposed by MacLeod for the period, preconquest population would have been around 2,800 people. Of course, a greater or lesser presumed percentage loss changes the estimate up or down, respectively. The Verapaz administrative area, which included Sacapulas at that time, suffered a severe epidemic in 1571, the effects of which are reflected in the 1572 population figures. The *tributarios* were enumerated as part of a litigation in 1572 (AI Leg. 5942 Exp. 51995). This time they numbered 200, for a total population of six *parcialidades* close to 900. Based on negative evidence alone, this 1571 epidemic, rather than those immediately preceding the conquest or in the 1540s, appears to have been the first to radically affect the Sacapultecos. If this is the case, then doubling the 1548–50 estimate for a preconquest figure of 2,800 would be excessive. A figure of less than 2,000 would seem more justifiable. One may note that intra- and intercommunity disputes over land increased in the later eighteenth century when population appears to have topped 1,600 people. Therefore, the estimate of the preconquest population at about 1,800 people may not be too far off.

In 1664, 204 *tributarios* were listed for a total population of just over 900 (Solano 1974, 110). For the same year other records indicate 221 *tributarios* and thus a population of 984 (A3.16 Leg. 1601 Exp. 26391). The latter figure includes only four *parcialidades* (perhaps five) that were subject to crown tribute. The others were presumably paying their tribute to an *encomendero.* We might expect, then, that this figure represents only between 65 and 85 percent of the total population, perhaps about 1,200 people.

By 1692 there were 195 *tributarios* for four (again, perhaps five) *parcialidades,* no longer *encomendadas* but paying crown tribute. Two others present at the time were not listed, presumably because they were still *encomendadas.* If we add a total average of 96 *tributarios* for the two unlisted *parcialidades,* we arrive at a figure of 291 *tributarios* for a total population of just under 1,300. Fuentes y Guzmán cites 223 *vecinos* and 892 *habitadores* (inhabitants) in his *Recordación Flórida* (Fuentes y Guzmán [1690] 1932–33, 3:56). Using the population formula developed here we arrive at 911 people, a minimal difference but suggestive of the possibility that he did not have complete tributary figures.

There is a gap of nearly fifty years until the number of *tributarios* is listed again for Sacapulas. From 1725 through 1741 documents record the amount of tribute paid per *tercio,* rather than the number of *tributarios.* However, in 1741, 596 entries (*partidas*) were cited for Sacapulas as part of a land dispute with neighboring Aguacatán-Chalchitán (AI Leg. 5979 Exp. 52518: 42v–44). These entries were evidently of individuals of tribute-paying age and not the number of *enteros.* Thus the 596 figure included all adults except *reservados.* In this instance, then, computation of the population estimate does not require the initial doubling of the figure as normally done. The population estimate for the period is thus just over 1,300, which is only a very slight increase in fifty years. The explanation here may lie in an epidemic of smallpox or typhoid that occurred in 1733, (MacLeod 1973, 100). Recovery appears to have been rapid since, as will be recalled, the population numbered 1,623 by 1769. The latter figure is also in general agreement with the 1,608 people noted by Archbishop Cortés y Larraz for Sacapulas during his visit sometime between 1768 and 1770 (Cortés y Larraz [1770] 1958, 40). With regard to the 1768 and later figures, it must be borne in mind that women were exempted from tribute obligations in 1756, causing the *tributario entero* unit gradually to disappear. From mid-century on, population figures were usually given as totals. Thus for 1779 a total population of 1,936 was reported (AI Leg. 6097 Exp. 55507).

Population fell as a result of a smallpox epidemic in 1780 that affected Uspantán and Cunén in addition to Sacapulas. The priest of Uspantán made an official report stating that the three towns lost a total of 300 people, plus seven "ladinos" in Sacapulas (AI.24 Leg. 6097 Exp. 55507); however, population figures for 1783 show some recovery (AI Leg. 6097 Exp. 55507). By the early 1790s, for reasons unknown to us at present, the population had actually declined; numbering 358 *tributarios* for a total population of about 1,600 (AI.80 Leg. 6040 Exp. 53305: 26). A more detailed census was made in 1795 (ibid., 29–29v). The 366 *tributarios* and 83 *reservados* still made for a population of only just over 1,600 people (for distribution by *parcialidad* see Table 1). The population seems to have increased rapidly thereafter, since, according to Juarros (Solano 1974, 179), the population in 1808 numbered 1,792.

The entire tribute system was abolished three years later in 1811 by the Cortes de Cádiz (Villacorta 1942, 144). With it went the tribute rolls and population figures used in its reckoning. However, the archbishopric of Guatemala continued to maintain records of the number of souls in its care and for the year 1812 recorded a total population for Sacapulas of 2,408, including 85 non-Indians lumped together as Spaniards, *ladinos,* and Negroes (AGI Guatemala 529). The figure seems incongruous with the earlier population data, there being an apparent increase of one-third in only four years. One might expect that the church's figures would be more reliable since records were kept by each town's friar or priest, yet the 1812 figure is out of agreement with later figures as well. In 1821 a newly independent Republic of Gautemala conducted a census of the country (B 84.3 Leg. 1134 Exp. 26011). At that time the population of Sacapulas was still only 1,920, and was approaching its colonial period high. Otherwise, very little documentation is available for Sacapulas in the nineteenth century until near the century's end. Unfortunately, once figures again become available, Sacapultecos are not differentiated from immigrant Indians from

Santa María Chiquimula who began arriving in significant numbers at that time. Both groups were classed together simply as Indians, a trend that has continued down to the present.

Processes

More important to this study than merely tracing the extent of population loss or growth is the reaction of the Sacapultecos to the changing situation. Did they become totally disorganized socially and culturally and thus susceptible to Spanish attempts at directed change and reorganization along Peninsular lines? Evidently not. The Sacapultecos responded to both drastic population loss and slow increase in terms of their *parcialidades.* As population growth approached the preconquest threshold, competition for land developed between *parcialidades* that had previously been united as *amaq'.* Such a breakdown of an *amaq'* was precisely the nature of the litigation between Santo Tomás and San Francisco over their common boundary (this dispute and its implications are the subjects of Chapter 8).

The Sacapultecos appear to have dealt with severe population loss through the incorporation of remnant groups within the existing *parcialidad* structure. Apparent examples include the Bacín, Iztapaneca, and Sitalá *parcialidades,* and the Uchabajá *amaq'.* The former would appear to have been incorporated into Santiago and San Sebastián along with the Uchabajá. The latter two were evidently incorporated into San Francisco. A definite, documented example is that of *parcialidad* Santa María Magdalena.

Information about the incorporation of Santa María Magdalena comes from a legal case that ran from 1786 to 1790 (AI Leg. 6037 Exp. 53258). Four individuals who claimed to be *"calpulis",* or heads, of the Magdalena *parcialidad* attempted to gain control of the group's former landholdings for their own purposes. The four were opposed in this by the *Gobernador* of Sacapulas and others who stated that the four *"calpulis"* were really not of Magdalena at all and therefore should have no part of the defunct *parcialidad*'s land. As a result of the official investigation the land was declared *realenga* (part of the royal patrimony) and offered at auction. The four *"calpulis"* had expected to receive the land gratis and so were unprepared to purchase it. The municipal authorities made no attempt to buy the land either, so the situation returned to the status quo ante.

While the case itself is not especially instructive, some of the testimony presented does shed considerable light on the incorporation process. Andrés Henríquez, the priest at Sacapulas, was asked by the *Alcalde Mayor* to make a report on the claims made by the disputants in the case. He stated that the *calpul* of Magdalena, like the other five *calpules* of the town, was one of the small groups which had been brought together to form the town of Sacapulas.

> El Calpul de Magdalena (como los otros cinco de este Pueblo)—fue y fueron pueblos pequeños, que por Superior Orden se juntaron a constituir el Pueblo de Zacapulas; y mediante el matrimonio están hoy todos los Calpules mezclados entre si. (ibid., 5)

Despite the supposed mixing mentioned by the priest, people still knew to which *parcialidad* they belonged. That this was true even in the case of an incorporated remnant is shown by the statement of twenty descendants of Magdalena in the proceedings. Although they were born in the *calpul* of San Sebastián, they still knew they were descendants of Magdalena and still maintained the *cofradía* of their patroness:

> Solo nos metemos en servir a María Magdalena y nosotros no sabemos lo que ellos hacen por estar en otro Calpul como nosotros estamos en el Calpul de San Sebastian descendientes de Magdalena por nuestros antepasados . . . (ibid., 8)

More enlightening as to the incorporation process itself is the testimony presented by the *Gobernador* and *alcaldes* of Sacapulas to the *Alcalde Mayor.* They stated it had been more than 150 years since the Magdalena people were nearly annihilated by a terrible disease (that is, c. 1639). The few survivors came to live in the town of Sacapulas and in neighboring Santa María Cunén, in which was kept the image of the group's patroness. The survivors continue to reside and marry among the two towns, but they are so few as to number only perhaps thirty. Of these were Francisco Ramírez (the key litigant in the case) and his three associates. Yet these men had no separate *parcialidad,* but were mixed among the other five *calpules* of the town which all contained a few survivors.

> Hace mas de ciento y cincuenta años que dicho Pueblo de Magdalena se aniquiló pues no sobrevive nadie de sus naturales porque en aquel tiempo parecieron una formidable peste y los pocos vivos que escaparon se avecindaron en éste Pueble de Sacapulas y en el de Santa María Cunén, en donde existe la Santa Titular de dicho Pueblo. Que aquellos indios avecinados y casados en estos Pueblos han tenido sucesión pero tan escasa que apenas—hay treinta decendientes de los cuales es uno Francisco Ramires y los otros tres que se decoran en el escrito incerto en el Despacho que rige. Que estos no tienen parcialidad,

sino que están mesclados a los Calpules de éste Pueblo que son—cinco y en todos hay de ellos. (ibid., 18)

Other testimony given by the *Gobernador, alcaldes, regidores,* and *principales* of Sacapulas provides additional information. They stated that it had been many years since the Magdalena people had been destroyed. Some of the survivors went to live in Cunén and others in Sacapulas. The latter group was divided and adopted into the five *calpules (parcialidades)* that compose the town. Most of the survivors affiliated themselves with the *calpul* San Sebastián, and continued to celebrate the image of Magdalena without assistance in defraying the cost of the celebration from those survivors who divided themselves up among the other *calpules*.

> Es un Pueblo de Magdalena que ha muchos años que se destruyó y acabó pasando sus individuos a vivir unos al Pueblo de Cunén y los dema a este de Zacapulas, los que se dividieron y proahijaron por todos los cinco barrios o Calpules de que se compone nuestro Pueblo, afiliándose la mayor parte al Calpul de San Sebastián quienes con dicho Calpul celebran hasta hoy la Imagen de Magdalena,—sin que concurran en lo mas leve, los que se esparcieron por los demas calpules a los gastos que ofrece una celebridad. (ibid., 6)

What is the nature of the incorporation process described here? In terms of the time involved, it was asserted that the Magdalena *parcialidad* ceased to exist about 150 years previously, or c. 1639. However, the *parcialidad* is still listed by name in 1692 and even through 1725. Perhaps the Sacapultecos were exaggerating to improve their case. This is doubtful, however, since their opponents never disputed the time frame presented. It is perhaps more likely that the Magdalena people were already incorporated socially into Sacapulas, but continued to be assessed by and pay tribute to the Spaniards as a separate group. If such were the case, then the Spaniards' policy of assessing tribute by *parcialidad* would have served to preserve the group's identity. In any event, the key factor in the incorporation process seems to be severe population loss. In the Magdalena case there were only ten to twelve *tributarios enteros* left. Whatever total population figure this converts to, we are clearly dealing with a group too small to remain endogamous and survive. Rather than have the group die off completely, the Maya of this area chose to incorporate and thus preserve the survivors. The survivors gave up some of the privileges attached to being a *parcialidad*. In particular, they ceased to control their former lands; this was, logically, divided between Sacapulas and Cunén, the two towns that absorbed the survivors. However, the memory and the identity of the people, as descendants of the *parcialidad* Magdalena, persisted, perhaps helped in part by the official recognition and tribute obligations imposed by the Spaniards. Another factor affecting continuity of group identity, at least for those people incorporated into San Sebastián, may have been the survivors' and descendants' continued celebration of the cult of their patroness.

So far as can be told, the process of incorporation or remnant groups was a purely Maya response to a crisis, and not directed by Spanish authorities. While some groups may have been brought to Sacapulas by the Spaniards, the way they were incorporated appears to have been worked out by the Sacapultecos themselves. Possibly this process occurred occasionally in preconquest times as well. Population loss due to famine or warfare might easily have destroyed individual *chinamitales*, whose survivors would then be taken in and absorbed by neighboring groups, the land being divided among them.

While incorporation involved only a minor exception to the generally closed nature of the *parcialidad* unit, the general population loss seems to have required a more far-reaching change: a shift from *parcialidad* endogamy to intermarriage among the *parcialidades* forming Sacapulas. Having noted that the Magdalena group was small, it must be borne in mind that the population of *all* the groups was quite low until the eighteenth century. Thus, in order for the groups to survive, the closed nature of the individual *parcialidades* was changed to allow intermarriage. However, the change does not appear to have weakened the principle of *parcialidad* in the social organization of the Sacapultecos.

Summary

Two processes seem to characterize the history of the sociopolitical groups in Sacapulas. The first process, associated with population growth, was the gradual disappearance of the larger *amaq'* associations and their replacement for most purposes by the individual *parcialidades*. While strong in 1572, later in 1645 and even in the early eighteenth century, by mid-century the formerly united *parcialidades* San Francisco and Santo Tomás were engaged in an almost epic litigation over land they had once held together. The Santiago and San Sebastián *parcialidades*, on the other hand, did not engage in litigation against each other, so the phenomenon of *amaq'* breakdown was by no means a universal process.

The other process, associated with population decline, was one of continuing incorporation of remnant groups. Only groups allied with

(Uchabajá, Santa María Magdalena, Sitaltecas) or subordinate to (Iztapa-necas?) leading *parcialidades* seem to have been accepted. Members of the group introduced by the Spaniards, *parcialidad* San Pedro, were left to fend for themselves. The process of incorporation resulted in changes in terms of the number, origins, and heterogeneity of the *parcialidades* and, early in the colonial period, rules of *parcialidad* endogamy (to the extent they ever existed) had broken down. However, most other characteristics of the preconquest *chinamit* endured through time. As will be illustrated in the chapters that follow, *parcialidades-cantones* in Sacapulas remained as (1) primary, corporate landholding units; (2) nexuses of political, legal, and religious rights and duties; and (3) foci of solidarity and allegiance for their members. The *chinamit*-cum-*parcialidad* principle itself was not aban-doned but continued to be used in the social organization of the Sacapulas people.

Preconquest Political Geography

While the sources used in Chapter 2 give us some idea of the composition and functions of a preconquest *chinamit,* and while the data from Saca-pulas allow us to estimate a range of preconquest population figures, none of the sources by themselves tell us much about the size of the territories occupied or the distribution of the population per se. Yet by combining the documentary and archaeological records of the Sacapulas area, it is possible to reconstruct the *chinamitales'* territories, their settlement patterns, and some of the concerns these reflect. The reconstructions presented here serve as a baseline for evaluating changes in territorial extent and settlement patterns. They also serve as models of territorial organization that may be of use to archaeologists in interpreting the distribution of remains in other highland Maya areas.

It is due almost entirely to the efforts of A. L. Smith in the 1940s that anything is known about the archaeology of the Sacapulas area (Smith 1955). Smith identified and mapped ten sites during his month's stay in the area. He made collections of surface ceramics for comparative dating, and conducted limited excavations at three of the sites (Xolchun, Xolpacol, and Chutixtiox). However, numerous questions remain. Some concern the antiquity and sequence of human occupation (How far back was the area occupied? When was the salt first exploited?). Others are raised by statements made in the course of colonial period litigation reports (Were there other sites not seen by Smith? What was their relation to the preconquest *chinamitales?*). Until more complete archaeological investigations are undertaken, many questions must remain only partially answered. However, from the information at hand, a tentative outline of at least the immediate preconquest political geography of the area can be made, though future work will undoubtedly revise or refine our understanding.

The earliest-known occupation of the area was in Late Preclassic times, on the basis of ceramics recovered from the site of Río Blanco, referred to locally and in the documents as Xolcoxoy (ibid., 24). Classic period ceramics were noted at Xolchun, Xolcoxoy, and Chuchun. Most, if not all, of the known sites appear to have been occupied, or reoccupied, during the Late Postclassic period. It is this immediate preconquest period that most concerns us here, since it is for this time that the colonial references are most specific and continuity of sites with their former

inhabitants most direct. Statements made in colonial-period litigation proceedings make fairly clear the relationship between the former politico-
religious centers (now archaeological sites) and the *chinamitales* residing
in the area before the Spanish conquest. Significantly, the case records
allow at least partial reconstruction of what a preconquest *chinamit* looked
like "on the ground," thus providing a baseline for assessing the changes
in territorial holdings and settlement patterns.

The placement of the archaeological sites in the Sacapulas area clearly
demonstrates that the overriding concern of the preconquest inhabitants
was to utilize and defend the valley bottomlands (see Map 1-2). However,
based on the information contained in the records of colonial-period land
disputes, the Sacapulas *parcialidades* also controlled large tracts of mountainous land away from the rivers. Because of the documentary record and
the Maya way of defining territory, it is possible to reconstruct the territories of the different *chinamitales*.

As with all highland Maya people, the Sacapultecos have traditionally
defined their land in terms of named boundary markers called *q'ulbat* in
Quiché and *mojones* in Spanish. For a people lacking surveying equipment,
a system of *mojones* was probably the best way to demarcate boundaries.
They were probably adequate in most cases since people presumably knew
their respective *parcialidades'* boundaries from long experience, as they do
today. Some *mojones* are prominently placed on major mountains and are
locations for religious observances. In preconquest times there was the
added possibility that patrols were sent from the main centers to keep
watch on the neighboring groups. In most cases, however, defense of
boundaries was probably not a problem. Except for the valuable bottomlands, most of the *parcialidades'* territories would have been useful only for
supplying firewood and perhaps for some hunting and gathering. While
trespassing undoubtedly occurred, there was really no need or means by
which one group could successfully usurp the upland portion of its neighbor's territory.

Most of the information about *mojones* was presented in the course of
eighteenth-century land disputes, though in some cases earlier documents
were presented that dated back as far as the late sixteenth century in which
the names of some of the *mojones* were given. However, the question of
boundaries only seems to have become important in the eighteenth century when populations had finally recovered from conquest- and disease-
induced decline so that pressure on the limited arable land increased. It is
during this period, then, that the first formal, detailed surveys of the *mojones* were made by Spanish officials. Yet the boundaries thus recorded are

not arbitrary creations of the Spaniards. In all cases the surveying teams simply followed the information provided by their guides, who were the *principales* of the groups concerned. At boundaries between *parcialidades,* or between *pueblos,* representatives of all sides had to be present and agree as to the location of the *mojon* in question. The *mojones* so recorded in the eighteenth century appear largely unchanged since preconquest times. These *mojones* are still present and carry basically the same names today. Changes appear to have occurred only where the *municipio* has increased in size on the north and west. On the north the old *mojones* continue to be used to mark the limits of the *aldeas* which have developed there.

Map 1-2 contains the *mojones* listed for Santiago-San Sebastián and San Pedro in a 1776 survey, and for Santo Tomás and San Francisco in a survey of 1794. Because of the relative crudeness of the maps produced from the eighteenth-century surveys, the *mojones* were all visited and located on a 1:50,000 map of the area. The only exception was at the western end of the *municipio* where the boundary has changed through the addition of territory. For the Río Negro *mojón* this does not present a problem, since its position can be closely approximated from the colonial-period survey maps, and also because of its proximity to a major archaeological site (Xoltinamit) located close to the traditional boundary.

Chinamit-Parcialidad Reconstructions

SANTO TOMÁS (ZACUALPANECAS)

Because of two lengthy eighteenth-century litigations, Santo Tomás, or the Zacualpanecas-Lamakib, is the best-documented Sacapulas *parcialidad* in terms of our ability to reconstruct the territory and sites occupied by its members in preconquest times.[1] The Zacualpanec holdings centered on the fertile lands and the confluence of the Ríos Blanco and Negro. The important site of Xolchun (Department of El Quiché) occupies the low bluffs above the juncture (see Figure 4-1). This land was irrigated in colonial times, though it is at present unknown if irrigation was practiced there before the conquest. The eastern and southern borders were secured by the readily defensible sites of Xolpocol and Pacot, respectively.

In ancient times the holdings of the Zacualpanecas extended all the way up the Río Blanco, almost to its source in the present-day *municipio* of Aguacatán, Department of Huehuetenango. This northwestern border was marked by another site called Xolchun, also known locally as Tenam (short for *tinamit?*) (Smith 1955, 15; Fox 1978, 101). No site is mentioned in

Figure 4-1. Reconstruction drawing of Xolchun, Department of El Quiché. View is toward the south, with the site of Pacot (Chucot) on the hill beyond. (Drawing by Tatiana Proskouriakoff, from A. L. Smith, *Archaeological Reconnaissance in Central Guatemala,* Carnegie Institution of Washington Publication 608. Reproduced by permission of the Carnegie Institution and the Peabody Museum.)

the documents that might have been on the border with the Ixil and Santa María Magdalena people to the north and northeast, respectively, although remains are reported in the area (Anthony P. Andrews, personal communication; Fox 1978, 90). However, on the west, along the Río Negro, the documents do mention parcels of land with the Maya word *tinamit* (meaning town or city) as part of their names. During a reconnaissance of the area in 1983 a site was in fact found. Called Xoltinamit by the local people, it was built—with an eye for defense—on a knoll at a sharp bend in the Río Negro (see Figure 4-2). Placement, architectural details, and surface artifacts all indicate a Late Postclassic occupation (Hill n.d.).

Figure 4-2. Xoltinamit viewed from the south. Although largely overgrown and in a poor state of preservation, terraces that probably supported residential structures can be seen on the upper third of the knoll.

To this point, only sites with major architectural features (presumably occupied by the socially elite leadership of the *chinamit*) have been discussed. Whether or not the bulk of the population of the Sacapulas-area *chinamitales* also resided at or near the main centers is a question for archaeological research, though extensive terracing at sites such as Chutixtiox, Chutinamit, Pacot, Xoltinamit, and Xolchun (Department of Huehuetenango) suggest sizable resident populations. However, one site, Xolcoxoy, is mentioned as pertaining to the Zacualpanec. As noted earlier, the main occupation of this site appears to have occurred in Preclassic times. Based on ceramics he collected, Smith believed a Late Postclassic reoccupation may have taken place though he identified no corresponding construction (Smith 1955, 19). It may be, then, that Xolcoxoy was an area of residence for some of the common members of the *chinamit;* it was close to two elite centers and was as well the most productive agricultural land.

SAN FRANCISCO (COATECAS)

Neighbors to the Zacualpanecas on the south and east were the Coatecas (later *parcialidad* San Francisco). The only site identified with them from documentary sources is the impressive Chutixtiox. In addition to the legal records, Fr. Francisco Ximenez, during his stay in Sacapulas in the early eighteenth century, also noted this as the capital of the San Francisco people (Ximenez 1929, 191). Chutixtiox is located on a triangle of land on the north side of the Río Negro held by the Coatecas. Immediately to the west of the site is the valuable agricultural tract called Patzagel, while on the east is a similarly valuable tract called Xetzagel. Southeast across the river is a third tract, Ixpapal. Together, these formed the bulk of the Coatecas farmlands (see Figures 4-3, 4-4, 4-5, and 4-6). That these were sensitive areas before the conquest is evidenced by the placement of sites of three different *chinamitales* in close proximity: Xolpacol of the Zacualpanecas, Chutixtiox of the Coatecas, and Papsaca (Smith's Chuchun) of the Ah Canil-Ah Toltecat (Santiago and San Sebastián). Most of the Coatecas' territory lay to the south, following a small, steep valley through which the road to Quiché now passes. Evidently, however, these lands were not considered worth actively defending as no additional sites are known in the area traditionally controlled by the Coatecas.

Fortunately, in the 1790s a detailed survey was made of the land traditionally claimed by Santo Tomás and San Francisco in connection with a dispute over boundaries (see Chapter 8). The two *parcialidades* and the Spanish authorities recognized that it was arable land rather than just gross area that was the important issue, so all workable plots were mapped and their extent computed. The surveyor reported that of two hundred *caballerías* (about 8,989 hectares) only slightly fewer than twelve *caballerías* (about 530 hectares) were suitable for planting with the traditional techniques still in use at the time (AI.80 Leg. 6040 Exp. 53305: 14; AI.80 Leg. 6042 Exp. 53327). Thus, at most, only about 6 percent of the group's holdings could be exploited for agriculture. While precise survey data of this nature are lacking for the other *parcialidades,* given the nature of the terrain it would seem that the 6 percent figure would apply equally well to their holdings. Another Spanish report of the same period provides additional details on the land and agricultural techniques of the Sacapultecos

Figure 4-3. Reconstruction drawing of Chutixtiox, viewed from the south. (Drawing by Tatiana Proskouriakoff, from A. L. Smith, *Archaeological Reconnaissance in Central Guatemala,* Carnegie Institution of Washington Publication 608. Reproduced by permission of the Carnegie Institution and the Peabody Museum.)

generally (AI.80 Leg. 6042 Exp. 53327: 42v). The Spanish official stated that the Indians called land useful only if it could be planted. Such land was scarce and even then was sandy and dry. For the Indians to achieve even a moderate harvest, double cropping was necessary. Also needed were abundant rains during the winter and a short *canícula* (a dry period in August) or the *milpas* would dry out and the Indians' work would have been wasted. Aside from the cultivatable *vegas* the rest of the land consisted of sterile hills. Thus, not only was good land limited, there had to be a delicate combination of factors for the Indians to have agricultural success even on these plots. In this light, the prominence of land disputes in the colonial period is easy to understand.

Figure 4-4. Patzagel, viewed from Chutixtiox.

SANTIAGO AND SAN SEBASTIÁN (AH CANIL, AH TOLTECAT, AND
UCHABAJÁ)

The ancient dwellers at the site of the town of Sacapulas proper were the
Ah Canil and Ah Toltecat. They controlled several sites along the Río
Negro, the names of which were recorded in the documents. Beginning
at the western boundary with the Coatecas there is mentioned a site called
Papsaca the location of which coincides with the site of Chuchun visited
briefly by Smith (Smith 1955, 25). Across from the town of Sacapulas is the
major site of Chutinamit. Evidence of occupation on the town side exists
in the form of buried masonry tombs (Charles Ward, personal communication). Otherwise, little remains on the south bank. East of Chutinamit
on the north bank of the Río Negro lies the site of Xecatloj, which probably marks the boundary of the two groups on that side. Another site,

Figure 4-5. Xetzagel, viewed from Chutixtiox.

Chulubalya, is mentioned in the documents but has not yet been identified.

The Uchabajá were a *parcialidad* living and allied with Santiago and San Sebastián during the colonial period. A statement by a member of the group, made in 1600 while on what he believed to be his deathbed, suggests that the Uchabajá were politically dependent on or subordinate to the Ah Toltecat. However, no archaeological sites are known to be associated with the Uchabajá.

SAN PEDRO (BEABAC)

As has been noted in Chapter 3, the San Pedro people do not seem to have been indigenous to the immediate Sacapulas area. Therefore, no archaeological remains are associated directly with them.

Figure 4-6. Ixpapal, viewed from Chutixtiox.

Patterns

Several patterns emerge based on the associations between archaeological sites and the preconquest political geography of the Sacapulas *chinami-tales*. Like the present-day Sacapultecos, the preconquest people of the area seem to have been solely concerned with defining and defending the river valley bottomlands. Sites are never far from one of the main streams, and no sites are known from the surrounding mountains. To whatever extent the uplands may have had economic significance in terms of hunting and gathering, or religious significance in terms of possible supernatural associations of different peaks, they were evidently not of a nature to require any permanent presence. Except for the Coatecas, each *chinamit* occupied or controlled more than one center, with a view toward marking and presumably defining their borders. The reason, then, for the concentration of sites in the area is not its natural richness—which is in fact very limited—or even a large population, but is instead the convergence of so many of the *chinamitales'* borders along the Río Negro.

The particular pattern of site placement was dictated by the nature of the *chinamit's* landholdings. The Zacualpanec land was strung out for a considerable distance along the courses of the Ríos Negro and Blanco. No one center would have been in a position to guard such holdings or respond quickly to encroachment by neighboring groups. The Zacualpanec solution was to place their main center near the middle of their territory (Xolchun-Department of El Quiché), with secondary centers at the limits of their river-course holdings (Xoltinamit, Xolchun-Department of Huehuetenango), and others to define their territory at the rivers' confluence (Pacot, Xolpacol).[2]

Slightly different problems were faced by the Ah Canil and Ah Toltecat. They were not concerned only with defining their territory, but also with safeguarding a localized resource, the *salinas*. Accordingly, a major site, Chutinamit, was constructed in an impregnable location close to the *salinas*. Another site, Papsaca (perhaps only a small settlement by Late Postclassic times), defined the western boundary with the Coatecas. A third settlement, Xecatloj, was located on the east, though not at the limits of the territory. Here, the topography dictated the placement of the site. Xecatloj occurs at the only place in the territory large enough to contain a settlement and still leave room for agriculture. This does not seem to have been a problem with regard to defense, however, since the next series of Late Postclassic archaeological sites (indicating the presence of other groups) begins some fifteen kilometers downstream, away from the Río Negro itself, along the drainages of the Sajcabajá-Canillá area. The nearest Late Postclassic site situated along the Río Negro occurs at Chimul some fifteen kilometers further downstream (Ichon 1975, 12).

The Coatecas were in a different situation. Their best land was three tracts of level ground (Patzagel, Xetzagel, and Ixpapal) closely spaced along the Río Negro. While the Coatecas evidently controlled considerable land to the south, it was mountainous and broken by numerous washes. The land worth defending was along the river. The Coatecas' answer to their security problem was to maintain just one site at the center of their holdings, Chutixtiox, but make it large and practically unassailable.

External Relationships

At this point it would be appropriate to place the groups inhabiting the Sacapulas area within the political structure of the preconquest highlands generally. Unfortunately, it is impossible to do so in a meaningful way. Despite several attempts at synthesis, our understanding in anthropological terms of higher level political organization is limited (but see Carmack 1981, Miles 1957). Given the sparseness of documentation, it is unlikely the situation will dramatically improve. What is known is that the most powerful polity of the immediate preconquest period in the Maya highlands centered on the Quiché of Utatlán, some forty kilometers south of Sacapulas. Carmack has argued that the structure of this polity was similar to the segmentary lineage system found among some East African pastoralists, and that shortly before the conquest it had become a state (Carmack 1981, 156−63, 368−69). The juxtaposition of these radically different forms of organization makes both of these interpretations difficult to accept.

The alternative interpretation suggested here is that this Quiché polity, like its rivals the Cakchiquels of Iximché and Tzololá and the Tzutujils of Atitlán, was a confederation of *amaq'* and *chinamitales*. Some groups, such as the Cavek of Utatlán, whose history is continued in the *Popol Vuh,* claimed to control the confederation (hence perhaps its interpretation as a state), but there is little corroborating evidence. Perhaps exceptional leaders could dominate for a time, but such control does not appear to have been institutionalized. Each component *chinamit* evidently had numerous dependent *chinamitales,* though it is difficult to determine the nature of the relationship. It is tempting to suggest that the relationship was feudal, that as a way to control their territory the Utatlán leaders placed subordinate groups in specific areas, ceding local control in return for loyal support. Certainly the conditions in the Maya highlands at that time were conducive to feudalism. Because of several competing polities, an overarching state organization did not exist. Warfare was a constant threat. Communications were poor, making administration difficult. Knowledge of writing—in whatever form it may have taken at the time—was surely limited to a small elite and we do not know if it was used at all for administrative purposes. General-purpose money does not seem to have existed except for cacao beans, which would have been used only for certain exchanges (see Chapter 8). Thus, it would have been difficult to pay salaries. The way to maintain subordinates would have been to give them land.

On the other hand, subordinate *chinamitales* may have had more of a client type of relationship with their superiors. In this case, the groups involved would have applied to a militarily more powerful *chinamit* or *amaq'* for protection, pledging loyalty and perhaps labor and tribute in return.

Unfortunately, the data on Sacapulas do not allow us to clarify the situation or indeed even characterize any relationships that may have existed between the local *chinamitales* and their powerful neighbors at Utatlán. As a salt-producing center, control of the Tuhalhá *amaq'* would have been of obvious value to the Quiches. Some sort of Quiché suzerainty is in fact suggested by the *Anales de los Cakchiqueles*. In this chronicle it is claimed that the Cakchiquels conquered the Tuhalhá and Uchabajá *amaq'* for the Quiches some time before their split with the latter in the late fifteenth century (Villacorta 1934, 229–30). The *Popol Vuh,* however, contains no mention of this conquest on the part of the Quiches' former allies, though it does contain a claim that the Tuhalhá and Uchabajá people were required to render both service and tribute to the rulers of Utatlán (Edmonson 1971, 246–47). The only evidence for a Cakchiquel presence is linguistic and consists of the resemblances between that language and Sacapultec (see Chapter 1). Finally, in the seventeenth century, Tovilla recorded a story in which it was claimed that Sacapulas was indeed a Quiché dependency and that prisoners were sent there to work at salt making (Tovilla 1960, 217). Unfortunately, as no other corroboration of these claims can be found in the Sacapulas documents, they remain highly suspect.

Whatever the relationships of the Sacapulas-area *chinamitales* to the Quiché polity at Utatlán, the outlines of the local organization are clear. It was a desire to protect access to both water and fertile valley bottomlands against encroachment by close neighbors that prompted the construction of so many centers. In preconquest times, diplomacy backed by the threat or actual use of forces permanently located at border points probably kept the boundaries stable. With the disappearance of the higher-level native political system as a result of the Spanish conquest, local diplomatic and military means for maintaining boundaries lapsed. The only recourse for the people of the Sacapulas *parcialidades* then was legal action in Spanish courts, a recourse they were to utilize extensively in the succeeding centuries.

Initial Contacts and Formation of the *Pueblo*:

Congregación in Sacapulas

Military Conquest

It is unclear what role the various groups that later formed Sacapulas played in the drama of the Spanish conquest. If they were subject to the Utatlán Quiché, as claimed in the *Anales de los Cakchiqueles* and the *Popol Vuh,* we should expect them to have participated in the disastrous campaign against Alvarado, culminating in the burning of the Quiché capital and the execution of its rulers. There is, however, no hard evidence of any Sacapulteco resistance to the initial Spanish conquest in 1524, though Sacapultecos do seem to have figured in a subsequent campaign to pacify the Uspantán area in 1529–30.

Our only source of information about the Uspantán campaign is Fuentes y Guzmán ([1690] 1932–33, 3:58–64), who credits Uspantán with being the political center on which the area of Sacapulas depended. He supports this by noting that in the *libros de Cabildo,* where the records of the expedition are contained, it was Uspantán and not Sacapulas that was cited with a *título de guerra.*

The campaign itself was two-phased. The first phase took place in 1529 when sixty Spaniards and three hundred Indian allies under Gaspar Arias entered Uspantec territory and carried out inconclusive operations for six months. At that point, the onset of the rainy season and the lack of provisions began to take their toll, especially among the Spaniards' Indian allies. Also, political enemies of Arias had arranged his replacement as *Alcalde* of the capital, necessitating his departure from the field and placing the command in the hands of Pedro de Olmos. An incautious assault on Uspantán ordered by Olmos resulted in an ambush and defeat for the Spaniards, with the loss of many Indian allies to the Uspantecos as prisoners for sacrifice. The Spanish force subsequently retreated south toward the capital by way of Chichicastenango. At some point between Sacapulas and Chichicastenango, the Spaniards were again ambushed. As a result, all their supplies were lost and they arrived in great distress at Santa Cruz del Quiché. The Spaniards' route on the retreat must have taken them close to, if not through, Sacapulas territory, and one might suppose that Sacapultecos participated with the Uspantecos in the successful ambush on the way to Chichicastenango.

The failure of this first attempt to pacify the Uspantecos and their allies reflected badly on Governor Orduña, ruling in Alvarado's absence. In an effort to remedy the situation before the *adelantado's* return, Orduña commissioned Francisco de Castellanos in 1530 to try again. His troops were to consist of forty Spanish infantry and thirty-two cavalry, along with some four hundred Tlaxcalan and Mexican auxiliaries (ibid., 3:61). The force made its way to Chichicastenango from which ambassadors were sent to persuade the Uspantecos to give up fighting and submit to the Spanish Crown. The ambassadors were killed as a sacrifice, and the Spaniards now felt fully justified in doing their worst. It is from this second phase of the campaign that more direct evidence of the participation of the Sacapultecos is available.

The force left Chichicastenango and proceeded for seven leagues "leaving Sacapulas on the right hand" (ibid., 3:62). They arrived at the south bank of the Río Sacapulas (Río Negro) where the swift current made the construction of a bridge necessary. Interestingly, the crossing was not opposed by the Sacapultecos in whose territory the bridge was almost certainly erected, even though, as Fuentes y Guzmán himself notes, the Spaniards could easily have been stopped.

After crossing the Chixoy, the Spanish forces subjugated the Ixil, who were allies of the Uspantecos, at Nebaj and Chajul. With the elimination of the Ixil, and with their flank effectively turned, the Uspantecos prepared for a final battle against the Spaniards, calling in allies from Verapaz, Cunén, Cotzal, and, in Fuentes y Guzmán's words, "what is now the territory of Sacapulas." The battle resulted in victory for the Spaniards; many Indians were captured and enslaved.

With regard to Sacapulas, several features of Fuentes y Guzmán's account are interesting. The Sacapulas area did not automatically fall to the Spaniards' control with the elimination of the Quiché polity at Utatlán. This indicates a degree of political and administrative independence at odds with the Quiché claims voiced in the *Popol Vuh*. Fuentes y Guzmán's assertion that the Sacapulas territory was subject to Uspantán is based on flimsy evidence: the lack of a *título de guerra* for the former. It may have been that the Sacapulas area was never completely or exclusively subject to either Utatlán or Uspantán but rather maintained some relationship with both. Alternatively, the relationship between the Sacapulas' polities and Utatlán may have been such that the latter's demise allowed or induced the Sacapultecos to seek a new relationship with Uspantán. Finally, Fuentes y Guzmán's description of "what is now the territory of Sacapulas," with its inhabitants dispersed in small settlements "of twenty to thirty people," contrasts with his references to Nebaj, Chajul, Cotzal, and Uspantán as distinct centers each controlling an area. The view of Sacapulas from Fuentes y Guzmán's description, and its role in the Uspantán campaign as an area of small polities lacking overarching organization and control, agrees with the legal documents. The experience of these groups in opposing the Spanish military conquest of Uspantán probably accounts for the spectacular early successes of Spanish missionaries, to be examined next.

Missionary Activity

The Sacapultecos seem to have been left alone by the Spaniards at the conclusion of the Uspantán campaign in 1530 until Bartolomé de Las Casas and the first Dominican friars in Guatemala made efforts to convert them in 1537. The main source for this well-known story is Remesal ([1615–17] 1964–66, 1:215, 227–34). As noted in Chapter 2, there are considerable questions as to the role of the Sacapulas people in Las Casas' efforts to pacify the Verapaz, with at least one scholar asserting that *cacique* Don Juan was not from Sacapulas but Rabinal, an area further east (Carmack 1973, 179). In fact, Sacapulas does lie rather too far west for the seemingly easy communications with the Verapaz described by Remesal. A more likely candidate for the center where Don Juan was contacted may be the important Late Postclassic site of Cauinal (Ichon et al. 1980). The site lies a short distance to the northwest of Rabinal, along a tributary of the Río Negro. Using Cauinal as the focus of Remesal's narrative rather than Sacapulas, the action and geography appear to coincide more closely. Nonetheless, Remesal's account is presented here as an example of what initial missionary contact could have been like, if not representative of the actual events in Sacapulas.

The four friars, Las Casas, Rodrigo de Ladrada, Pedro de Angulo, and Luís Cancer, are all credited by Remesal with an understanding of the Quiché language, which he states was spoken throughout Quiché and Sacapulas (Remesal [1615–17] 1964–66, 1:215). They composed a number of verses in Quiché treating various religious themes: the creation of the world, the fall of man from grace, the death of Christ and his resurrection, among others (ibid., 1:215). Las Casas then sought out four Indian merchants, presumably Cakchiquels since they are described as "de la provincia de Guatemala" (ibid., 1:215). Remesal gives the impression that Las Casas wanted these merchants because they regularly went to the Sacapulas area to trade. If this is so, the reason for choosing Sacapulas as the focus of missionary activity is unclear. Perhaps its remoteness from the Spaniards made Sacapulas attractive as a place for Las Casas to put his ideas of peaceful conversion and "civilization" of the Indians into effect. In any event, the four Indian merchants were taught the verses and how to put them to music on native instruments, and then were sent on to Sacapulas. In addition to their normal merchandise, Las Casas also gave the merchants Spanish-made combs, knives, small mirrors, and bells as gifts (ibid., 1:228).

Remesal credits the Sacapulas area with a single ruler: "un cacique poderoso, hombre de buen juicio y razón, emparentado con lo mejor de la tierra" (ibid., 1:228). This statement is clearly at odds with other sources which indicate a great degree of political fragmentation. Perhaps one *cacique* was first among equals. Perhaps the *cacique* in question is simply reported as being important since he was the one with whom the merchants—and the friars—had to deal. In any case, the merchants arrived in the Sacapulas area and, following preconquest custom, stayed in the house of the *cacique*, giving him some of their Spanish goods as presents in return for his hospitality. Remesal asserts that this custom was necessary since there were no inns (*mesones*) or *Casas de Comunidad* where travelers could stay (ibid., 1:228). The *cacique* was enchanted with the gifts and the merchants conducted a day of trading. That evening the merchants entertained the *cacique* by singing the verses they had memorized. The novelty of the presentation—musical instruments plus voices in harmony—appears to have impressed the *cacique* as much as the message conveyed. He ordered a repeat performance the next day and each day thereafter for eight days. Their repertoire exhausted, the merchants answered the *cacique's* request for more verses by saying it was not their office to compose, but that of the friars.

Who were the friars? The *cacique* had never seen or heard of them. The merchants painted a picture of them and described their rigorous way of life: they ate no meat, they wanted no gold or *mantas* or feathers or cacao, they were not married and had nothing to do with women, and day and night they prayed to God before beautiful images (ibid., 1:229). The friars were so good, in fact, that if the *cacique* would send for the friars, the friars would come and teach him more fully the meaning of the verses. The *cacique* was pleased and determined to send his younger brother with the merchants to the capital along with some presents for the friars.

The *cacique's* brother was well received in the capital and shown how the Spaniards lived. Fr. Luís Cancer was selected to return to Sacapulas with the *cacique's* brother, bringing gifts of crosses and saints' images. Cancer was met at the entrance to the "town" by the *cacique* who deferentially averted his eyes as he would do with the Maya priests (ibid., 1:239). According to Remesal, Cancer had a church constructed (probably a temporary structure) and began to preach. His message was taken to heart, especially by the *cacique*—who was later baptized Juan—and his brother, the latter being the first to throw down and burn the idols (ibid., 1:230–31). Shortly thereafter, Cancer returned to the capital to report to his associates on his success.

Acceptance of the new faith by Don Juan and his brother was the cause of immediate friction between them and their unconquered, unconverted neighbors in the Verapaz. A marriage had been arranged for the brother with a daughter of the *cacique* of Cobán. As part of the ceremonies, the bride's and groom's parties would meet at a river dividing the two territories. The bride's party would cross and birds would be sacrificed to determine if the omens were good or bad. Don Juan, however, had sent a message to the Cobán party that, while they were welcome in his territory, they were requested not to conduct the sacrifices, as these were all vain and false according to his new religion. The request was an affront to the Cobán party but it also frightened them. If Christians brought the death and destruction to Sacapulas they had already brought to the Quiché and Cakchiquel, surely Cobán would be next. When a delegation of Cobaneros went to Sacapulas, however, they saw that Don Juan was not involved in any conspiracy with Christians against Cobán, nor were there any Christians about. Reconsidering their position, the Cobaneros felt that Don Juan was too valuable a potential ally, or too dangerous a potential foe, to let a small thing like the bird sacrifice interfere. Besides, the idols in Cobán could be consulted for the omens instead, either by sacrificing deer or, if necessary, a number of men. The marriage took place.

Other conflicts arose within Sacapulas itself. Many of Don Juan's "vassals" were unhappy with his abandonment of the idols and sacrifices and they burned Cancer's church. Don Juan had it rebuilt in time for a visit from Las Casas and Angulo in December 1537 (ibid., 1:231). The two friars toured Don Juan's domain and, with an escort of sixty Sacapultecos, pressed on to some settlements in Cobán territory. They returned to Don Juan at the beginning of 1538 (ibid., 1:232). Later that same year, when Las Casas asked for his help in bringing scattered Indian settlements together in a town, Don Juan negotiated with the Rabinales and the town of Rabinal was formed. It is interesting to note that a town was not formed at Sacapulas and that Las Casas was directed to Rabinal. Don Juan may have been wary of giving too much control to the friars, or both he and Las Casas may have sensed the opposition to Christianization in Sacapulas and were afraid to push too much.

When Las Casas returned to the Spanish capital to report on his progress to Bishop Marroquín, Don Juan accompanied him. The Sacapulas *cacique* was greeted by the bishop and by Alvarado, who made a present of his own feathered hat (ibid., 1:238). Marroquín and Alvarado also guided Don Juan on an extensive tour of the capital, especially to the various merchants and craftsmen, so that the *cacique* could better understand Spanish culture and what it offered. The bishop instructed the tradesmen to offer Don Juan anything he expressed an interest in; the bill would be paid by the church. Although curious and attentive, the only object to move the *cacique* was an image of the Virgin. This was given him by Marroquín and treated with great veneration by Don Juan. All members of the party were given gifts of Spanish goods before finally returning with Las Casas and Ladrada to Sacapulas. From there Las Casas and Ladrada were to continue their missionary efforts in Cobán territory.

Don Juan reportedly met with Las Casas for the last time in 1538 when Las Casas and Ladrada made their return to Mexico, and ultimately Spain, via Rabinal, Cobán, and Sacapulas. The *cacique* expressed his sorrow that he would never see the friars again. On a practical level he expressed his fear that, left alone, the enemies he had made by throwing down the idols and embracing Christianity would rise up against him. The friars mollified Don Juan by assuring him of their prompt return. Apparently satisfied, Don Juan accompanied the friars to the limits of his territory and provided bearers for their goods to Chiapas. Partly because of the Dominicans' success in converting Don Juan, and his subsequent assistance in gaining entry for the friars to Cobán territory, Las Casas was able to obtain a royal order prohibiting the entrance of Spanish nonclerics for five years. During this period the Dominicans would initiate their experiment with the peaceful conversion of the people and the formation of a truly Christian society.

If Remesal's account is accurate, no further encounters are reported between the Sacapulas people and the Spaniards until 1545. Again the contact is with friars, though this time Franciscans rather than Dominicans. This episode probably represents the first corroborated historical contact with Spanish missionaries. The two friars in question were Gonzalo Méndez and Pedro Betanzos. Méndez was one of the first six Franciscans to enter Guatemala in 1539–40 (Torquemada [1615] 1975, 3:338). Betanzos was with the second contingent that arrived with Motolinía as their guide in 1542 (ibid., 3:339). Both Torquemada and Vázquez credit Betanzos with being one of the foremost Franciscan linguists. He reportedly perfected and added to the Parra system of orthography for writing Maya languages, and wrote one of the first grammars of Cakchiquel (ibid., 3:339; Vázquez [1714–17] 1938, 2:171–78).

According to Vázquez, Méndez began his missionary career in Guatemala in 1540 among the Tzutujil of Atitlán where he helped found a Franciscan convent. In 1541 he was recalled to the capital after the calamitous earthquake of that year (Vázquez [1714–17] 1937, 1:71–100). From about 1545 onward Méndez shifted the field of his activities to the northern sierra area, including Sacapulas. Although Vázquez speaks in terms of "founding" many towns (among them Sacapulas), it is more likely that Méndez spent his time traversing the difficult countryside and contracting and baptizing the groups he encountered (Vázquez [1714–17] 1938, 2:32). The Dominican Ximenez specifically credits Méndez with bringing the Sacapulas *parcialidades* of San Francisco and Santo Tomás into submission (Ximenez [c. 1729] 1929–31, 1:191).

Betanzos' participation is not attested to by the religious historians and is mentioned only in passing in one of the archival documents. Testifying in a land dispute case in 1740 the priest of Sacapulas, Reimundo de Herrera, stated that he knew from old papers pertaining to the foundation of the *pueblo* that the Santo Tomás *parcialidad* was originally known as the Inaquip (Lamakib), who were brought into submission, and into the town, from their capital, Xolchun (now in the Department of Huehuetenango), by both Gonzalo Méndez and Pedro Betanzos.

Méndez, at least, continued to work among the sierra towns until about 1553 when the Dominicans, with additional personnel, began to found convents among the Indians. The Franciscans maintained their hold on the populous Quetzaltenango area, ceding the difficult sierra country to Dominicans. Sacapulas was chosen as the site of the convent, from which the resident friars (four were recommended) would make regular *visitas* to the towns in their charge (Remesal [1615–17] 1964–66, 2:259). Judging from the *caciques* to whom the *Presidente de la Audiencia* wrote announcing the new convent, the Dominicans would be responsible for a huge and difficult area. Besides Sacapulas, the groups and towns included were the Aguatec of Aguacatán, Chalchitán, and Balamihá; the Ixil area including Nebaj, Ilon, Huil, and Acul; and Cunén and Sajcabajá (ibid., 2:260). The convent at Sacapulas retained its preeminent position until

1649 when the center of Dominican administration was moved to Santa Cruz del Quiché (Ximenez [c. 1729] 1929–31, 2:259).

Colonial Policies and the Formation of a *Pueblo*

With the founding of the Dominican convent in 1553, the religious chroniclers move on to other topics in their histories. They mention Sacapulas from time to time but only as the site of regular meetings of the clergy (*capítulos*). The policies and events that shaped the town's foundation go unreported and we are forced to turn to other sources. Fortunately, a series of litigation proceedings about land, communal property, and the election of officials throws considerable light on the town's formation, especially the problems associated with accommodating the disparate *amaq'* and *parcialidad* groups.

The impetus for town formation came in the 1540s and 1550s from the Spaniards and their *congregación* program. As its name implies, the aim of the program was to bring together or congregate the many small Maya settlements into a few larger ones. According to Murdo MacLeod (1973) the program was motivated by the convergence of several Spanish interests. From the missionaries' standpoint, congregation of the dispersed Maya population would considerably simplify evangelization. The limited number of friars simply could not effectively minister to the widely scattered population. The process of Christianizing and civilizing the Maya would be easier and more effective if towns could be formed under the direct supervision of missionary friars. The civil authorities and colonists agreed, though for reasons of their own. The internal security of the *Audiencia* would be enhanced as the Maya were gathered from their defensible preconquest hilltop centers to much less defensible valley-bottom *pueblos,* which were easily policed by the limited Spanish military resources. Tribute collection would be simplified by reducing the number of stops collectors would have to make and making it difficult for individuals to live in isolated areas and thereby avoid their tribute obligations. Spanish officials would know just where to find the Maya if they all lived in towns. For the area of the *Audiencia* generally, the decreasing Maya population was another reason for *congregación*. The Maya were declining in numbers, but demand for their labor and tribute was growing. Labor in particular would be easier to exploit if towns were formed (MacLeod 1973, 120–22).

With the establishment of Spanish administration, Sacapulas, like other communities of indigenous Mesoamerican peoples, theoretically became subject to a range of colonial institutions designed to extract money and labor from the Indians for the benefit of the Crown and colonists. Yet its distance from major Spanish centers and apparent unattractiveness for Spanish commercial enterprises seems to have spared the Sacapultecos from the worst effects of some of the more abusive Spanish practices. Tribute of some form was unavoidable and was paid to the Crown and/or a grantee or *encomendero*. As noted in Chapter 3, tribute was assessed on the basis of the population of a *parcialidad* or town, but its payment was the responsibility of the group not the individual (very similar to the preconquest custom *nut;* see Chapter 2). This fact alone may have been of considerable importance in maintaining the Sacapulas *parcialidades* which, at least by the late seventeenth century, were given individually as *encomiendas*.

The *encomienda* is one of the most extensively described institutions of Spanish colonialism in the New World.[1] It was essentially a trusteeship granted by the Crown as a reward to one of its servants, entitling that individual to the tribute and/or labor of a certain number of Indians. Again, as noted in Chapter 3, the Sacapulas people were subject to this system, or at least partially. However, at the time of their first listing as *encomiendas* in 1549 and 1550 Sacapultecos were able to obtain exemption from their labor obligations through payments of cacao (AGI Guatemala 128).

The *encomienda* system was subject to many abuses with regard to labor demands made on the Indians. In an effort to rectify the situation, *repartimiento* was introduced.[2] Under this new system, Spaniards needing Indian laborers were required to operate through a royal official—the *juez repartidor*—who would distribute the available Indians in his district. Pay and conditions of work were specified. However, this system was also widely abused, with overdrafts of Indians, nonpayment of wages, and bad working conditions. Yet again, presumably because of their relative isolation the Sacapultecos appear to have been largely spared; at least there is precious little mention of the subject in the documents.

The picture of Sacapulas that emerges is of a town definitely within the colonial regime but at the same time at arm's length from it. Tribute obligations had to be met, but as long as they were met, Spanish officialdom was not concerned. The apparent absence of labor drafts left the Sacapultecos free to concentrate their efforts on their own purposes. Trade in salt and other commodities and crafts certainly integrated Sacapulas into the region—as it does today—but small-scale commerce was of little interest to the Spaniards. Indeed, the main contact between the Sacapultecos and the colonial government seems to have been via the legal system where inter- and intracommunity conflicts were played out.

Once congregated in their new towns, the Maya were to be politically reorganized along ideal municipal lines imported from Spain. The basic institution was to be the municipal council called the *cabildo* or *ayuntamiento*, staffed by one or two *alcaldes* and several *regidores*, all selected annually. The council would have the responsibility for everyday affairs as well as tribute collection and other obligations imposed by the Spaniards. It is significant that the newly introduced municipal offices did not displace the native Maya aristocracy's hold on power for some time. In 1573, for example, one each of the two *alcaldes* and *regidores* of Sacapulas were *caciques* (the Spaniards' term for indigenous leaders) of *parcialidades* and thus entitled to the honorific title of *don* (AI Leg. 5942 Exp. 51995:32v–38). Collins noted a similar pattern for colonial Jacaltenango, where a more complete record demonstrates continuity of such practices down to the early eighteenth century (Collins 1980, 229–45). Her data suggest that the gradual decline in office holding by *caciques* is attributable in large part to continued population decline (ibid., 237–38).

Through the cooperation of the civil and ecclesiastical authorities the *congregación* program was carried out. Smaller groups were brought together and sometimes moved some distance from their former homes. Officially, the program was a complete success. As MacLeod notes:

> Most of our information comes from reports written by friars or other clerics and these are usually little short of rhapsodic in tone. The whole massive operation, they felt, had been conducted with a minimum of fuss and disruption. . . . (MacLeod 1973, 122)

At the same time, however, "It is hard to tell what the Indians' reactions were to *congregación*" (ibid., 122). In Sacapulas, we are afforded a view of the reactions of some Maya groups and what a "minimum of fuss and disruption" meant on the local level.

The litigation began in 1572 and was based on various complaints filed by members of the three "foreign" *parcialidades,* the Sitaltecas, Zacualpanecas, and Coatecas. These groups appear to have been known collectively before the conquest as an *amaq'* called the Lamakib. The status of these groups as, to a certain extent, foreigners in the town was recognized by all parties, including themselves, the indigenous *parcialidades,* the clergy, and the courts. They were understood to have been brought to Sacapulas against their will and as a result were at a distance from their preconquest lands.

The "native" Sacapultecos consisted of the Ah Canil, Ah Toltecas, and Uchabajá. The former two at least appear to have formed the Ah Tuhal or Ah Tuhalhá *amaq'*, with the Uchabajá as subordinates or dependents in the late preconquest and colonial times. According to the native Sacapultecos this process of *congregación* or forced incorporation had begun only seven or eight years before the 1572 litigation (that is, 1564–65), considerably later than the claims of town formation made by Vázquez for Gonzalo Méndez (late 1540s) or by Remesal at the time of the founding of the Dominican convent (1553). From the indigenous and foreign groups the friars formed one community; they also built a church and a jail. For the purposes of defraying costs of community necessities the newly formed community bought a number of brood mares whose offspring would later be sold. The problems began when the corporateness of the *parcialidad* units asserted itself and the foreign *parcialidades* claimed foals for themselves, removing them from the community *estancia* without permission from the Sacapultecos.

According to the three foreign *parcialidades,* the question of dividing the community's horse herd was only one of several they had petitioned the courts to address. The other questions included (a) allowing them to divide the funds in the *caja de comunidad,* (b) allowing them to elect their own *alcalde* and *regidores,* and (c) allowing them to maintain legal possession of their lands. Strangely, these requests were granted by the *Audiencia* in 1572, though they were plainly counter to the Dominicans' aim of forming a single community. The third point on the list of requests amounted, in fact, to setting up another municipal unit, and was recognized as such by the participants: "piden . . . se haga jurisdicción en la dicha población de Citalá" (AI Leg. 5942 Exp. 51995:12).

However, when the three foreign *parcialidades* attempted to notify the native Sacapultecos of the decision, trouble ensued. The Sacapultecos would not listen to the reading of the court's order and took the papers away. Subsequently, the Sacapultecos ran horses through the foreigners' fields, destroying crops, and actually took a number of the foreigners prisoner. Some of the prisoners were fined while others received corporal punishment.

At this point the Dominicans appear to have stepped in to try to effect a reconciliation and to preserve the town they had worked so hard to form. The attempt consisted of a six-point contract, countersigned by two friars, to which both litigant parties would have to adhere. This is a fascinating document for what it reveals about the concerns of the Maya involved.

First, the Sacapulas people agreed to pay the foreigners three foals each year as recompense for their maintenance of the fences around their *milpas,* which prevented the community's horse herd from damaging them. Second, both parties agreed to cooperate in building the fences and corrals necessary for maintaining the *estancia* where the herd was kept. Third, they agreed not to antagonize each other further; they would not, for instance, attempt to take each other's lands and fishing areas. Punishment for trespass would include confiscation of the guilty party's tools and payment of a fine for any damages. Fourth, both sides promised not to tamper with or remove horses from the herd (that is, presumably, without first consulting with each other). Fifth, it was agreed that the community would have one *caja de comunidad* for its funds, but three keys would be needed to open it; two of the keys would be held by the *alcaldes* (presumably two) of Sacapulas, the third by the *alcalde* or *regidor* representing the three foreign *parcialidades.* At the same time both sides agreed to collect separately among themselves for the patronal *fiesta* of Santo Domingo. Sixth, it was agreed that the *alcaldes, regidores,* and *principales* of both groups should govern the town without being partial or keeping track of who was from which *parcialidad.*

The *Audiencia* approved the six-point contract with two modifications. The first was that the Sacapultecos and the three foreign *parcialidades* would each elect one *alcalde* and one *regidor* instead of the two *alcaldes* for Sacapulas in the contract. The second change was to divide the foals of the horse herd equally each year between both parties.

The proposed election of only one *alcalde* for the Sacapultecos and the equal partition of the foals brought an immediate response. According to the Sacapultecos the three foreign *parcialidades* had a population of only 40 *vecinos* among them while the Sacapultecos numbered more than 120 *vecinos.* Since the brood mares were bought as common property, and since the Sacapultecos put up proportionately more of the purchase cost, they argued that they should receive a division of the foals commensurate with their population. It also seemed unjust to the Sacapultecos that the Sitaltecos should be able to elect an *alcalde,* since they had a population of only 20 *vecinos.*

The subsequent revised sentence clarified that an equal division of the foals should be understood to mean equal according to the number of *vecinos* in each group. The question of *alcaldes* was not addressed, leaving the Sacapultecos with only one.

The first and only partition of foals for which we have records occurred in 1573. Prior to the division a census was taken which gives interesting population data for the period. The Sacapultecos numbered 143 *vecinos,* including a group of 21 "Yztapanecas," while the Sitaltecas numbered 31 *vecinos,* the Zacualpanecas 19, and the Coatecas 7 (ibid., 37v–38v). We find the object of all the litigation to be sixteen animals. Three were given over to the foreign *parcialidades* as per the Dominican-sponsored contract: the remaining thirteen animals included eight two-year-olds and five yearlings. The Spanish official sent to preside over the division of the herd made the following distribution: six of the two-year-olds were awarded to the Sacapultecos and two to the foreigners, while three of the yearlings were awarded to the Sacapultecos and one to the foreigners. The remaining yearling was sold for eight *tostones* of cacao, of which six went to the Sacapultecos and two to the foreigners (ibid., 40–41). The animals were to be branded with distinctive irons by the two groups, but only the Sacapultecos actually did this (ibid., 73).

As far as can be told from the documents, the contract was adhered to and relations between the Sacapultecos and the foreign *parcialidades* were relatively calm through the years until 1645. One reason for this may have been that the Sacapultecos were involved in a boundary dispute with San Andrés Sajcabajá in 1600–1601 (AI Leg. 5926 Exp. 51914). By 1645, however, problems had developed. The foreign *parcialidades,* represented by the Sitalá, petitioned the court for help in maintaining the "custom" (established in 1572) of the Sacapultecos and Sitaltecos each electing an equal number of *alcaldes* and *regidores*. The problem was not stated explicitly, but it appears that the Sacapultecos were agitating for, or had found, a way to influence the elections.

The Sitalá people also requested a legal guarantee of their rights of possession of a piece of land called Ixpapal. This particular area was important to the Sitaltecos because in it they made their *milpas,* retrieved firewood, *ocote,* and "other things" for their subsistence. The problem was that the three component groups of Sacapulas (named for the first time as the Toltecas, Ah Canil, and Uchabajá) were trespassing on the Sitaltecos' land and keeping animals on it that harmed the *milpas*. On several occasions the Sacapultecos came upon some Sitaltecos cutting wood in Ixpapal; they relieved them of it against no resistance from the Sitaltecos.

Both these actions on the part of the Sacapultecos were in contravention of the 1572 agreement. The court, therefore, duly granted the Sitaltecos' requests by issuing an order to maintain the custom of elections and to guarantee their rights to Ixpapal. No information is available concerning the implementation of the orders, nor of the reactions of the Sacapultecos. Some modus vivendi must have been found, however, since no further litigation occurred between the two parties.

Discussion

What do these sixteenth- and seventeenth-century litigation proceedings reveal about the *congregación* program? How should its impact on Maya principles of social organization be assessed? First, the Spaniards were indeed able to bring *parcialidades* together in their *congregación* program, either through the gentle persuasion of friars or the threat of military force. However, at least in this case, the Maya were not passive actors complying meekly with Spanish demands. Second, these Maya preserved the identities and functions of their *amaq'* and *parcialidad* units in the face of reduced populations and the introduction of a model of Spanish town organization. Third, not only was the preconquest *amaq'* principle maintained, it was also used to structure relationships between previously unaffiliated groups thrown together in the new social and political environment of the *pueblo*. As a result of the dispute, each *amaq'* group of three *parcialidades* was allowed to select its own *alcalde* and *regidor* to the town government. While the offices are clearly Spanish introductions, the groups' desire for political autonomy (or at least parity) vis-à-vis each other was an expression of a traditional Maya concern. This is especially clear when one considers that the aim of the Spaniards was to form a single municipal unit along Peninsular lines from diverse native groups. In any case, the introduced offices were initially controlled in large part by the native aristocracy. Finally, with church and state sometimes working at cross purposes, the *parcialidades* were able to press successfully for a redress of their grievances and a settlement based firmly on preconquest Maya concepts of *amaq'* autonomy and *parcialidad* association and control. Cultural change in the principles of sociopolitical organization as a result of *congregación* was extremely limited, since the new forms introduced by the Spanish were greatly modified in their application at the local level to conform with preexisting cultural principles.

CHAPTER SIX

Boundary Disputes: "Range Wars"

In the previous chapter we saw how *parcialidades* attempted to adjust to each other and to a new municipal arrangement, the result of Spanish programs for reorganizing highland Maya society. During the same period another element was introduced, apparently intentionally: the keeping of livestock. In preconquest times, the Maya did not have domesticated animals, with the exception of turkeys and dogs. Herd animals were entirely unknown. Yet, as the last litigation described in Chapter 5 indicated, by the 1560s the Sacapultecos were already breeding horses for sale in order to help meet community expenses. Because of the heavy involvement of the Dominicans in the formation of Sacapulas, it seems likely that they were the ones to introduce livestock breeding into the area. Gibson reports a similar pattern in the Valley of Mexico beginning during the sixteenth century and continuing through the eighteenth, during which time "some towns supplemented their incomes by herding animals on the community lands. The animals were town properties and herding became a communal enterprise under the direction of the town government" (Gibson 1964, 211).

Livestock provided a means of exploiting land that was hitherto either marginal or unusable in terms of agriculture, especially for the Sacapultecos. As we shall see, in addition to supporting the municipal government, livestock herds were also being kept by *cofradías* by the eighteenth century in order to help defray the costs of *fiestas*. This pattern was repeated elsewhere in Guatemala but was by no means universal, as is demonstrated by Collins's data on Jacaltenango, a town in the Cuchumatanes mountains (Collins 1980, 212). Here, unlike the area to the south of Sacapulas, large, Spanish-owned ranches were not created. According to Carmack, the Spaniards took over unoccupied Indian lands in the Santa Cruz del Quiché area in the early eighteenth century (Carmack 1981, 328–29). The growth of large Spanish ranches seems to have been a common colonial pattern in both Mexico and Guatemala, but one which did not obtain in the Sacapulas area. The Spaniards evidently did not find the region north of Santa Cruz attractive. As a result, large herds among the Sacapultecos and their neighbors were kept by town governments and *cofradías*. Individual Maya may also have kept herds; however, these are not attested to in the records.

Figure 6-1. The plain of Mixcolajá, viewed from the west, in the middle distance around the pond.

Evidently, the very success of livestock raising created problems. Some of these difficulties were noted in the last chapter, especially the need to control the animals so that crops would not be damaged. As we shall see, as both animal and human populations grew, and as more farm- and grazing-land was needed, disputes also arose when herds were kept near the mutual borders of different towns.

An early symptom of the problem was a litigation in 1601 between the Ah Canil and Ah Toltecat *parcialidades* of Sacapulas and the neighboring Indians of San Andrés Sajcabajá. The latter were accused of usurping Sacapulteco land around Mixcolajá (see Figure 6-1) for livestock grazing. The suit was not even answered by the Sajcabajá people, who also boycotted the proceedings. The two Sacapulas *parcialidades* won their suit at a cost of sixty-one *tostones* (AI Leg. 5936 Exp. 51914). Unfortunately for all involved, such problems were not so easily solved as the colonial period wore on.

Parcialidad and *Pueblo* Attempt Expansion

Another, more complex litigation began in January 1739 with a petition filed with Don Francisco Orozco Manrique de Lara, the *Juez Privativo del Real Derecho de Tierras,* by the *procurador* for Sacapulas on behalf of the entire town. Through their *procurador* the Sacapultecos stated that some of their land was bordered by land belonging to the *pueblo* of Chalchitán. The Sacapultecos were disturbed by the Chalchitanes' attempts to control some supposed Sacapulas land, known as Pichiquil, to which the latter allegedly had no right or title. The petition closed with a request that a Spanish official be sent to examine the *títulos* of both sides, verify what land pertained to each group, and enliven (*avivar*) the *mojones* separating them. If this were done, the Sacapultecos and their *procurador* felt the trouble would stop (AI Leg. 5978 Exp. 52518:1–IV).

In response to the petition, the *Juez Privativo* commissioned Don Juan Martínez de la Vega, the *Maestre de Campo* of Huehuetenango (the administrative unit to which Sacapulas and Aguacatán/Chalchitán both pertained at this time), to examine the papers of both groups, verify their land claims, enliven the *mojones,* and report back to his superior (ibid., IV–2). Two weeks later, at the end of January 1739, the *Maestre de Campo* received his instructions and made preparations to carry them out. Only one of these preparations was recorded. Significantly it was the naming and swearing-in of Joseph González, a Spaniard from Chiantla who spoke the languages of both groups, as interpreter for the proceedings (ibid., 12–12v).

Evidently, however, no action was taken, because the Sacapultecos filed another petition on 1 April 1739, restating the problem, requesting the inspection be carried out, and presenting evidence to back their land claims. This time they alleged that the Indians from Chalchitán *and* Aguacatán had transgressed their boundaries and had stolen livestock from the *estancias* (ranches) of the *cofradías* of Santo Domingo, San Francisco, and Santísimo Sacramento. The Sacapultecos also presented a listing made in 1595 of *mojones* for the *calpul* of Santo Tomás (ibid., 3–5v).

The *Maestre de Campo* was evidently moved to action. Ten days later a petition arrived from the *parcialidad* of Chalchitán in the *pueblo* of Aguacatán. The Chalchitanes requested an affidavit to the effect that, since their *título* was old and fragile and they were afraid of losing it, they would

Figure 6-2. The valley of Pichiquil, viewed from the north.

prefer to present a transcription instead. The request was granted. The document, dated 1691, indicated that trouble had been brewing between the Chalchitanes and Sacapultecos since at least that time. Because of disputes over land, thefts of livestock, and trespass of livestock, the officials of the *parcialidad* were committing the names of their ten *mojones* to writing. This copy of their *título* was duly included with the papers pertaining to the dispute (ibid., 8–10).

Three days later the Chalchitanes formally presented a petition to *Juez Comisario* Don Valentín Laso de la Vega in Aguacatán in which they told their side of the story. They asserted that their *título* proved their immemorial possession of Pichiquil, the parcel of land about which the dispute revolved (see Figure 6-2). The place was the original home of a *parcialidad* called Baijoon, which in 1739 composed (in part?) the Chalchitán *parcialidad;* the latter also claimed to have houses there. The Chalchitanes claimed that it was the Sacapultecos who, a few years previously, had begun an attempt to gain control of the land. Such a move would hurt the Chalchitanes since they claimed it was the only good land they had for planting, the proceeds of which went to pay their tribute and support *cofradía* activity. The same land was used in the summer to graze their mules and horses, animals that served the town of Huehuetenango in the daily transport of people and cargo. Additionally, the land was used to graze the more than four hundred head of livestock belonging to the *cofradía* of the titular cult of the *pueblo,* Nuestra Señora de la Encarnación. The Chalchitanes further stated they had no other serviceable lands for their support; all they had were some stony hills that lacked water and that were useless for any purpose (ibid., 6–7).

Arguments for both sides were thus clearly drawn. The Sacapultecos claimed encroachment by the Chalchitanes, who were stealing cattle from the *cofradías'* herds. The Chalchitanes asserted it was the Sacapultecos who had transgressed the traditional boundaries, endangering the farmers' control over their most productive piece of land.

Meanwhile, the *Juez Comisario* prepared to conduct the survey of *mojones* as per his instructions. He required both disputants to appear at their *mojones* with whatever papers or titles they felt gave them rights to their land. The same order applied also to the town of Santa María Cunén, which, because many people from the abandoned village of Magdalena resided there, had control of land bordering on both Sacapulas and the Chalchitán *parcialidad* (ibid., II–IIV, 13–14V). As a result of his survey, the *Juez Comisario* discovered a discrepancy in the *mojones* recognized by the two groups, resulting in more than a league (approximately 4.18 kilometers) of overlap. The judge stated that the two parties had agreed in principle to divide the difference in land in order to avoid future disputes, and they had promised to abide by whatever boundaries he would set. Part way through the process of resighting the boundaries the judge was forced to call a halt as the people of Aguacatán claimed they had received word from their priest to return to town to celebrate a *fiesta.* It would be five days before they could resume the boundary survey. In the meantime, the judge went to stay in Sacapulas, whence he would leave to finish setting the boundaries at Pichiquil and the *estancia* of Santo Domingo *cofradía* (ibid., 15–16).

Renewing his survey on 20 April 1739, the *Juez Comisario* visited the *estancia* of Santo Domingo *cofradía* and the land once belonging to the Magdalena people, which now pertained to Santa María Cunén. Since they were far from the town, the judge spent the night in the *estancia,* arriving at Pichiquil the next day. There, through an intrepreter, the *Juez Comisario* told the assembled delegations from Sacapulas, Cunén, Chalchitán, and Aguacatán that he could find no *mojones* listed in the papers they had presented and that anyway these were unofficial papers without any legal validity. Because of their surplus holdings, they should conform to the boundaries he would set and thus avoid litigation. The representatives responded that they would abide by his disposition of the *mojones*. Under the new boundaries, the Chalchitanes were given Pichiquil, while the Cunén people and the Sacapultecos agreed to divide the Magdalena land, since half the survivors of the group had gone to each town. The people were ordered to erect masonry markers to prevent future disputes. The Chalchitanes were further ordered to dig trenches around their *milpas* to prevent the Santo Domingo *cofradía* livestock from damaging them. The Chalchitanes were also told to abandon five *milpas* they had made along the Río Blanco in Sacapulas land, which they agreed to do. With all sides in apparent agreement, the *Juez Comisario* concluded the proceedings and filed his report (ibid., 16v–19v).

What seemed to be an amicable agreement was, for some unknown reason, canceled by the *Juez Privativo* in the capital. He issued a decree in January 1740 that called for the people of Aguacatán to be evicted from Pichiquil; the land was to be given to the Santo Tomás *parcialidad* of Sacapulas. Pichiquil is here explicitly stated as pertaining to the Santo Tomás *parcialidad,* which may indicate that this group had taken a direct part in the dispute, bypassing the formal municipal government. Perhaps the Tomases were not in accord with the agreement made by the municipal officers in April 1739. The *Juez Comisario* was to inform the Aguatecos that they could appeal to the *Juez Privativo,* but he was to proceed with the eviction (ibid., 23–25). This he did, notifying the Chalchitanes who, while stating they currently had no goods at the site, refused to listen to or sign the formal notification (ibid., 25–25v). The same day the *Juez Comisario* met with the Tomases to set the *mojones* and give them formal possession of the land. Evidently, the *mojones* listed in the Tomases' old papers were followed this time, which extended their boundaries far beyond those set in 1739.

Though there is a gap in the documentation of the case from April 1739 to January 1740, the Chalchitanes were aware that the Tomases were up to something, inasmuch as four days after their eviction they presented testimony from a Spaniard and two *mestizos* taken on 12 January 1740 that supported the Chalchitanes' claim to Pichiquil. The Chalchitanes mentioned that their witnesses were the oldest (non-Indian) people in the town of Huehuetenango. The two *mestizos* claimed to be seventy and eighty-five years old; the Spaniard fifty-eight years old. In their sworn testimony they all agreed on the main points. As far back as they could remember, Pichiquil had always belonged to the Chalchitanes. The Chalchitanes had no other land on which to plant. They had never heard that that same land belonged to Sacapulas. The three witnesses knew the land was cultivated by the Chalchitanes since, at one time or another, they had passed through Pichiquil on their way to Nebaj (ibid., 51v–56). Along with the testimony, the Chalchitanes presented their formal appeal of the decision awarding Pichiquil to the Tomases (ibid., 50–51v). As a result of the appeal, the *Alcalde Mayor* of Huehuetenango was ordered to verify the accuracy of the statements made and, if necessary, to remeasure the land in question.

In early March 1740 the Tomases made a similar claim to Pichiquil, which they said pertained to their old (preconquest) center of Xolchun (Department of Huehuetenango). The Tomases argued that while the witnesses presented by the Chalchitanes may have been telling the truth so far as they knew it, the Tomases' own occupation was still more ancient. The Tomases requested a letter of *amparo* for their possession of the land, and requested another order again forcing the Chalchitanes to leave Pichiquil (ibid., 20–20v). Once more, the *Alcalde Mayor* of Huehuetenango was instructed to investigate and make such adjustments as he found necessary.

In mid-March 1740 the *Juez Privativo* suddenly reversed his decision on the dispute, granting the Chalchitanes possession of Pichiquil and allowing the Tomases to appeal. The immediate reason for the reversal appears to have been still another petition submitted by the Chalchitanes in which they reminded the court of their witnesses' testimony, which showed that for more than thirty years they had been in possession of Pichiquil. They requested that the Tomases be ordered to leave the land free and clear for the Chalchitanes' use. If the Tomases had anything to present to the court with regard to the dispute, the Chalchitanes stated they would be ready to contest it. The petition was granted and the Sacapultecos notified (ibid., 48–48v).

The rest of the Sacapultecos seem to have become interested in pursuing the matter again, for in November 1740 the municipal officials named Don Thomás Mora as their *procurador* (ibid., 61–61v). The next day, Mora's first action was to present a letter from *Teniente General* Ordoñez to the *Padre Provincial* (head of the Dominican order in the area) in which, among other things, Ordoñez stated he believed that the land in question did not belong to either party but was *realenga* (that is, belonging to the Crown). Accepting this to be the case, Mora suggested that the court officially declare the land to be *realenga* and offer it at auction to the highest bidder. Mora's tactic recognized the fact that the Chalchitanes numbered only fifty tributaries and the Sacapultecos some nine hundred (apparently including all adults). The latter, then, should have been able to top any bid the former might make. The *Juez Privativo* accepted both Mora's interpretation of the land being indeed *realenga* and his suggestion that it should be offered at auction. Don Manuel Lardízaval y Llosa was duly commissioned to officiate at the auction as well as to gather information about the Sacapultecos' claim of lack of land (ibid., 28–30v).

Lardízaval y Llosa did not carry out his instructions until mid-January 1741 when he presented a warrant to Ordoñez. Formalities for the auction began in Aguacatán the same day. Interpreters of both the Aguatec and Sacapultec dialects were named and sworn in. The *alcaldes* and *principales* of Sacapulas and Chalchitán were notified to appear with their *títulos* or other documents for an inspection of Pichiquil, which was to take place several days later. Surveyors who would measure the plot were named and sworn in. On 25 January 1741 both sides appeared with their papers, which were adjudged to have no legal value. The land was declared *realenga*. The surveyors determined Pichiquil to be six *caballerías* and five *cuerdas* in extent (about 270 hectares) (ibid., 29v–35). Two days later, testimony was taken from three Spaniards of Huehuetenango as to what value should be placed on the land as a floor price for the bidding. All three agreed on six *tostones* per *caballería,* which was set as the minimum opening bid (ibid., 35v–37v). Since the proceedings were taking place in Huehuetenango, *defensores* who would enter the bids were named for both parties. On 30 January, the auction began; it lasted until 10 February. Each day Lardízaval y Llosa publicly announced the auction and waited for bids. The first bid did not arrive until 7 February, when, through their *defensor,* the Chalchitanes bid seven *tostones* per *caballería.* The next day the Sacapultecos' *defensor* bid eight *tostones.* On 9 February, the Chalchitanes upped their bid to fifteen *tostones,* but again the Sacapultecos countered, this time on the same day with a bid of twenty *tostones.* On 10 February, the Chalchitanes tried again, bidding twenty-five *tostones.* This bid must have been their limit because when the Sacapultecos' *defensor* stated they would bid one *toston* more than the highest other bid, the auction ended (ibid., 37v–39v).

Following his instructions, Lardízaval y Llosa next prepared to gather information about the Sacapultecos' need for additional land. Two *mestizos* from Nebaj and a Spaniard from Santa Cruz del Quiché gave testimony.

When asked whether the Sacapultecos had enough land to support themselves, all three witnesses agreed they did not. The witness from Quiché stated that the Sacapultecos could plant only along the rivers, and from this land they had lost about a *caballería* of crops the year before to floods. The two Nebaj witnesses stated that they knew the Sacapultecos had to live on corn purchased from other towns (ibid., 40–42). The Sacapultecos also submitted a petition to Lardízaval y Llosa asking for two Spanish officers in Huehuetanango to certify, as individuals who knew the area well, that the Sacapultecos were indeed in great need of land on which to plant. Both men did so certify (ibid., 46–47v).

On 13 February, Lardízaval y Llosa notified the Sacapultecos that they must go to the capital within forty days to have the formalities concluded by the *Juez Privativo de Tierras* (ibid., 42). In his concluding report, Lardízaval y Llosa stated that the Chalchitanes really did not need Pichiquil, having already as much workable land as the Sacapultecos. In addition, only the year before a number of idols had been found in Pichiquil by a Spanish official. Presumably he meant to imply that the Chalchitanes were practicing their traditional religion there and, therefore, were not deserving of the land. Finally, in terms of population, the Chalchitanes numbered only 135 tributaries while Sacapultecos had a total of 596. He further stated that the Tomases had taken him to a place containing buildings of their ancient town, which was near the Río Blanco (Xolchun) and where there was no other place nearby where they could have had farmland except Pichiquil—just a league away. When he asked the Tomases why they did not have the land under cultivation, they replied that at that time (just before or more likely after the conquest) they were few in number. Now (in 1741) the population had grown and they needed land to work, especially since there was a dearth of workable land other than along the river banks.

With regard to their religious and tribute obligations, Lardízaval y Llosa reported that the Sacapultecos maintained the divine cult very well while the Chalchitanes celebrated mass only twice a month and supported only one *cofradía* (de Nuestra Madre y Señora de los Mercedes). The Sacapultecos also paid more tribute and were very punctual. With this summary he ended his investigations and remitted the paperwork to the *Juez Privativo* (ibid., 42v–44).

Through their *procurador* the Chalchitanes appealed. The key to the appeal was that Pichiquil had been declared *realenga* in violation of Spanish law. Citing chapter and verse, the *procurador* argued that with regard to the sale of land, the Indians were to be left the land that belonged to them. With regard to Indians moved to towns (*reducción* or *congregación*), a royal *cédula* of 1692 explicitly stated they were not to be deprived of the land that they had formerly held, and that furthermore they were to be officially confirmed in their possession of such land. The implication of the laws quoted was clear. The Chalchitanes had proven their possession of the land through the testimony of witnesses, some of whom were over eighty years old. It was an error, therefore, to declare the land *realenga* only because the Chalchitanes lacked a legitimate title. The law cited made no mention of the evidence needed to sustain a claim (*justificación*) that their land should not be taken, only that they be confirmed in the possession of land occupied prior to the date of the *cédula*, 1692. The memories of the oldest witnesses extended back beyond that date, so the Chalchitanes had proven their possession and satisfied the legal preconditions for official confirmation of their holdings. The *procurador* went on to state the familiar problem: that the Chalchitanes had no other good land to plant. Apparently they presented a sworn statement to that effect from the resident priest of Chiantla. Also noted by the *procurador* was the fact that Sacapultecos were many and the Chalchitanes few in number. The former were rich, with ten *haciendas* of livestock, various parcels of land, and their *salinas,* but, being away from the royal highway, they were free from the *téquios* to which the Chalchitanes were subject. The idea here was that while the Sacapultecos paid more tribute, the Chalchitanes gave more direct service (ibid., 64–65v).

An undated order from the *Juez Privativo* to the *Alcalde Mayor* of Huehuetenango appears next in the records, instructing him to divide the Pichiquil land equally between the Chalchitanes and Sacapultecos as a way of ending the dispute. The order also forbade the admission of more documentation under pain of a twenty-five-*peso* fine (ibid., 67). There is no evidence of the order's having been implemented. In fact, in early March 1741, the Sacapultecos' *procurador* again petitioned the *Juez Privativo*, this time asking for two judges to decide the case and award Pichiquil on the basis of a survey of both parties' territories, which would prove who needed land more (ibid., 67–67v). The continuity in documentation of the case is broken at this point and no further actions are recorded.

We learn of the dispute's settlement when it unfortunately reerupted in 1808 (AI.45 Leg. 2924 Exp. 27326). In the new dispute the Chalchitanes presented a letter of *ámparo* from the *Juez Privativo* dated 11 December 1742 that secured their possession of Pichiquil. The land's boundaries were set officially in 1759; the paperwork for this contained the Sacapultecos' agreement to the boundaries between both groups' territories (ibid., 7v).

More problems began in 1808 when a Spanish official attempted to renovate the boundaries of the Santo Tomás *parcialidad*. As a result of their split with *parcialidad* San Francisco in the 1790s, and the accompanying division of the groups' land, the Tomases either believed Pichiquil was included in the new boundaries or were professing such a belief as a new tactic in their campaign for control. The Aguacatán-Chalchitán people refused to participate in the inspection of the *mojones*, and the matter was once again referred to the world of Spanish officialdom. Two years later, in 1810, the case was finally settled. The letter of *ámparo* granted by *Juez Privativo* Orozco in 1742 was recognized as the most legal document presented by either party, and the Hidalgo survey of the Tomases' land in 1794 (see Chapter 8) was determined not to have included Pichiquil. Names of the *mojones* dividing the two parties were officially listed, and an order was given that title to Pichiquil be issued to the Chalchitanes in order to avoid any further disputes (AI.45 Leg. 2924 Exp. 27326:1–20v).

Discussion

By the end of the sixteenth century, boundaries that had been of little concern since the conquest were becoming important again as herding assumed a greater role in the economies of towns in the Sacapulas area. Without fences (and seemingly without much supervision), animals easily passed across boundaries, eating what they found on the other side. The problem was a new one for the Maya; now it was animals rather than people that were violating the landholdings. The response was becoming more familiar: a complaint to the Spanish authorities through counsel. Yet, at least on the Sacapulas side, the social units concerned—the *parcialidades* that formed the ancient Tuhalha *amaq'*—demonstrated considerable continuity in the organization they used in administering land and in responding to threats to its continued occupation.

To a great extent the dispute with the Aguacatán-Chalchitán people seems to parallel the one between the people of Sajcabajá and of Santiago and San Sebastián in 1601. Livestock, introduced by the Spanish into the economy of the Sacapulas Maya, was being used to support various *cofradías*. Yet, as this was an addition to, rather than substitution for, traditional undertakings, the Sacapultecos—like the Sajcabajá people earlier—had to find suitable areas for grazing. From the Sacapultecos' standpoint Pichiquil was an appropriate place, suitable for grazing, watered, and away from areas already used for agriculture. Unfortunately, the Chalchitanes already occupied the place and depended on it for *milpa* as well as stock grazing.

However, in addition to reflecting problems of livestock introduction and perhaps population resurgence, the dispute may also indicate renewed attempts at expansion—at least by the Tomases to the northwest. The Tomases claimed the site of Xolchun (Department of Huehuetenango) as theirs before the conquest, and this claim was never denied by the Chalchitanes. The site, quite far from the Tomases' land in the colonial period but right on the edge of the valley of Aguacatán, overlooks the archaeological site of Chalchitán. According to Smith, Xolchun dates exclusively to the very latest period of Maya prehistory, while the site of Chalchitán appears to span from the Pre- to Postclassic periods (Smith 1955, 15–16). Is it possible that Xolchun is evidence of a process of territorial expansion in immediate preconquest times? If so, the process was cut short by the conquest, by population loss, and by the *congregación* program. Over two hundred years later, when expansion was again desirable, the Tomases moved in the same direction as had their ancestors, and even used their ancestors' memories of Xolchun as their own in order to bolster their case. Perhaps before the conquest the area northwest of the Tomases was already in dispute, and Xolchun built to enforce the Tomases' claims. If the preconquest people had recourse to arms to settle their disputes (which is suggested by the defensive positioning of the sites), the matter appears not to have been decided before the conquest cut off the process. Later, when expansion was again attempted, the use of force was out of the question. Litigation in the Spanish courts was the only strategy.

Ejido and *Pueblo* versus *Parcialidad:*

An Attempt at Directed Change

Another litigation proceeding between *parcialidades* occurred in the eighteenth century, this time between the Sacapultecos of San Sebastián and Santiago and the San Pedro people. In the century and a half since the litigation involving the "native" and "foreign" groups, the Spaniards appear to have forgotten everything they had previously known about *parcialidades*. The *pueblo* was now to be the administrative and legal unit of importance; disputes within *pueblos* were simply bothersome. However, 250 years after the Spanish conquest, the *parcialidad* was still a basic principle of Sacapulteco social, political, and territorial organization. As a result of the Spaniards' inability to understand the basic Maya units (*chinamitales, parcialidades*), and their attempts to impose Peninsular institutions (*pueblo, ejido*), litigation dragged on for seventeen years before a compromise based on the *parcialidad* principle was finally agreed to.

The Litigation

The litigation was brought to court in 1775, but trouble had been brewing since 1762. The origin of the conflict is not clear from the documents, but two factors may have been causal. The first was apparently a land problem. The two Sacapulteco *parcialidades* of Santiago and San Sebastián had held large tracts of territory on both sides of the Río Negro since preconquest times. At some point after the conquest the San Pedro people were brought in. We do not yet know the origins of the group. The Sacapultecos allowed the San Pedro people to settle and use some land on the north side of the river, while they themselves appear to have been concentrated on the south side near their *salinas*. One cause of the litigation appears to have been the Sacapultecos' attempts to cultivate part of the land again themselves, against the wishes of the San Pedro people (AI.80 Leg. 6025 Exp. 53126:66).

The second factor was the San Pedranos' attempt to sell some of the land near Turbalya to the local priest; before he bought the property the priest wanted to see the San Pedranos' *títulos*. Not having any such documents the San Pedranos approached the Sacapultecos, offering them eight *pesos* if they would loan their *título* long enough to show and satisfy the priest. The Sacapultecos refused. In retaliation the San Pedranos began their suit. Though not explicitly stated, it would seem likely that the San Pedranos' attempt to sell land on loan to them from the Sacapultecos, and then to request the latter's *título* to legitimize the transaction, must have created feelings of considerable hostility and betrayal on the part of the Sacapultecos. Yet, in the documents, the San Pedranos always represented themselves as the injured party (ibid., 71).

It cannot be discerned from the documents just how the problem came to the attention of the courts. It is to be assumed that one of the parties lodged a complaint, but we cannot say with certainty which one. We do know that once the Spaniards became involved they greatly complicated the situation and were unable to impose a solution.

The Sacapultecos first appeared before the *Juez Subdelegado* of Totonicapán in November 1775 in response to his order to submit their *títulos* written in their native language. The *títulos* were to have served as the basis of the first official survey of land claimed by each of the five *parcialidades*. Once the value of the land was determined by Spanish officials, the Sacapultecos could then purchase their own land from the Crown and receive a *título real*. The additional complicating factor introduced by the Spaniards at this point was the institution of *ejido,* or royal grant of common land issued to a community as a whole for the use of its citizens.

The *Subdelegado* was instructed by the *Audiencia* in early December not only to conduct the survey of land claimed by Sacapulas, but also to determine whether the Indians had sufficient *ejido* land and enough other land for planting. The land was to be marked in consultation with the surrounding communities, and care was to be taken to verify that land outside the community (that is, *ejido*) was not privately titled. The *Subdelegado* was similarly given the authority to add to the *ejido* if, in his judgment, it was too small for the population. In this case the land and *título* would be made over to the community at no cost. However, if the additional land requested was not necessary on the basis of the population but had been in the community's possession, a "moderate adjustment" could be made. The right of final approval was reserved for the *Audiencia* after a review of the *Subdelegado's* reports (AI Leg. 6021 Exp. 53083:3–30).

At the least, the instructions indicate the Spaniards' lack of familiarity with the realities of Sacapulas social organization. The *ejido* institution could be applied successfully to simple communities with a single jurisdiction, and no doubt this is what the Spaniards believed Sacapulas to be. However, Sacapulas was an artificial, forced collection of preconquest groups. Each *parcialidad* held its own land and maintained a degree of social and political independence that were all jealously guarded against encroachment by the other *parcialidades*. Therefore, to give land to the "community" was impossible in this context. The situation was made still worse by the Spaniards' choice of land for the *ejido*.

Seemingly in anticipation of the coming dispute, the Santiago and San Sebastián *parcialidades* petitioned in January 1776 to be allowed to remain in possession of the land that they together, as founders of the town, had held "anciently." Specifically mentioned were the salt flats, which were stated to belong exclusively to the Santiago and San Sebastián people (ibid., 5).

The Spanish authorities' answer came in February; it was to send Manuel Barroeta, *Subdelegado del Real Derecho de Tierras* of the *Alcaldía Mayor* of Totonicapán, to carry out the instruction previously described. His first act was to measure out the "royal league" that would constitute the community's *ejido*. Boundary markers were duly set and limits noted. The *ejido* grant was composed of a square of land on which the town itself was built, extending mostly south from the river, but also including a strip of land on the north shore (see Map 7-1). For a single community, not subdivided into smaller landholding *parcialidades,* Barroeta's designation of the *ejido* as the town proper and surrounding land might have been correct. In Sacapulas, however, the town and adjacent land belonged to the Santiago and San Sebastián *parcialidades*. Thus, in effect, Barroeta's action removed a considerable portion of the Santiago and San Sebastián land—including the valuable *salinas*—from the *parcialidades'* control and introduced the idea that this land and the *salinas* should be freely exploited by all members of the community. *Parcialidad* ownership and administration were to be replaced by individual initiative and exploitation. The ramifications of this act did not become evident immediately, especially since the rest of the *Subdelegado's* instruction remained to be carried out.

On the day after the *ejido* designation, Barroeta planned to begin his survey of the land claimed by the various *parcialidades*. However, trouble ensued at the first *mojón* between the San Pedro people and those of Santiago and San Sebastián. Both claimed that particular *mojón* (Barroeta's report does not specify what *mojón,* but we are later told it was Piedra Negra) and decided they did not want their land surveyed at the same time, but separately. In Barroeta's judgment, the situation went beyond his instructions. He therefore suspended the survey in order to file an

Map 7-1. Facsimile of the Barroeta survey map with north on the left.

interim report and await further orders. In his account, Barroeta included some observations. He stated that the *salinas* possessed by Santiago and San Sebastián was the only useful piece of land in the area except for four- teen *caballerías* owned jointly by Santo Tomás and San Francisco. The two Sacapulteco *parcialidades* had no instrument to back their claim to the *salinas* other than their *título*. This was the "Título de los Señores de Sa- capulas," which was presented for the first time to Spanish authorities in this case. Barroeta judged the document to be of no legal value, while the Santo Tomás and San Francisco people had had an official title granted by the Spaniards in 1707. On the other hand, the *Subdelegado* reported that the San Pedro people had nothing but "rocky hills and ravines," used mostly for pasturing livestock. In a confusing final statement Barroeta gave some idea of the impending problems, stating that he could not con- vince the Indians that the pasture and hills (of the *ejido*?) were common land. According to their viewpoint, since the *salinas* were not common land, neither should anything else be (AI.80 Leg. 6025 Exp. 53126:15). This initial failure of the Sacapultecos to understand the implications of *ejido* did not last long.

In March 1776, Barroeta returned to Sacapulas to continue his work, specifically to survey the land claimed by Santiago and San Sebastián, and San Pedro. His first step was to take sworn testimony from local witnesses to determine the precedents for claims to the land. At this point we get the first indication that all is not right with *Subdelegado* Barroeta. While his assignment was to look into San Pedro and Santiago and San Sebastián land, he called one witness from San Pedro and one each from Santo Tomás and San Francisco. One begins to question Barroeta's competence and/or honesty. The three statements themselves are nearly identical, being made by elderly individuals of ninety (San Pedro), one hundred (San Francisco), and over one hundred (Santo Tomás) years of age. All stated that they had heard it said and (except for the man from San Pedro) had read in papers left by their ancestors that their respective groups had been in possession of the land they now claimed since before the conquest. They further stated that no judge had previously measured any part of the land except for the fourteen *caballerías* owned jointly by Santo Tomás and San Francisco.

After lengthy formalities of selecting personnel and equipment, the survey was finally carried out. Another travesty of justice occurred when Barroeta decided, seemingly arbitrarily, that the river would be the *mojón* dividing the land of San Pedro on the north bank from that of San Sebastián and Santiago on the south. The decision was counter to preconquest precedent, the latter two *parcialidades* having controlled considerable land on the north bank (see Chapter 4). Only later in the official correspondence do we learn the reasons for Barroeta's decision. It was made on the basis of Santiago and San Sebastián's failure to comply with the *Subdelegado's* order to plant *milpas* (in the disputed north bank land?), despite his admonishments. He goes on to say, however, that this "disobedience" on the part of the two *parcialidades* resulted from the request of the San Pedro people that the Santiago and San Sebastián people stay out of the land in question. This decision, along with Barroeta's earlier exclusion of representatives of Santiago and San Sebastián from testifying, points to a bias on the *Subdelegado's* part in favor of the San Pedro people and suggests some sort of collusion between them.

The next phase of the proceedings was to assess the value of the land claimed so that the Spaniards would know how much to charge the Indians for a royal title. The Spanish concept was that, with the conquest, all land had passed into the royal patrimony. Granting title to a piece of land decreased the patrimony; therefore compensation must be made to the Crown for the favor. To the Sacapultecos it simply meant they had to purchase their own land.

Witnesses were called to give assessments of the land's value under oath. Unlike on previous occasions, the witnesses were identified by name and *pueblo* (Sacapulas) only. No *parcialidad* affiliations were given. In view of Barroeta's behavior up to this point, the omission may be significant. Perhaps all the witnesses were San Pedro people. The three witnesses all agreed that San Sebastián and Santiago land was of little use except for the *salinas*. Nonetheless they valued it at from three to four *pesos* per *caballería*. The San Pedro land was agreed to be worse still, and worth only from four *reales* to one *peso* per *caballería*. Based on this information Barroeta concluded that Santiago and San Sebastián should be charged five *pesos* per *caballería* and San Pedro two. His assignment in Sacapulas completed, the *Subdelegado* left the area. His name continues to be mentioned, however, in the complaints filed against him by Santiago and San Sebastián.

Difficulties arose almost immediately with the Spaniards' attempts to implement their land-apportionment scheme. Manzanares y Zerezo, the *Alcalde Mayor*, went to Sacapulas in August 1778 as part of his *visita* or inspection tour. The situation had apparently not changed greatly since Barroeta's survey. After explaining that the land was now common land (just *ejido?*) and could be used by all for planting, the San Pedro people asked for this to be put in writing so they would have a document for future use. They were opposed by the people of Santiago and San Sebastián, who said they would agree only if it was made clear that the San Pedro people were to have no part of the *salinas*. The San Pedranos replied that everyone had a right to the *salinas* now because they were all of the same *pueblo* and that the *salinas* were within the *ejido* of that *pueblo*. The San Pedranos had learned quickly how to adapt the Spanish concepts to their own uses. The *Alcalde Mayor* made no decision, but referred the problem to the *Fiscal* (AI 80 Leg. 6025 Exp. 53126:40v–41).

Shortly afterward, also in August 1778, the two *parcialidades* of Santiago and San Sebastián sent a letter to the *Juez Privativo del Derecho de Tierras* registering their complaints against Barroeta's actions. Here the degree of the *Subdelegado's* incompetence or collusion with San Pedro was made known. The first complaint pertained to the examination of the *parcialidades'* boundaries and explained why the river was chosen as the boundary between San Pedro and Santiago and San Sebastián. On the second day of his stay, they said, Barroeta called the *principales* of the town together and, after measuring the royal league of *ejido,* went on to walk over their land. However, upon arriving at the *mojón* on the Río Negro called Piedra Negra, Barroeta did not wish to go on. The document is not unequivocal on this point, but we assume the Sacapultecos meant that he did not wish to go on across the river to the north bank and continue the survey. Barroeta maintained his position even when advised by the two *parcialidades' principales* that he should cross, asking disdainfully, "What do you want with hills?" (ibid., 42–42v). According to Santiago and San Sebastián, Barroeta followed the advice of San Pedro and did not continue the survey.

After the aborted survey Barroeta went to the *parcialidad* house of Santiago where he was asked to register their old *títulos*. He said the *títulos* were worthless because they were written in Maya. Next he was asked to register their royal warrant to their land and *salinas*. After registering it, Barroeta asserted that while the warrant had been issued by the king, he had forgotten to sign it! The *Subdelegado* said he would take it to the capital so the king could sign it. Not being able to read and thus verify Barroeta's assertions, the Sacapultecos entrusted their papers to him. This would account in part for the fact that the royal warrant was never presented to the authorities for consideration in the dispute.

Later, when they went to retrieve their warrant, Barroeta told them not to be foolish, that he would not release the warrant to them, that they would have to bring all the papers of the five *parcialidades* to him so that the king could sign them. He assured them that they could retrieve the papers once he received the appropriate letters from the capital and the *Alcaldía Mayor*. These never arrived and, in fact, all the papers had secretly been turned over to the San Pedro people.

With all the community's documents now in their hands, the San Pedro people were well placed to continue their efforts to expel the people of Santiago and San Sebastián from land on the north bank of the river. The latter, however, would not give up their ancestors' land. Seeing this, the San Pedro people stated that they had title to the land, but when the two *parcialidades* called San Pedranos' bluff and demanded to see the *títulos* (knowing them to be forgeries) the San Pedranos answered that the *Audiencia* had taken all the titles. Asked what they had done with the royal warrant, the San Pedro people laughed and asked "What warrant? There is no more warrant!" (AI.80 Leg. 6025 Exp. 53126:43).

When representatives of Santiago and San Sebastián went to Barroeta to ask for his permission to plant (presumably on the north bank), he denied them, saying the land was no longer theirs. Later, he summoned the San Pedro people to tell them to plant.

The Santiago and San Sebastián people closed their August 1778 letter to the *Juez Privativo* by asking him to right these wrongs by (a) returning their land on the north bank and *salinas,* although they were within the *ejido* grant, (b) sending them a copy of their *Despacho,* (c) forcing the San Pedro people to present their supposed *título,* and (d) sending them another judge to resurvey their land.

Later in the history of the dispute, the tactics of the San Pedranos are clarified. According to the people of Santiago and San Sebastián, an individual from San Pedro who wished to change his affiliation to their side confessed that his group had no *títulos,* that all of their claims had been lies. Furthermore, to support their claims, the *principales* of San Pedro had forged a *título,* inventing its contents, which task must have been considerably simplified once the San Pedro *principales* had been given the Santiago and San Sebastián *título* by Barroeta and thus could use it both as a model and for information about specific *mojones.*

Incredibly, the Spanish authorities accepted Barroeta's findings and supported his recommendations. He even received orders through August and September 1778 to return to Sacapulas to oversee the placement of boundary markers as dictated by his survey. Santiago and San Sebastián were to be reimbursed for the loss of any crops on the north bank of the river. Otherwise, the land was to pass to San Pedro. In spite of the fact that the *salinas* belonged to Santiago and San Sebastián, they were in the future to be held in common for the use of the entire community because they were included in the *ejido.* The only action from which the Sacapultecos received satisfaction was the order to return all documents presented in the case to their rightful owners. But even this order was addressed to Barroeta who, as we have seen, turned all the papers over to San Pedro. Finally, Barroeta was to expedite the issuance of royal titles to the different *parcialidades,* an action that would effectively institutionalize his survey (AI 80 Leg. 6025 Exp. 53126:44–48v).

The Spaniards' thinking was summed up by the *Fiscal,* or state's attorney, who, ironically, quoted Barroeta's report about *parcialidad* land in general and the Sacapulas *salinas* in particular. The *Fiscal* asserted that the land should be declared common land for the entire *pueblo* without reference to *calpules, barrios,* or *parcialidades.* He hoped these subgroups would disappear gradually in all areas because of the discord, disagreements, and enmity they caused between residents of the same *pueblo.* The Spaniards clearly felt they could and should extirpate the institution of *parcialidad* through creating *ejidos.* Litigation proceedings between groups would thus decline and *pueblos* would be strengthened as the basic units of colonial administration.

Barroeta did not return to Sacapulas to carry out his orders. The last record of his activities is a note he sent to the *principales* of San Pedro in March 1779 advising them of an impending visit by the new *Alcalde Mayor*, who would settle matters. After this, Barroeta drops from sight. Perhaps the new and, as we shall see, conscientious *Alcalde Mayor* relieved him of duty. Whatever the case, while Barroeta himself was gone, his survey continued to haunt the Sacapultecos and ultimately formed part of the basis for settling the dispute.

That same month, the new *Alcalde Mayor*, Don Francisco Geraldino, went to Sacapulas, not only to familiarize himself with the case but also to implement the *Audiencia's* orders with regard to land division and *ejido* among the *parcialidades*. Geraldino's first action was to ascertain that the *salinas* were not in fact common property of a *calpul* (*parcialidad*) but were owned by individuals. The people had always bought, sold, and inherited them from their ancestors. He reported this to the *Audiencia* and went on to compile a list of the owners' names and titles, and the extent of their holdings.

The *Alcalde Mayor* decided not to name *defensores* (lawyers) for the parties in the case in order "to more simply produce the truths" (ibid., 49v). Geraldino had the *parcialidades* restate their complaints against each other, but no new information was produced. He also visited the disputed land on the north bank of the river, across from the chapel of San Francisco. Unfortunately, Geraldino's final decisions and recommendations to the *Audiencia* are not found in the documents. Geraldino himself was called away on other business and apparently never returned. Judging from the tenor of the continuing dispute, the *salinas* appear to have been removed from the *ejido* and returned to their owners' control, though San Pedro continued to claim them. However, litigation continued over the disputed north-bank properties.

There is a gap in the documentation from 1779 until 1786. In March 1786 the people of Santiago and San Sebastián requested that the *Fiscal* order the return of their *título* and other papers originally entrusted to Barroeta. The *Fiscal* was inclined to grant their request and so ordered the *Alcalde Mayor*. However, the San Pedro people protested the order, and the papers remained with the authorities.

The entire dispute was brought to a head in April 1788 when, with the time of preparation of the *milpas* for planting at hand, the question arose of who would do the planting on the disputed land (AI 45 Leg. 2906 Exp. 26938). This appears to have been a problem because the San Sebastián people had worked the land the year before. The initial decision was to allow the San Pedro people to plant if they would reimburse the other *parcialidad* for having already cleaned the plot. Instead, however, as an interim measure while awaiting the final disposition of the case, *Alcalde Mayor* Don Nicolás Ortiz de Letona decided it would cause less disturbance to divide the plot equally among the three *parcialidades*.

Simple as it appears, this sensible interim solution represented a fundamental change in thinking on the part of at least one important Spanish official connected with the case. One is tempted to believe that the *Alcalde Mayor* was becoming acculturated, or at least conditioned, to view problems according to Maya principles. While previous officials had talked about land being for the common use of the entire *pueblo*, Letona now almost unconsciously saw that it was logical to divide the plot among the three *parcialidades,* accepting them de facto as the proper units to hold the land. This position represents quite a turnaround in the Spanish policy of forming single municipal units. Don Nicolás' decision was accepted even by the *Audiencia*. He sent orders to this effect to his lieutenant in Sacapulas. While Santiago and San Sebastián were more than willing to accept the temporary division, San Pedro was not. Nonetheless, the division was publicly made in May, though it was boycotted by the San Pedro people.

No further action was taken until November 1788, the delay being due to the death of the *Fiscal* and the need of his successor to familiarize himself with the *Fiscal's* affairs. Ultimately, the new *Fiscal* recommended to the *Audiencia* that it should simply reissue the orders for the original solution of 1778 to the *Alcalde Mayor,* Ortiz de Letona. However, Don Juan Hurtado, *Secretario de Cámara de la Audiencia,* seems to have wanted additional information before making a decision. He commissioned a map based on Barroeta's survey of 1776. Despite the objections previously made by the Santiago and San Sebastián *parcialidades,* the survey was again accepted as valid by the *Audiencia* in December 1788. The *ejidos* plotted by Barroeta were reaffirmed, including the *salinas*. All other land within the *mojones* surveyed by Barroeta was declared *realenga*, purchasable from the *Audiencia* at the prices established in 1776 (four *tostones* per *caballería*) (AI 80 Leg. 6025 Exp. 53126:88v–96).

In January 1789 the San Pedro people were able to pay the *Audiencia* the necessary 151 *pesos* and 1 *real* for the land they claimed outside the *ejido* and a title was duly issued. The people of Santiago and San Sebastián followed suit in April of the same year, paying 89 *pesos* and 7½ *reales* for their land not in dispute, minus the *ejidos*.

Early in 1790 the San Pedro people made new appeals to the *Juez Privativo del Derecho de Tierras*. They complained bitterly that the Santiago and San Sebastián *parcialidades* had kept them from using the *salinas* and *ejido* land on the south side of the river. However, they recognized this as the state of affairs, they said, and were petitioning the court only to make the other group recognize the river as the dividing line. Such an action would leave San Pedro in control of a small strip of *ejido* land along the north bank, which of course was the original object of their litigation back in the 1760s.

Based on recommendations from the *Alcalde Mayor* and *Fiscal,* the *Audiencia* was initially inclined to grant the San Pedro people's request because it seemed the quickest way to resolve the dispute. No action seems to have been taken until June 1792, though. At that time the San Pedro people responded, for the first time through their *procurador,* that they would agree to recognize the river as the dividing line. Orders were sent in 1792 to *Alcalde Mayor* Ortiz de Letona to implement the plan.

San Sebastián and Santiago acknowledged the order but openly ignored it for several weeks. Through their *procurador,* the San Pedro people then petitioned the *Audiencia* in August, asking it to proclaim that the two *parcialidades* were in rebellion (AI Leg. 603 Exp. 53257:17). The *Audiencia* declined to take such a drastic step.

Finally, on 13 September, the *procuradores* for both parties informed *Secretario de Cámara* Hurtado that the three *parcialidades* had worked out their own compromise to divide the north bank *ejido,* and that their leaders had even come to the capital to have the compromise approved. The agreement itself was simple and obviously based on the interim division of the land in 1788. Immediately after harvesting the corn and sugarcane the San Pedro people currently had growing there, the land would be divided into two parts. The eastern part would go to San Pedro, the western part to Santiago and San Sebastián.

As a final answer, however, the proposal was unacceptable to the *Audiencia* which stubbornly held to the letter of the law with regard to *ejido* (ibid., 25). In the *Fiscal's* opinion, neither the *procuradores* nor the *principales* of the *parcialidades* involved had the power to make such an agreement nor were they authorized to compromise the rights of their respective groups. These arguments were logical in view of the *Audiencia's* need to retain ultimate authority in legal decision making. However, the *Fiscal's* third argument against the agreement indicated a significant shift of thinking on his part. He stated that, in addition to the other problems just mentioned, the proposed agreement had not been approved by all the interested *parcialidades,* which totaled five in number. Since the land in question was part of the *ejido,* there should be common use for all five without one being able to hinder (*embarazar*) another. This intransigence is surprising in view of the fact that the south-bank *ejido,* including the *salinas,* had been conceded to Santiago and San Sebastián. Nevertheless, a proper agreement would have had to include a statement that all five *parcialidades* had common use of the north-bank plot.

Thus even the legal adviser to the *Audiencia* had become almost conditioned to thinking in terms of *parcialidades'* rights as opposed to individuals' rights. This thinking was accepted by *Secretario de Cámara* Hurtado, who declared the north-bank plot to be for the common use as part of the *ejido.* In addition, he empowered the *Alcalde Mayor* to divide the plot among the five *parcialidades* if they so desired, in order to avoid future disagreements. When notified of this option on 16 October, the five *parcialidades* were unanimous in their desire that the plot be formally divided among them and requested that the *comisionado* of the *pueblo* oversee the process. This was immediately ordered by the *Alcalde Mayor* and the division was made the same day.

As a result of some three decades of effort, each *parcialidad* was awarded a piece of land measuring about 205 *varas* wide (1 vara = 0.83 meters), and agreed not to worry about the variable depth of each piece that resulted from the river's uneven course. Final approval by the *Audiencia* came in mid-January 1793.

Discussion

For the San Pedro people the litigation proved to be something of a disaster. As a "foreign" *parcialidad* they had been settled as guests on Santiago and San Sebastián land on the north bank of the Río Negro. They had no *títulos,* either from preconquest times or from the Spanish authorities. This was of no consequence for many years, but with the passing of time the San Pedro people forgot their status and came to consider the land their own. The Sacapultecos did not forget, however, and, for whatever reason, began to use some of the north-bank land. Initially, the San Pedro people's only aim was to secure their north-bank holdings. Their objectives changed when the Spaniards introduced the *ejido* concept to the *pueblo.* The idea of the *ejido* as the common land of an entire *pueblo,* as opposed to a single *parcialidad,* combined with Barroeta's criminal survey, which incorporated much Sacapulteco land and the *salinas* in the *ejido,* presented new possibilities for the San Pedro litigation. Instead of merely securing the north bank, the San Pedro people could attempt to gain access to the economically important *salinas* as well as other south-bank land. For a while they were able to press their demands successfully, thanks largely to what must have been Barroeta's collusion with them. Ultimately, though, the just precedent for Santiago and San Sebastián's claim, at least to the *salinas* and south bank, was recognized. In the end the San Pedro people did not gain access to the *salinas* or the south bank. In fact, they lost four-fifths of the north-bank holdings for which they had begun the litigation.

Inexplicably, the north-bank plot remained *ejido* in the minds of the Spanish officials. This is doubly strange when one considers that they made no attempt to enforce common exploitation of the south-side *ejidos* after the San Pedro people had given up all claims to the south bank. Thus by 1790 the complex struggle was over a small strip of land only about one kilometer long and, at most, a few hundred meters deep. While the plot remained as *ejido* in the Spaniards' minds, the unit they felt should control and exploit it changed. By 1788 the official closest to the scene, the *Alcalde Mayor*, was proposing a temporary settlement based on the *parcialidad* principle. By 1792 even the *Fiscal* had come around and was taking the line of reasoning to a logical conclusion: *Parcialidades* hold the land, but since the land in question is *ejido* all the *parcialidades* must hold it. In the meantime, the three *parcialidades* had been allowed to purchase other lands from the Crown, to which they were granted confirmed titles. This lapse on the Spaniards' part only served to reinforce and revivify the *parcialidad* principle in Sacapulas.

In terms of cultural continuity the case is instructive. Two and a half centuries after the conquest the ancient *chinamit*-cum-*parcialidad* principle had not only survived but continued to be the key to the Sacapulas people's social organization and land tenure systems. A concerted effort to dismantle the *parcialidad* principle through the introduction of *ejido* and *pueblo* as mutually supporting counter-principles failed. To affect a final solution, the Spaniards were forced to change their concept of *ejido* to conform to Maya principles. *Ejido* would be common land for all the *parcialidades*, but each *parcialidad* would control its own section.

An *Amaq'* Breaks Down

By the eighteenth century, two *parcialidades* survived of the three that had composed the Lamakib *amaq'* from preconquest times down to the 1580s. Santo Tomás and San Francisco *parcialidades* appear to have maintained a high degree of political association, similar to that of Santiago and San Sebastián, presumably based on a shared sacred geography and, perhaps in the colonial period, intermarriage. Down through the early eighteenth century the relationship changed little, if at all. They jointly received limited title to their land in 1591 and again in 1707. Yet, by the second half of the eighteenth century, the situation had changed. Population growth was certainly one factor. In 1776, when the dispute first came to official attention, Sacapulas' population was at its colonial zenith—at or beyond preconquest levels (see Chapter 3). Difficulties in controlling livestock herds also increased. The Sacapultecos dealt with these pressures in several ways.

Hitherto unused or previously abandoned portions of the *parcialidades'* territories were reoccupied, but since agriculturally useful land was limited in extent, expansion to traditional boundaries must have been rapid. Once these were reached, one option was to encroach on the land of a neighboring *pueblo,* which was precisely the nature of the dispute between Santo Tomás (and later all of Sacapulas) and Chalchitán and Aguacatán, reviewed in Chapter 6. Another alternative was to encroach on the land of a neighboring *parcialidad.* Such a tactic would have been limited, of course, by the tenacity with which *parcialidades* defended their territories. In Sacapulas, yet another alternative was developed, perhaps as a result of acculturation to Spanish customs: the surreptitious "sale" or "rental" of both *salinas* land and agricultural plots, with transactions of farmland sometimes occurring between individuals of different *parcialidades* without the knowledge of their respective leaders. In the short term, an individual with an excess of land could make a profit by "renting" or "selling" a portion of it to someone else who had no plots in which to plant. Again, in the short term, individuals would survive and inequities in land distribution among an increasing population could be ameliorated.

Even this tactic was of strictly limited help and, in the case of Santo Tomás and San Francisco, the pressures resulted in an open rift between the two, a lengthy litigation, and the eventual partition of the land they had once jointly controlled. However, the attempt by Spanish officials to arrive at an equitable division of the land was enormously complicated by claims of private ownership to various plots and the resulting need to decide if the claims were valid and whether or not to deduct the plots thus claimed from the total area to be divided. As a result of the dispute the *amaq'* broke down as a landholding unit, while individual land owning was effectively prohibited and the *parcialidad* principle was reinforced.

The Litigation

The dispute was first brought to the attention of Spanish officials in April 1776 when a complaint was registered with *Subdelegado* Barroeta by the Santo Tomás *parcialidad* against their neighbors, the *parcialidad* San Francisco. According to the Tomases, the Franciscos had recently begun encroaching on that part of the fourteen *caballerías* of land that had been titled to both groups in 1707 but traditionally used by the Tomases. The reasons for this intrusion were not given, but population pressure must have been one. In 1794, San Francisco numbered 455 people, Santo Tomás only 255 (AI Leg. 6040 Exp. 53303:37v); although this was a generation after the case was begun, one can only assume the relative proportions of the two groups' populations were still similar.

In response, the Tomases presented a translation from Maya of a *título* (or a list of *mojones*) dated 1595 that marked the boundaries of their territory. Barroeta simply ordered both sides to return to their own territories and remain there without disturbing one another.

Barroeta's orders seemingly were not obeyed. In June 1779 *Alcalde Mayor* Geraldino issued similar commands. He directed that four Franciscos who had planted crops in the Santo Tomás portion of the fourteen *caballerías* be removed from the land, but that they be paid the value of their crops, as assessed by the first *alcalde* of Sacapulas, who belonged to neither group.

Geraldino's decision was based on a perceptive and revealing report by Captain Pedro Henríquez, who had been commissioned by the *Alcalde Mayor* to investigate the case. To support his decision that each *parcialidad* return to and remain in its respective traditional territory, Henríquez presented seven points reflecting local customs and conditions.

First, he asserted that each *calpul* (*parcialidad*) had immemorially recognized its own territory without members of one group trespassing into the land of another. It followed that the "ancient" *principales* of both *calpules* would have made a just division of the fourteen *caballerías*. It would also follow that the record of the division would be in the papers of each *calpul,* which listed the *mojones.* While the Indians called these papers *títulos,* they were not legal titles in the Spanish sense. For that reason, the authorities ignored the native *títulos,* fixing their attention instead on titles awarded by the Spanish authorities; those titles made the land common to both groups in regard to its legitimate possession, but did not address the question of its traditional use.

Second, Henríquez thought it certain that the divisions of *calpul* land and its exclusive use by a particular *calpul* without transgressions by others were derived from preconquest practices. The specific divisions of the land were ratified after the conquest and acquisition of a royal title. However, the title made the land common to the two groups only in regard to its possession; how the land was to be used was never implicitly or explicitly stated. Because of the antiquity of these practices, any attempt to vary the groups' rights of land use would certainly bring discord.

Third, while the independent use of a *calpul's* land by its members was one of ancient practice, and not transgressing into the land of other *calpules* was another, it was also true that from the moment the land was first titled both *calpules* had sold many pieces of land to individuals of different *calpules.* According to papers Henríquez examined, such sales had been occurring for a hundred years without either *calpul* being aware of the sales made by the other. Over the years the illegally alienated pieces of land, which he stated were numerous, were inherited and sold until individuals of other *calpules* held them privately. Again, this change of land use and possession practices was sure to cause trouble.

Fourth, Henríquez examined the land of two *calpules* used for *milpa.* He stated that the Santo Tomás people had a beautiful plain called Chicumatz and both banks of the Río Negro. Not only did the Santo Tomás people live along the Río Negro, but also located there were the gardens purchased or rented by individuals of all the *calpules* of Sacapulas.

Fifth, the San Francisco people had three tracts of level ground named Ixpapal, Xetzagel, and Patzagel. Ixpapal, it will be remembered, was in contention in the 1572 suit between the "foreign" and "native" *parcialidades.* The Franciscos had sold and rented plots on this land to individuals of other *calpules.* According to Henríquez, if the San Francisco people were to plant the three areas simultaneously, they would not have the strength to work them. If they did plant them, they would harvest enough maize to provide for half the *pueblo* of Sacapulas. The Franciscos also left plots unplanted, possibly to rest the land. This need to rest the land for a number of years after a few seasons' use may account in large part for the San Francisco peoples' inability to plant all their holdings at once, as Henríquez had suggested, and for individuals' renting and/or buying plots of land where possible. Henríquez felt the confusion was exacerbated by the San Francisco *principales'* ability to impede the planting of the land the *maseguales* (commoners) had selected for that purpose, although he did not know by what right the *principales* did this. Also, in the event a *masegual* or *principal* died, leaving a plot of land, the *principales* would claim it, saying the land belonged not to the deceased but to the *calpul*.

Sixth, an additional source of disagreement was that the San Francisco people claimed the Santo Tomás people had grazed their livestock on San Francisco land during the last planting season. Henríquez dismissed this as a serious complaint; the numerous *barrancas* in the area would easily serve as places to fence in cattle, and both groups had livestock that pastured indiscriminantly in both territories. He suggested the *Alcalde Mayor* simply order the *alcaldes* of Sacapulas to require owners of animals to corral them.

Finally, Henríquez recommended that the best way to solve the problem was to reissue Barroeta's decision. He also suggested that an *Auto* be extended to the Santo Tomás people in order to defend their land.

Although there is a gap in the documentation from 1779 to 1794, Geraldino's orders do not seem to have had much effect in quelling the dispute between the two *parcialidades* over their jointly held land. On 30 July 1794, the *principales* of San Francisco addressed a complaint to the *Juez Privativo* stating that, based on extracts from old *títulos,* the Tomases were now claiming all the land that both *parcialidades* had always held together like holders of a common *ejido*. The Franciscos asserted that such claims were against the sovereign's wishes that the *ejido* land of a *pueblo* should be enjoyed by all its inhabitants. They petitioned the *Juez Privativo* to confirm their possession of the land.

The Franciscos' interesting use of the *ejido* concept to justify their complaint probably derives from their experience during the partially contemporaneous dispute over *ejido* land between San Pedro and Santiago and San Sebastián (see Chapter 7). In any case, the *Juez Privativo* responded by sending *Subdelegado* Domingo Hidalgo to investigate.

Arriving at Sacapulas on 18 December 1794, Hidalgo had representatives of the two groups brought into his presence and questioned them extensively, retrieving the essential points of the case from the long arguments. To Hidalgo, the most significant point was that the land in question was not in fact part of the town *ejido,* as asserted by the San Francisco people, but a fourteen-*caballería* plot to the west of town that both *calpules* held jointly under a *título de composición*.

To understand the bases of the claims, Hidalgo ordered the litigants to present their *títulos*. The San Francisco people presented a thirteen-page document copied by *Alcalde Mayor* Geraldino in 1780 from the broken fragments. The document contained a *título* given by the *Presidente de la Audiencia* Don Alonso Oviedo de Castilla to Don Rodrigo de Cárdenas, dated 13 April 1591.[1] The two *parcialidades,* called by the preconquest names of Saqualpaneca and Quateca, are stated to have asked for a remeasurement of their land. This was done, but Hidalgo expressed dissatisfaction with the lack of specifics recorded in the survey. Only some thirty lines of the document were given over to the particulars of the survey, and they did not provide directions, give the number of *cuerdas,* or describe *mojones* (with two exceptions). The document concluded with an estimation of the area involved: fourteen *caballerías.* In Hidalgo's opinion, the document proved nothing but the good faith with which both groups had previously held the land. As with all old *títulos,* the 1591 *título* had no legality.

The documents presented by the Santo Tomás people consisted of copies of those already produced in the current dispute: the Barroeta survey, Geraldino's order to remain on their own land, the priest's report in favor of the two groups' remaining on their respective land, and Barroeta's order to peacefully maintain the boundaries. Hidalgo felt that this set of documents did not add any information on which to base a decision. Hidalgo subsequently suspended the proceedings since the Franciscos mentioned some *mojones* as their boundary with Santo Tomás while the Tomases claimed other *mojones* as their boundary with the Franciscos. There was no impartial way to decide who was right.

At this point the Franciscos presented Hidalgo with a formal request for a survey of all the land they held in common with the Tomases, and suggested that a line dividing the holdings in half be made the new boundary. Hidalgo stated that the obscure nature of the *títulos* would only perpetuate disagreements. The only way to forestall this would be to establish fixed *mojones* along a line such as the one requested by the Franciscos.

During the course of Hidalgo's brief inspection (*vista de ojos*) on 19 December 1794 the Franciscos presented Hidalgo with a four-page *título* to nine *caballerías* of land granted in 1678 to one Don Antonio Ramirez, *Gobernador* of Sacapulas and a member of the Franciscos. When he died, the *parcialidad* had inherited the land. The Franciscos understood the nine *caballerías* to be part of the fourteen in question and asserted that they had rights not just to half but to the full nine *caballerías*. Hidalgo was not sure that the nine *caballerías* in the *título* corresponded in whole or in part with the land disputed in the present case because of the *título's* lack of precision in identifying the area. Accordingly, he told the Franciscos to keep the document in case they would need to present it later to higher authorities.

The outer boundaries of the two *parcialidades'* land were surveyed from 20 to 24 December without further incident and at a cost of three hundred *pesos,* which was evenly divided between them. However, trouble arose when Hidalgo attempted to trace the internal boundary between the two groups. The Franciscos asserted that the line from Río Negro to Piedra Canoa was the dividing line between the two *calpules,* giving them both fertile land on either side of the Río Negro.

With the survey completed, Hidalgo made the surprising revelation that the area jointly occupied by both *parcialidades* was not 14 but 200 *caballerías* in extent, encompassing the entire area claimed by the groups. Of the total, Santo Tomás controlled some 121 *caballerías,* including the fertile banks of the Ríos Negro and Blanco, leaving San Francisco with only some 78 *caballerías.* If the dividing line of the Franciscos were legalized it would change the balance in their favor, 92 *caballerías* versus 107 for Santo Tomás (see Map 8-1). While not achieving parity in terms of actual area, the Franciscos would have gained essentially both banks of the Río Negro, at the Tomases' expense (AI.80 Leg. 6040 Exp. 53305:14v).

The Tomases vehemently opposed this proposed division, stating that the land in question along the Río Negro had been bought in small portions by the present users and that since ancient times the land had then been sold and inherited. The Franciscos disagreed, stating that all the land was held jointly under the old *título* for fourteen *caballerías.* Therefore, it should be divisible in quality and quantity; the Tomases should not possess land on both the Río Negro and the Río Blanco, as was now the case.

Hidalgo referred the matter to his superior for decision. In his report, however, he offered his opinion that the title to nine *caballerías* granted to Antonio Ramirez in 1678, recording as it did the payment for the land to the Crown, gave the Franciscos the right to half the land held with the Tomases, or at least the Río Negro portion.

The dispute dragged on from early 1795 through September 1798, both parties filing tedious claims, counterclaims, and appeals in order to determine their joint interior boundary as advantageously as possible vis-à-vis each other. In the process, two additional detailed surveys and evaluations of both groups' land and a census of their respective populations

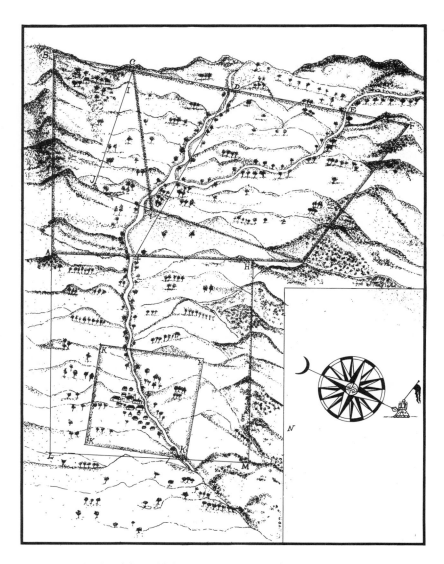

Map 8-1. Facsimile of the Hidalgo 1794 survey map.

were made by Spanish officials at a cost of 210 *pesos*. In addition to the procedural complexities, the other major complicating factors in the case were claims that some of the disputed land was in fact privately owned or rented.

The Santo Tomás people sent a formal appeal to the *Juez Privativo* in May 1795 asserting, among other things, that several pieces of the disputed land along the Río Negro had been purchased from the Franciscos and other private individuals. Thus, the present "owners" had their land by virtue of purchases made by their forefathers. The Tomases presented a book noting the land purchases to the value of seven hundred *tostones*. Since it would be impossible to divide the land as the court ordered without grave consequences to the owners, who would lose not only the land but the crops growing on it, the Tomases requested justice. They asked to have their claims recognized.

Growing increasingly exasperated by the *Audiencia's* inability to end the dispute, the *Fiscal* advised that Hidalgo's proposed settlement be temporarily suspended and that *Alcalde Mayor* Aguirre determine if the two groups could find a mutually agreeable compromise. He also suggested that a certain fact be used to pressure the two groups into agreement: the land was legally owned by the Crown, not by the two *calpules,* and therefore theoretically salable to other individuals. The *Juez Privativo* took this advice and in June 1796 orders were sent back to Aguirre (AI. 80 Leg. 6042 Exp. 53327:43–44). These actions amounted to a recognition of the *Audiencia's* inability to impose a settlement and a relinquishing of sovereign authority. The officials of the *Audiencia* themselves recognized their inability to adjudicate the dispute and, essentially, threw it back at the litigants to settle themselves. Now, all the *Audiencia* could offer was a thinly veiled threat to sell the land to others.

Representatives of both *parcialidades* went to Totonicapán in July 1796, where the *Alcalde Mayor* (through an interpreter) explained the court's desire for them to come to an agreement among themselves; he hinted that the land could be sold by the Crown to others. However, the Tomases were still adamant in their rejection of the Spaniards' proposed settlement. Aguirre gave the parties another day to examine all the documents pertaining to the dispute and to work out their differences. Finally, both groups agreed to divide equally the fertile and irrigable land on both sides of the Río Negro. The *Alcalde Mayor* communicated this news to the *Juez Privativo* and stated that, as soon as other business was taken care of, he would see to the measurement of the land and put the two *calpules* in possession of it (ibid., 47–48v).

Aguirre made his second trip to Sacapulas in March 1797. He duly surveyed all the land claimed by the two *parcialidades*, especially the *vegas* of the two rivers, which he reported were held in much greater quantity by the Tomases (ibid., 51v–52). He asked for a census of the population of both groups to aid in dividing the land. During this inspection Aguirre was made aware (as Hidalgo had been before him) of the Sacapultecos' practice of buying, selling, and inheriting plots of land along the rivers. Both the Franciscos and individuals from other *parcialidades* owned such plots along both the Río Negro and the Río Blanco. The Franciscos, believing these plots were not held in common, were anxious that they not be counted as common land subject to the division in settlement of the dispute (ibid., 52). The *Alcalde Mayor* explained that such sales were invalid since the land belonged to the Crown and was not theirs to sell. The two *parcialidades* replied that it had long been their custom to make such sales and to inherit specific plots, and they had papers to prove it. These arguments were rejected by Aguirre since they were not specific about when the plots were acquired or their extent. The Indians replied that they had been ignorant of the fact that they could not sell their land and had always assumed such transactions to be valid. Because of this they felt that individuals who had in good faith acquired, possessed, and invested work in plots should not have them taken away (ibid., 53).

Aguirre decided to measure the valley bottomland, including individual holdings that would be subtracted from the total holding of each *calpul*. The resulting figure would represent the commonly held land of both groups and from it the equal division would be made (ibid., 53–53v). The survey determined that, aside from individually owned plots, the Franciscos owned 305 *cuerdas*, 29 *varas* planted in sugarcane. The Tomases, aside from private holdings, owned in common 470 *cuerdas*, 40 *varas;* for an excess of 154 *cuerdas*, 30 *varas*. As a result, Santo Tomás would have to cede 77 *cuerdas*, 40 *varas*, to San Francisco. The pieces of land to be turned over were agreed upon and included Chibulbux and Xecu in addition to some smaller pieces. During the proceedings Aguirre also made sure the two groups understood that they were not to buy, sell, or otherwise alienate the land granted them under forfeit of payment. He promised to send all the documents to the *Juez Privativo* so that he could have their respective titles prepared and thus put an end to the present dispute and forestall any resumption of it in the future (ibid., 63v–65).

This was not, however, the end of the story. *Subdelegado* Hidalgo was assigned the task of reviewing Aguirre's reports and drafting a map. He found that Aguirre had not correctly calculated the extent of the various

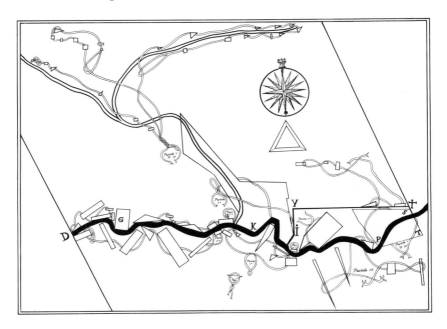

Map 8-2. Facsimile of the Hidalgo 1798 survey map.

plots surveyed (ibid., 77–78). The resulting error in apportioning the land
had been noticed by the Franciscos, but they had no recourse since the
Alcalde Mayor had sent the papers directly to the capital. The Franciscos
also felt the division was uneven. Since their population was greater than
that of Santo Tomás, they felt themselves entitled to a larger share of the
land (ibid., 75–75v). Aguirre was eventually ordered by *Juez Privativo* Villa
Urrutía to return to Sacapulas, accompanied by Hidalgo, to resurvey the
land in question. The two were also given broad powers to resolve the
dispute (ibid., 102–102v). Aguirre claimed other pressing duties would not
permit him to go to Sacapulas, but he did promise to have his subordinate,
the *comisionado* of the *pueblo,* aid Hidalgo (ibid., 103v–105). Nevertheless,
Hidalgo arrived alone to begin his survey on 20 June 1798 (ibid., 115v) (see
Map 8-2).

As part of the survey and inspection in June 1798 (see Map 8-2), Hidalgo also informed himself about the private sale of land to individual
Indians. The information he presented was significant both for the course
of the litigation and for illustrating the Indians' attitudes about private
land. His statement began by discussing the nullity of such sales. The
documents used by the Indians to record the sales were simple statements,

not legal documents. A more basic difficulty was that many of the plots changing hands were on officially unappropriated land that no one but the *Real Fisco* could sell. Even if the *parcialidades* obtained title to the land they could not in turn sell or alienate it, since the title only granted them limited rights of possession (*precaria posesión*).

He went on to state that the wish of the Tomases had been to convince the authorities that they had purchased the seven pieces of arable land on the south bank of the Río Negro, and that this factor would add weight to their case. However, their argument could be nullified by the simple fact that the land had not been purchased from the only legitimate (in the Spaniards' eyes) authority, the *Real Fisco*. The Tomases might also assert that they had bought the land from the Franciscos and claim that the Franciscos ought to lose the land in any settlement of the case, but they could never prove that the Franciscos even had possession of the south-bank land, especially since the boundary survey (approved by the Tomases) demonstrated that the Franciscos never had had any possessions on the Río Negro except below the confluence with the Río Blanco. Therefore, the Franciscos could not have sold something which they had never possessed. The land had always been controlled by the Tomases. If the individual members had sold their land, they should, as members of an indivisible body, lose possession of those plots and be assigned another piece of the groups' common land (AI. 80 Leg. 6042 Exp. 53327:137v).

Based on his survey, and despite deducting "privately owned" plots from the *parcialidades'* total landholdings, Hidalgo reasserted that his original plan for dividing the jointly held land was the most equitable. To wit: the Franciscos would be given the entire south bank of the Río Negro and its north bank below the confluence with the Río Blanco and the Tomases' *cañaverales* (that is, the land planted with sugarcane around Chutixtiox); the Tomases would keep all of the Río Blanco land and the north bank of the Río Negro above the small section granted the Franciscos.

Predictably, the Tomases objected to the reapportionment plan and refused to pay their half of the survey costs (which totaled 210 *pesos*) (ibid., 140, 152). Further, they accused Hidalgo of conducting the survey improperly, of showing favoritism to the Franciscos, and ultimately of collusion with them (ibid., 162–63). The priests residing in Sacapulas also addressed letters to the *Alcalde Mayor,* stating that the enmity between the Tomases and Franciscos was getting out of hand. Fights had erupted between the serving boys of the two *parcialidades* who worked in the priests' kitchen (ibid., 149). The charges and complaints were forwarded by the *Alcalde Mayor* to *Juez Privativo* Villa Urrutía. Hidalgo easily deflected the charges against him and justified his actions to his superior's satisfaction. He also requested that the Tomases be ordered to pay him their share of the survey costs (ibid., 164–66v).

In September 1798, with all complaints against Hidalgo dismissed, *Alcalde Mayor* Aguirre was ordered to see to the redistribution of land and the collection of Hidalgo's fee (ibid., 166v–167). Aguirre once again begged off, sending *Comisionado* Henríquez in his stead (ibid., 167v). Only two problems arose. First, the Franciscos had always possessed three small plots north of the road to Huehuetenango (the new dividing line between the two *parcialidades* on the north side of the Río Negro). Were these to be ceded to the Tomases as part of the settlement? Second, what was to become of plots owned by individuals of other *parcialidades* within the land ceded to the Franciscos (ibid., 169v)?

With regard to plots owned by members of other *parcialidades*, Hidalgo recommended that the current owners remain in possession of their plots. However, each of two *parcialidades* being granted limited possession rights (*precaria posesión*) could through time (and in an unspecified manner) reincorporate into their respective common holdings the plots of individuals of other *parcialidades*. Concerning the Franciscos' plots north of the road to Huehuetenango, Hidalgo stated that these would indeed have to be ceded to the Tomases. The Franciscos agreed to this since the road served as a constant and secure boundary marker (ibid., 170v).

Finally, the *Alcalde Mayor* compelled the Tomases to pay their half of the costs of Hidalgo's survey (ibid., 171). Titles were duly drawn up for both groups, thus ending—at least for the authorities—an unnecessarily complex and lengthy litigation.

Discussion

In two of three eighteenth-century disputes, the question of individual Sacapultecos' buying, selling, and inheriting land arose and complicated the already difficult process of arriving at acceptable agreements. In the dispute between Santiago and San Sebastián and San Pedro, the fact that the *salinas* or salt flats were divided in plots purportedly "owned" by individuals who had "bought" or "inherited" them was used to justify the removal of this resource from consideration as *ejido*. The move aided Santiago and San Sebastián while hurting San Pedro's attempt to gain access to more land. In this case the question of sales may not be significant since the transactions were all among members of the same group. However, in the litigation involving Santo Tomás and San Francisco, reckoning of the extent of both groups' land and its equitable division were complicated considerably by claims of private ownership by members of the groups in question, as well as by individuals of the other *parcialidades*. Such claims were not made in earlier disputes or in another contemporaneous case in the eighteenth century. How can this apparent change in the principle of *parcialidad* ownership be interpreted? What was its impact?

One interpretation is that the Sacapultecos were being innovative as a result of acculturation. As they gained experience with Spanish concepts of land ownership, some individuals may have implemented similar practices locally. In addition to exposure to Spanish practices, it must be remembered that during the eighteenth century the Indian population approached preconquest levels and competition for scarce land increased. In that case, the *parcialidad* principle, which had proven unassailable by direct Spanish actions and change-oriented policies, was being challenged by the Sacapultecos themselves as individuals attempted to adapt to increasingly unfavorable man/land ratios.

Unfortunately, it is difficult to ascertain if the Sacapultecos were indeed adapting thusly. In their recorded statements, the Sacapultecos used Spanish rather than Maya terms. Spanish officials, even when investigating the subject of land sales, made their reports using Spanish terminology alone; no attempt was made to understand Maya concepts of buying and selling. The Spaniards were concerned only with the question of the validity of such sales vis-à-vis Spanish law. We do not know with any certainty about the existence or extent of Indian concepts that approximated the idea of private property or of rights gained through purchase in preconquest times.

Based on resemblances noted in Chapter 2, it might be fair to assume that the Maya *chinamit* administered land in ways similar to the Aztec *calpulli*. As will be remembered, the members of a *calpulli* had inheritable rights to a piece of land, though not the right of alienation. Failure to cultivate a plot or the lack of heirs resulted in the land's reversion to the *calpulli* for reapportionment by its leadership. Land could be "rented" to outsiders, though presumably this was arranged by the *calpulli* heads. According to the statements of Henríquez, practices in Sacapulas had been similar. He noted that the Sacapulas "*calpules*" recognized their own respective territories and avoided trespass. He also commented upon the ability of the *calpul* leadership (the *principales*) to decide where members could plant, and on the custom whereby when a member died (either a *principal* or a commoner) his land reverted to the *calpul*. Thus, all indications are that a *parcialidad's* members held only usufruct to their plots.

Perhaps the preconquest aristocracy was allowed personal holdings, but precise information is lacking. If renting of land had been a preconquest practice administered by the *principales,* by the eighteenth century it seems to have become an unregulated private matter.

Entries in colonial-period Maya-Spanish dictionaries indicate the Maya had a sophisticated cultural taxonomy describing a variety of transactions. The most abundant information is contained in the Coto [c. 1690] dictionary.

TIN YA. Arrendar, dar, prestar (ibid., 37, 108, 362)

TIN K'EX. Comprar, mercar cosa de poco precio de 20 cacaos abajo (ibid., 86); trocar una cosa por otra, feriar (ibid., 85, 471)

TIN LOQ'. Comprar, mercar alguna cosa y a de ser que suba el precio de 20 cacaos arriba . . . (ibid., 86)

TIN YAC. Cuando mercan una cosa para revender (ibid., 285)

TIN KAH. Alquilar casas, solar, tierras de otro (ibid., 20)

For the Spanish linguist-friar, *Tin ya* included or approximated renting or leasing (*arrendar*), giving (*dar*), and loaning (*prestar*). Purchases were distinguished according to price: those costing less than twenty cacao beans (*Tin k'ex*) and those costing more (*Tin loq'*). The use of cacao as a medium of exchange and the vigesimal unit as a cutoff point strongly indicate the preconquest origin of the distinction. Purchases were also distinguished if intended for resale (*Tin yac*). Finally, one entry (*Tin kah*) indicates that houses, house lots, and land could all be let or hired out (*alquilar*). All of these could be distinguished from gift giving (*Tin loq'oh—dadiva: la cosa que graciosamente se da . . .*; ibid., 108).

Unfortunately, the dictionary data are only suggestive. The entries do not describe which people may do these things. They do not specify the sorts of things that may be rented, loaned, or given, or the kind of rights and obligations to which the parties may have been subject. What did it mean to "rent" something? How much did twenty cacao beans buy? What things cost more than twenty cacaos? Who could rent how much land to whom and for what payment? All these questions remain unanswered. The data demonstrate the existence of a taxonomy of transactions but do not provide much detail. In any event, the Maya terms, if used, were never entered into the official record of the litigation proceedings. If a term such as *Tin loq'* had been used, however, it would suggest that the eighteenth-century Sacapulteco claims of private ownership were less a borrowing from the Spaniards than a conservative innovation, the adaptation of a custom already in their culture to a new opportunity made possible by the Spanish presence.

While some change was clearly taking place, we also lack any indication of the Sacapultecos' reactions to claims by some of their fellows to private ownership of some land. If an overwhelmingly negative opinion had been recorded for the Sacapultecos, we might be more inclined to see individual holdings as a borrowing from the Spaniards that was heartily disapproved of by a conservative majority. Lacking such, we must examine how widespread the practice was, how much land and how many people were involved. Thanks to the Aguirre survey of 1797 and Hidalgo survey of 1798, we are able to make such an examination for the lands of Santo Tomás and San Francisco.

According to Aguirre, twenty-two individuals claimed to be owners (*dueños*) of plots in the territory of *parcialidad* San Francisco. Of these, seventeen were members of the *parcialidad,* with three from San Pedro and two from San Sebastián (AI Leg. 6042 Exp. 53327:58–58v). By the Hidalgo survey, this meant that of a total of 910⅝ *cuerdas* of arable land, 210½ *cuerdas* were claimed by individuals (ibid., 132–134). Twenty-six individuals claimed lands in Santo Tomás territory: eleven from the *parcialidad* itself, six from San Sebastián, five from San Francisco, and four from San Pedro (ibid., 58–58v). Of 2,119⅜ arable *cuerdas* of land, 324 were claimed by individuals (ibid., 132–34). During the same period there were eighty-three heads of households in Santo Tomás, including widows, widowers, and men over fifty exempt from tribute; for San Francisco there were 148 (ibid., 54–57v). Thus, some 13 and 11.5 percent of the household heads were claiming individual ownership of agricultural plots in Santo Tomás and San Francisco, respectively. Because of differences between the Aguirre and Hidalgo surveys we are unable to assess the extent of individual holdings and thereby characterize their importance in relative terms. We might assume that individuals were uniformly gaining access to more land on a per capita basis, but this is impossible to verify. Aguirre identified plots and their claimed owners (if any), but he failed to make a map or note the shape of individual plots. In any case, he calculated their area by *adding* the dimensions rather than by multiplying (in the case of a rectangle) or multiplying and then dividing by two (in the case of a triangle). Hidalgo noted this error in his review of Aguirre's work and was sent to Sacapulas to conduct a new survey. He correctly figured the areas of the plots, and made a detailed map of them, but failed to note those that were claimed by individuals. There is thus no way to accurately compare the surveys of the two Spanish officials.

However, from the Spaniards' point of view (as well as that of the authors), the claims of individual ownership either through purchase or inheritance and the amounts of land in question were of secondary importance. Whether representing innovation resulting from acculturative experience or not, the interpretation of such claims and the reaction of Spanish officials operating under their legal system served to suppress the division of communal land into individual holdings, and thus unintentionally reinforced the *parcialidad* principle. According to Spanish law, all land, except that granted as *ejido,* was part of the royal patrimony. All the land claimed by the *parcialidades* outside of the *ejido* was officially held through only limited rights of possession (*precario*), granted by a magnanimous sovereign through his representatives. None of the Sacapultecos could claim to have any private ownership (*dominio directo*) of land unless they had purchased it from the Crown. The only example of such a purchase revealed in the litigation was made in 1678. At that time, Don Antonio Ramirez, a member of San Francisco and *Gobernador* of Sacapulas, paid 180 *tostones* for nine *caballerías* of land in the southwest portion of his *parcialidad's* holdings, in the area of the Xechiley and Chuicajbab *mojones* (and thus away from the river valley land under dispute). However, the fact that the land reverted to the common ownership of the *parcialidad* after Don Antonio's death, rather than being inherited by an heir, suggests that he may have purchased the land on behalf of his *parcialidad,* perhaps using funds collected from among its members. It may simply have been that Don Antonio, as *Gobernador,* had more experience with Spanish legal concepts. By acting through him rather than as a group, the San Francisco people may have thought that Don Antonio's official position would help them receive preferential treatment, since the Spaniards may have wanted to please or reward one of their native appointees. One assumes some such plan on the part of the San Francisco people, since the land later passed to the *parcialidad,* not to an individual. On the other hand, reversion of Don Antonio's land to his *parcialidad* may reflect the general custom described by Henríquez by which ownership of land reverted to the *parcialidad* upon an individual's death, regardless of his rank. In any event, according to the Spanish viewpoint, aside from those nine *caballerías,* no one in Sacapulas had a legal right to claim ownership of land. Such claims within a given *parcialidad* were of limited concern to Spanish officials. In a report containing recommendations for settling the dispute, Hidalgo suggested that new lists be made of land that was legitimately alienated (or so claimed) to individuals of different *parcialidades.* He specifically stated that one should not consider as sold or alienated the plots enjoyed by members of a given *parcialidad* within their territory.

The real concern was the alienation of a *parcialidad's* land to non-members, even though they were all part of the same *pueblo*. In the dispute, such sales had seriously complicated the task of dividing the fertile valley bottomlands between Santo Tomás and San Francisco. As part of the final resolution of the dispute, and to avoid such complications in the future, the Spaniards insisted on issuing limited titles (*título de ámparo*) to the *parcialidades* involved. Individual claims were never recognized. A stern warning was also issued that the Indians were not to engage in the sale of land in the future, under pain of the purchaser's forfeiting his money.

Culturally, if the Sacapultecos' claims to individual ownership through purchase or inheritance do represent partial acculturation to Spanish practices, it is evident that they grasped or chose to understand only a portion of the Spanish legal concepts concerning land. Already feeling they had ownership based on immemorial possession, the Sacapultecos did not bother with the formalities and great expense of buying their own land from the Crown in order to receive a legal title. They simply began "buying," "selling," and perhaps "renting" and "loaning" land among themselves. Even if such activity does represent some continuity of preconquest practices, all the transactions were regarded as illegal under Spanish law, as well as complicating factors in the litigation. To set matters straight, settle the dispute, and avoid similar problems in the future, such transactions were outlawed. The only titles to be granted were limited in nature and issued only to *parcialidades* as units. The *parcialidades* were empowered to recover alienated plots as the current owners died, or perhaps as they were purchased by the *parcialidad* concerned. Rather than encourage individual ownership of land through purchase (thereby eliminating *parcialidades* as landowning entities), the policy pursued in settling the dispute served to preserve, even strengthen, the *parcialidad* principle in the face of possible growth of the idea of private property. The importance of the contradictions in Spanish policy and the limited adjudicative powers of Spanish courts again become apparent. While a Spanish aim (as noted in Chapter 7) was to eliminate *parcialidades* because of all the litigation proceedings and disputes in which they indulged, none of the officials involved suggested or tried to promote the idea that individual Sacapultecos be granted titles to their plots; using narrow legal criteria, the question of private ownership was dismissed and ultimately prohibited. The courts, unable to impose a settlement because of the litigants' rights of appeal, were forced to allow the two *parcialidades* to arrive at their own compromise. The result was a setback for private ownership (whether due to acculturation or not) and a strengthening of the *parcialidad* principle. The old Lamakib *amaq'* broke down, but—despite the potential of individual land ownership—not into total disarray. The combination of the continuing utility of *parcialidad* units to the Sacaultecos themselves, combined with the Spaniards' uneven policy enforcement and limited jural authority, fairly ensured that the breakup of the Lamakib *amaq'* would be only to the level of component *parcialidades*, not to that of individuals.

CHAPTER NINE

Continuity in Change

Unfortunately, there is little information from the nineteenth century that is of use in tracing specific developments in Sacapulas and the reactions of the component *parcialidades*.[1] Historically, it is known that *ladinos* began colonizing the western highlands in the late nineteenth century, encouraged by favorable laws regarding land acquisition passed by the "liberal" national governments of the period. It is also known that the development of *fincas* (large-scale commercial agricultural enterprises) in the later nineteenth century and the attendant need for labor on a seasonal basis resulted in a series of laws and labor practices that, by modern standards, were terribly unfair to the Indians. In the 1870s there was the *mandamiento,* effectively a revival of the colonial *repartimiento* whereby communities were ordered "to supply a given number of laborers at a set wage and for a specified amount of time" (McCreery 1983, 741). There were no limits on such drafts, so that communities close to the Pacific piedmont coffee zone were subject to more frequent demands. The *mandamiento* was ultimately replaced by debt peonage as a legally sanctioned institution. Under this system, planters, or their agents or middlemen, would advance money to Indians who agreed to "work it off" on a *finca*. The potential for abuse was immense. There was no limit on the amount of debt an individual could incur, so one's obligations could easily become perpetual. Also, although the law required that a record of each individual's debt be kept in his possession, few Indians knew how to read and, through fraud, debts could be perpetuated. Money was advanced to Indians while they were intoxicated, for instance, when they might agree to anything in order to buy more liquor. Money was also advanced at times when it was most desperately needed by the Indians, for example, at the end of the dry season when corn was scarce and before *fiestas* when social obligations required large expenditures. Finally, the nation's vagrancy laws could be and were manipulated to require Indians to work or face fines or imprisonment (see Jones 1942; McCreery 1983 for a historical overview; Bunzel 1952 for a description of practices). While these events must have had an effect on the people of Sacapulas, we cannot document them. However, by picking up the documentary thread again in the late nineteenth century, we can still find evidence of continuity in the functions of the *parcialidad*.

The Last Case (1885)

This final litigation on the part of a *parcialidad* as a landholding and social unit was against an individual member of the group and occurred in 1885 (JPQ 1890A, Doc. 22). On 5 September, the twelve plaintiffs who claimed to represent the *calpul* San Pedro (probably the twelve-man *ax waab'*, see Chapter 1) made an appeal to the *Jefe Político* of El Quiché. They stated that as agriculturalists they possessed all the land commonly called by the same name, that of San Pedro. They cited one Nicolás Gomez as a bad member of the *calpul* who knew the land in question was to be used for the general good but who nonetheless installed himself on a piece of land some two *caballerías* in extent that had been acquired as collateral for a loan of twenty *pesos*. Since the greater part of the land was used for pasturing cattle, the Pedranos asserted it was unjust that one individual, Gomez, should deprive their cattle of freedom of movement, especially when there were no just motives for his actions. As Gomez himself had no cattle, he did not bother to fence in his *milpa* plots. Instead, he blocked the paths used by the cattle to move from pasture to the river in order to protect his crops. This precaution was not sufficient and the Pedranos' animals repeatedly damaged the plots, which resulted in their owners having to pay damages. This continued in spite of the admonitions of the local (Indian?) authorities, which Gomez allegedly refused to respect.

Finally, the Pedranos accused Gomez of refusing to assist with the public work assigned to the *cantón*. They closed their petition with the request that the *Jefe Político* order the Sacapulas authorities to evict Gomez and offered to pay him an indemnity of the twenty *pesos* he had paid for the land and any other expenses he may have incurred.

The *ladino Alcalde* of Sacapulas was ordered to investigate the claims made by the *capul* San Pedro in the petition (ibid., 2). He duly made an inspection of the land in question and reported back to the *Jefe Político*. The *Alcalde* stated that the total extent of the land purchased (*comprado*) by Gomez was twenty-four *cuerdas*. The three cultivated plots had a combined area of some fifteen *cuerdas* and were largely unprotected, the only security being some sections of fence that Gomez had placed around the circumference of the area he claimed. The piece of land ran for approximately one-half league from the river to the crest of a hill. The poorly constructed fencing was located one-quarter league up the hill and it did indeed impede the passage of cattle to the river from this area, which was used by others as pasture. The *Alcalde* noted the suggestion that if the cultivated plots themselves were fenced off and protected from the cattle, the fences blocking the paths could be removed, thus restoring free movement to the area. He also stated that Gomez' plots, although several, were not large enough to justify the large area he left uncultivated (ibid., 3–4).

Based on this report, the *Jefe Político* decided in favor of the Pedranos. The small plots were in the *calpul* land and a hazard to the common field. The plots had been planted on land intended for pasturage and by an individual who did not have exclusive ownership of the property, which was in fact owned by many. The Pedranos were declared not to be responsible for any losses incurred by Gomez in giving up the plots. The latter was ordered not to cultivate the land, which was not only not properly his but which was intended for grazing (ibid., 4).

The next month, October 1885, the Pedranos made another petition to the *Jefe Político,* stating that Gomez had not ceased to occupy the land in question and had in fact gone to Guatemala City (AI Leg. 6024 Exp. 53119:13–14). The Pedranos thought he might look to the president for protection, using lies and deceptions. They were also now afraid because they had not originally presented the *título* to their land, which included the land claimed by Gomez. The *título* they now presented was from 1778 and included a copy of the Barroeta survey (ibid., 1–12; see Chapter 6). This document, the Pedranos asserted, proved that the land in question was not vacant or unoccupied as Gomez had claimed, but was rather the legitimate and exclusive property of the *barrio* of San Pedro. They closed their petition by asking the *Jefe Político* to order the *alcaldes* of the town to protect their property, order Gomez to vacate the land, and require him not to cause future disturbances.

This time, the petition and *título* (or a copy?) were ordered sent to the *Ministro de Gobernación y Justicia,* who had been informed of the case (by Gomez?) and would decide it.

The documentation of the case ends here; we do not know how the litigation was finally settled. However, the outcome is largely unimportant. What is significant is the evidence of continuity. Whether successful or not, the members of a *parcialidad* (called by the old term *calpul,* now also *barrio* and *cantón*) still claimed and defended their land as a group, and were still concerned with the conformity of their fellows to group standards. Also significant is the fact that *parcialidades* continued to be recognized formally as such and used as units of local and departmental administration. The Pedranos complained that Gomez refused to assist with the work assigned to the *cantón,* indicating that local public work was being assigned on a *parcialidad* basis. Also, both the *Alcalde* and the *Jefe Político* utilized the term *calpul* when referring to the Pedranos, illustrating their familiarity with such units and their recognition that *parcialidades* still existed and had to be dealt with as such, at least on a local level.

Strangely, no mention is made of *parcialidades* or *calpules* in any of the surviving documents from the later nineteenth and early twentieth centuries. It is probably more than a coincidence, however, that at the time when *parcialidades* are no longer discussed in the official correspondence the *ladino* presence increased in the area and assumed control of the municipal government. In any event, we are forced to jump to the ethnograhic record and rely on informants' memories as we follow the career of the *parcialidad* principle down to the present.

Sacapulas Today: A Reprise

CHANGES IN RESIDENCE PATTERN IN THE *PUEBLO*

Since the late 1930s the *pueblo* of Sacapulas has changed considerably. According to the official censuses, between 1920 and 1950 its resident population more than doubled, from 856 in 1921 to 2,218 in 1950 (República de Guatemala 1921, 2:431–32; *Diccionario Geográfico de Guatemala*, 2:102). This represents a rate of growth much higher than that in the rest of the municipality. The composition of the *pueblo*'s population has changed as well. While Sacapulteco Indians still make up the majority of the center's inhabitants, the percentage of *ladinos* in the population has increased, as has the percentage of non-Sacapulteco Indians. Several government agencies have established offices in town, providing the residents with a new source of employment. Also, very few of the Sacapultecos from the *cantones* San Pedro, Santo Tomás, and San Francisco still own houses in the *pueblo*.

Many of the changes in the *pueblo* can be traced to the period when the roads linking Sacapulas to Huehuetenango, El Quiché, Cobán, and Nebaj were constructed. The link to Huehuetenango was completed in 1937, to El Quiché in 1933–34, to Cobán in 1941, and to Nebaj in 1942. Sacapulas is now situated at the intersection of two of the main arteries for motorized transport in northwestern Guatemala, Ruta Nacional 15 and Ruta Nacional 7W. Soon after these roads were constructed, trucks and then buses began to carry passengers on them. What had been a two-day walk to El Quiché and a three-day walk to Huehuetenango can now be accomplished in a few hours. But perhaps the most immediate impact the roads had on the municipality was not in tying it more closely to the outside world, but in making travel to the town center much less difficult. By coincidence, the roads cut through the hearts of the San Francisco, San Pedro, and Santo Tomás *cantones*. Now, instead of spending all day Saturday carrying goods to the Sunday market from distant Santo Tomás, one can simply get up early on a Sunday morning, haul one's produce to the edge of Route 7W, load it on the top of a bus or in the back of a passing truck, and arrive in town in time for the start of the market. Not only has travel time been cut significantly, but more goods can be carried. The impact of this new mode of transportation has been heightened by the fortuitous location of the roads, which has made them accessible to large numbers of a given *cantón*'s population.

As of 1980 there are at least five Indian- and *ladino*-owned buses passing through Sacapulas on a daily basis, as well as numerous trucks. Of the three buses owned by local residents, one is used to make a daily trip to El Quiché and back, another to make a round trip to Huehuetenango four times a week, and the last to shuttle people between Santo Tomás and the town center for the Sunday market. This last makes seven or eight trips on an average Sunday, and the owner also charters his bus to wedding parties from the *cantones* that have to make the trip to the *pueblo* for a civil marriage ceremony (performed by the *alcalde* in his capacity as *juez de paz*).

Since the 1930s the ease of transportation facilitated by the new roads and buses has had an impact on the composition of the *pueblo's* population. Since *cantón* residents no longer need to spend most of a day traveling to fulfill service obligations or to attend the Sunday market, they no longer need to stay in town overnight. *Barrio* houses have slowly fallen into disuse and over the last forty years most of those belonging to the residents of the *cantones* Santo Tomás, San Francisco, and San Pedro have been sold off. By 1980 there were only three houses in the *barrio* of Santo Tomás owned by members of that *cantón*, four houses in the barrio of San Francisco owned by residents of the *cantón* San Francisco, and not a single house in the *barrio* of San Pedro owned by residents of the *cantón* San Pedro. Nearly all the houses are in a sad state of repair as they have not been occupied in years.

As improved transportation made the maintenance of a house in town unnecessary for those living far from the *pueblo,* the population in the *pueblo* increased dramatically. One source of population increase was the immigration of *ladinos* seeking employment in the government agencies that were newly established or expanded in Sacapulas after the roads were built. According to older *ladinos,* before this period there were only eight or ten *ladino* families living in the *pueblo*. Another source of the *pueblo's* population increase was the immigration of Indians from other municipalities. Some opened stores, and a few married into the families of local Indians. Finally, improved health care facilitated the town center's population increase. For the first time, according to residents, Western medicine has become readily available to local Indians.

The population increase in the *pueblo* meant a ready market for those who wished to sell their houses there. These houses were purchased not only by *ladino* and Indian immigrants from other municipalities, but also by members of the *cantón* Santiago and San Sebastián, who began to spill over the boundaries of their own *barrio*. Houses were made even more valuable by the shortage of lots for new construction in the *pueblo*. Because of its proximity to the mountains and the river, it is impossible to expand the *pueblo* in those two directions and the land lying in the other two directions is under cultivation. It has already been pointed out that agricultural land is at a premium in this area, and to build a house on prime farmland is an expensive proposition. For these reasons, houses put on the market by those living outside the center have been rapidly sold and the *pueblo* has taken on the appearance of a crowded town.

The improved transportation has made residence in the *pueblo* unnecessary for the people living in the outlying *cantones* who want to enjoy the benefits of market day and need to discharge their obligations vis-à-vis the municipal government. Paradoxically, with the constraints of travel lessened, the old tendencies toward *parcialidad-cantón* autonomy have reasserted themselves. The most determined in this regard are the people of *cantón* Santo Tomás who, even as far back as the 1570s, never had much enthusiasm for being part of Sacapulas.

Removing the Image of Santo Tomás from the *Pueblo*

In the early 1960s, the *ax waab'* of Santo Tomás made an unprecedented request. They petitioned the *ax waab'* of the other *cantones* for permission to remove the images of Santo Tomás from the *pueblo* and bring them to their own *cantón*. Two images were involved: one resting in a shrine in the church, and another in a house in the *barrio* of Santo Tomás (the *cofradía* image). The people of Santo Tomás had already secured the priest's approval for this move by constructing a large church at the *aldea* of Río Blanco in their *cantón*. However, since the *ax waab'* of all the *cantones* control the ritual buildings in the *pueblo,* their permission also had to be secured. After much debate, the *ax waab'* decided to allow the *cantón* to have the *cofradía* image, but the image in the church was to remain in place. Although the people of Santo Tomás did not win everything they requested, theirs was still a victory.

Upon the decision of the *ax waab'*, a large procession was organized and, with much fanfare, the saint's statue was removed from the house in the *barrio*. Rockets and fireworks were set off all along the route to the saint's new home. When the procession reached the new church in Río Blanco *aldea*, the image of Santo Tomás was placed on the main altar, and a *fiesta*, with music, dancing, drinking, and feasting was held in his honor.

Ever since the people of Santo Tomás removed the saint's image from their *barrio*, they have stopped coming into the *pueblo* to participate in public rituals. They no longer decorate their chapel for Corpus Christi, or celebrate their saint's feast day with a procession there. Instead, all *cofradía* rituals are held at Río Blanco. Santo Tomás' feast day is now claimed by members of the *cantón* to be their *fiesta titular*, on the order of the *fiesta* of Santo Domingo, and they boast that this *fiesta* is much bigger and better than any held in the *pueblo*.

The building of a new church at Río Blanco *aldea* has also changed the distribution of Catholic rituals. The *cofradías* and *Alcaldía Indígena* have often clashed with the priest over the use of the church in the *pueblo*. A few years ago, when the priest demanded the keys to the church from the *Alcaldía*, the Sacapultecos drew their machetes and troops had to be sent from the departmental capital to restore order. In retaliation, the priest performed only the rituals that were absolutely necessary in the town center. In contrast, he was allowed free access to the church at Río Blanco. The people of Río Blanco also paid him more for services performed on special holidays than for those in the *pueblo*. Thus, at the celebration of Corpus Christi in 1980 the people of Santo Tomás were able to persuade the priest to say mass in Río Blanco rather than in the *pueblo*. Not surprisingly, those in the *pueblo*, particularly the members of the Santo Domingo and San Francisco *cofradías*, were extremely upset at this. In short, the removal of the *cofradía* saint from the *barrio* of Santo Tomás and the construction of a church at Río Blanco allowed the *cantón* to achieve ritual independence. Santo Tomás no longer has any need of the ritual buildings, or more important, the ritual organization located in the *pueblo*.

The ritual independence of Santo Tomás was financed, in part, by the new sources of wealth created in the *cantón* through improved transportation, irrigation, and the introduction of new cash crops. These factors operated together to pour unprecedented wealth into Sacapulas, and particularly into Santo Tomás, which has the best farmland and contains one of the few areas in the municipality where extensive irrigation is possible. Coupled with the long growing season, Santo Tomás' irrigated land is ideal for the cultivation of sugarcane and onions. With the construction of roads and the improved transportation in the area, these crops could be taken quickly and cheaply to market. The new-found wealth meant the people of Santo Tomás were better able to afford the expenditures necessary to build and maintain an *aldea* church, sponsor rituals rivaling those of the *pueblo,* and outbid the other *cantones* for the services of the priest.

While changes leading to increased wealth provided Santo Tomás with the wherewithal to finance their successful drive toward ritual independence, it was not the only factor leading to the breakaway. Other factors were involved, the most important of which will become apparent as we examine a series of events concerning the location of a government-sponsored service.

The *Pueblo,* Río Blanco, and the Health Center

One of the things about the *pueblo* that the people of Santo Tomás seem to resent is that the benefits derived from the services they perform accrue primarily to the residents of the *pueblo,* the vast majority of whom are members of the *cantón* San Sebastián and Santiago. Members of other *cantones* do not come to Río Blanco and paint their church or sweep their plaza or repair their buildings, but the people of Santo Tomás must perform such services in the *pueblo.* In addition, almost all municipal expenditures are concentrated in the *pueblo,* primarily because these expenditures are controlled by *ladinos,* and most *ladinos* live in the *pueblo.* Thus, the municipality will borrow money to fix the streets in the *pueblo,* but will spend precious little for building or maintaining public works in the *aldeas.* Projects that originate at the national level, such as the one to provide Sacapulas with fresh water and electricity, begin in the *pueblo* and spread out slowly—if at all—to the surrounding areas. Thus, the *cantón* San Sebastián and Santiago is favored when it comes to both municipal and national government expenditures because the *pueblo* is located there. This favoritism has contributed greatly to the resentment the people of Santo Tomás feel toward the municipality and the people of the *cantón* San Sebastián and Santiago.

Favoritism in municipality and government expenditures is not the only reason for the hostility between Santo Tomás and San Sebastián and Santiago, however. Within each *cantón* there seems to be an underlying enmity for Indians of other *cantones*. For example, it is said that a wise man will not attend the *cofradía* celebrations of another *cantón* because his money may be stolen if he becomes drunk and the saint of that *cantón* may cause him harm. Several deaths of this sort have in fact been attributed to San Francisco by the members of other *cantones*. A sudden illness, especially if the sufferer has had dealings in a *cantón* other than his own, may be attributed to witchcraft performed by members of the foreign *cantón*. There is, then, a latent antagonism on every level of *cantón* interaction, an antagonism glossed over by the formal rituals carried out in the *pueblo* and by the formal greetings people exchange.

The members of the *cantón* Santo Tomás have attempted to counteract the favoritism shown the *cantón* San Sebastián and Santiago in government expenditures by attempting to capture for Río Blanco some of the government-sponsored services located in the *pueblo*. An illustrative case is the recently constructed municipal health center. In the early 1970s the national government offered the municipality of Sacapulas the funds to construct a health center and the personnel to staff it if the municipality would provide the land. The *juez de paz* balked at the offer, since he had already gotten the municipality deep into debt and could not borrow any more money without antagonizing the leading citizens. Somehow, the people of Santo Tomás learned of the government's offer, and the reluctance of the *juez de paz* to act on it, and proposed a site for the health center at Río Blanco *aldea*. They even went so far as to clear the lot for construction. The offer from Santo Tomás spurred those in the *pueblo,* both Indians and *ladinos,* to action. An open meeting was held and the situation was explained to the *pueblo* residents, most of whom were in attendance. Rather than let Santo Tomás have the health center, it was decided that each family should contribute five *quetzales* for the purchase of a lot. The money was collected, the land was purchased, and the health center was constructed in the *pueblo*.

This same pattern has developed in regard to other projects. Whenever the municipality of Sacapulas has hesitated about an offer, the people of Santo Tomás have been quick to try to capture it for their own *cantón*. They have only occasionally been successful at this, since those in the *pueblo,* led by the *ladinos,* have usually taken countermeasures designed to secure the project for themselves.

What is most interesting about the competition between the *pueblo* and the *cantón* Santo Tomás for government projects such as the health center is that in each case those in the *pueblo* have interpreted the actions of those in Santo Tomás to be directed toward the creation of a new *pueblo* at Río Blanco. If they are successful at this, it is believed that *cantón* Santo Tomás will be able to establish itself as a separate *municipio*.

Unfortunately, it was not possible to discover firsthand what the people of Santo Tomás' purpose has been in competing with the *pueblo*. However, their actions over the past twenty-five years do seem to have been directed toward breaking away from both the other *cantones* and the municipality. The removal of the saint's image is a case in point. By ceasing to participate in the rituals performed in the *pueblo*, Santo Tomás has pulled out of the overlapping service obligations that united the *cantones* in a single ritual organization. As pointed out in Chapter 1, it is only in the ritual organization of the *pueblo* and the *Alcaldía Indígena* that the activities of the separated *cantones* articulate. If the people of the *pueblo* are correct in their assessment, the people of Santo Tomás are now trying to add to their ritual independence by eliminating their service obligations to Sacapulas through the establishment of their own municipality. At this time it is only the vigilance of those in the *pueblo*, particularly the *ladinos*, that prevents the people of Santo Tomás from achieving their goal.

The removal of the *cofradía* image from the *pueblo* and the attempt to capture the new health center for Río Blanco reflect the tenuousness of the bonds holding the *cantón* Santo Tomás to Sacapulas. Other data suggest that, given the opportunity, the other *cantones*—with the exception of San Sebastián and Santiago—would also work toward independence in ritual matters in order to become separate *municipios*. In other words, cleavage lines within the municipality are marked by the boundaries of the *cantones*. These cleavage lines exist where they do for historical reasons: for most Sacapultecos, corporate right to land and other resources, most political rights and duties, and community sentiment lie with the *cantón* and not with the area defined by the *municipio*.

As has already been pointed out, the most important factor preventing the *cantón* of Santo Tomás from successfully breaking away from Sacapulas has been the vigilance of the *ladinos* in the *pueblo* and their ability to manipulate the national government in their favor. However, the efforts of the people of Santo Tomás may not always be destined to fail. In the 1930s and 1940s, the present-day *municipio* Jocotenango was administratively part of Sacapulas. Through a long and expensive period of litigation, the Jocotecos were able to break away from Sacapulas and become established as a separate *municipio* in 1951 (*Diccionario geográfico de Guatemala*, 136). Since this case was recounted by several Sacapultecos, it undoubtedly serves as a model for action for the people of Santo Tomás.

New Trends for the Future

What is in store for Sacapulas? How long can the *cantón* organization endure, even in its attenuated form? Attempting to answer such questions is a risky business, all the more so because of the inherently unstable national political scene. However, certain local trends can be identified that, if allowed to continue, will pose serious problems for both the *cantón* system and all the *municipio's* residents.

The tendency for Sacapulas' *parcialidades-cantones* to assert their autonomy has been shown to be inherent because of the origins of the *municipio* and the continuing role of these groups as landholding, administrative, and ritual units. The desire for autonomy is thus a traditional part of the internal dynamics of Sacapulas. At least in modern times, this desire has been reinforced by the siting of the *pueblo* in the territory of San Sebastián and Santiago. Probably for as long as *aldeas* have existed in the other *cantones,* there has been reluctance to serve in and contribute to the *pueblo*. The benefits of such participation appear manifestly to accrue to only one *cantón,* San Sebastián and Santiago. The development of motorized transport facilities simply proved to be a new factor in the ongoing interplay of *cantones*. In this light, the efforts of *cantón* Santo Tomás can be seen as traditional, and not in themselves a threat to the *parcialidad-cantón* principle. The attempts of the Tomases to break away is an old theme in the history of Sacapulas, now being played out in a slightly modified setting. In the unlikely event that the Tomases should succeed, the material damage to the rest of the *municipio* would probably be slight. After all, the land being removed from Sacapulas' jurisdiction has always belonged to the Tomases. None of the other *cantones* has ever tried to exploit it. Use by members of other *cantones* has always been arranged between individual lessors and lessees. However, the issue of the Tomases' achieving independence would appear to be moot, at least for the moment, since the national government is not currently creating new *municipios*.

In studying Sacapulas, however, one can see how pressures that encourage the formation of new *municipios* might develop, and in such a way that the survival of Sacapulas might be endangered. The main factor is the tremendous influx of Quiché-speaking immigrants from the town of Santa María Chiquimula. Initially, in the eighteenth century, the Chiquimulas were only seasonal visitors to Sacapulas, where they grazed their flocks of sheep on the uplands. By the later nineteenth century some of them had begun to reside permanently in Sacapulas, forming *aldeas* in the upland portions of the *municipio* and paying a small rent to the *alcaldía* for the lands they cultivated. Populations have grown enormously since then, however, and there are now roughly as many Chiquimulas as Sacapultecos (Dubois 1981, 10). The Chiquimula *aldeas* are now large, sometimes almost self-contained *pueblos* themselves. Incorporating the Chiquimulas socially into the *municipio* would be one way to avoid potential fragmentation of the *municipio,* but difficult in practical terms. The Chiquimulas in Sacapulas have never formed a homogeneous body like the preconquest *chinamitales* or colonial *parcialidades*. Unlike the *parcialidad* San Pedro, they were not—could not—be given an area of their own to occupy because neither tracts of good land nor the authority to grant them to outside groups existed. Even if the land and the authority to provide it had existed, the pattern of Chiquimula immigration has been to form *aldeas* which, the immigrants hoped, would continue to develop.

A most extreme case is the *aldea* of Parraxtut in the northwestern corner of the *municipio* (see Figure 9-1). By local count in 1983, over two thousand people occupied the *aldea* center, which is laid out in a regular grid pattern. Residents claimed that Parraxtut is itself composed of four *cantones:* Tierra Colorada, La Montaña, Paché, and Patzam. The latter are officially recognized as small settlements of the *caserío* category (*Diccionario Geográfico de Guatemala,* 2:103). Many of the institutions and services associated with *pueblos* are present, including a church with eight functioning *cofradías,* a *juzgado* that houses the *alcaldía auxiliar,* running water to a central *pila,* a large school, a newly built health center, and a well-attended marketplace. In fact, judging from published photographs, the *aldea* looks much like a *pueblo* did in the first half of this century. The people of Parraxtut do not really need Sacapulas and do not gain by contributing to or participating in *pueblo* affairs. This "apartness" from Sacapulas is so pronounced that several residents, including one in a position of authority, did not understand that they were in the *municipio* of Sacapulas and under its jurisdiction. Once the situation was explained to them, they found the arrangement unsettling. In such a situation, where *pueblo*-type services are present and where the people are poorly integrated into the *municipio,* it would seem to be only a matter of time before the Parraxtut people make a formal attempt to gain recognition as a separate *municipio.* One such attempt is already under way at the *aldea* of Rancho de Teja, though at present its success is doubtful. However, if the trend continues and some of the Chiquimula *aldeas* do achieve *municipio* status, significant harm could be done to Sacapulas. While little in the way of

Figure 9-1. The *aldea* of Parraxtut, viewed from the south. (Photograph by Ruben E. Reina.)

good, arable land (by Sacapulteco standards) would be lost by the *municipio,* forest reserves would be greatly reduced. With the increasing utilization of firewood by a growing population, problems could lie ahead.

Increasing population is in itself a factor that threatens the *municipio.* It has been estimated that, prior to the Spanish conquest, some 1,800 people inhabited the Sacapulas area, a few hundred more if the Santa María Magdalena *parcialidad* is included. During the colonial period a population zenith of 1,941 coincided with the spate of eighteenth-century disputes over land and boundaries. Clearly, the Sacapultecos were near the limits of their land's capability to support them with traditional technology. Yet population has continued to grow, reaching almost 11,000 in 1950 and over 16,000 in 1973 (Dirección General de Estadística, 1975), and shows no sign of levelling off. Thus, the present-day population is some seven to eight times what the land traditionally supported. Agricultural technology changed with the introduction of chemical fertilizers, which has allowed otherwise undesirable land to be brought under cultivation. Presumably there are limits to the land, even with the use of fertilizers. Once such limits are reached, serious problems await.

The ability of the Sacapultecos to deal with these impending challenges is threatened by yet another factor: the growth of evangelical Christian sects. North American missionaries were active in Sacapulas during the 1970s and succeeded in making a substantial number of conversions. But these *evangelistas* no longer wish to participate in community affairs or assist in defraying the costs of community-related expenses. This attitude was recently demonstrated when the Sacapultecos arranged to have their *título* (of 1883) registered. The municipality did not have the money on hand to pay the lawyers' fees and other attendant costs, so the *principales* took up a collection of a few dollars per household. However, many of the *evangelistas* refused to donate (at least initially) reportedly saying, "We are not for this any more" (*ya no somos para esto*). In some cases the *principales* were able to convince individual *evangelistas* that since their houses and *milpas* were on *municipio* land and their firewood came from the same source they were still obliged to assist, regardless of their new faith. The episode sounds like some colonial-period dispute, but this time the recalcitrant parties belong not to a *parcialidad* asserting its autonomy but to a religious sect whose adherents, as individual members of various *cantones,* want to withdraw from community obligations and participation.

While the missionaries win converts, part of the process seems to involve weaning those converts away from participation in wider community affairs. From the standpoint of practical evangelism this is necessary in order to remove converts from the traditional *cofradía* organization and the associated religious beliefs. But another aspect of this (perhaps unforeseen by the missionaries) appears to be nonparticipation in the civil aspects of the civil-religious system. At the same time, the missionaries do not offer new institutions that could replace or parallel the traditional organization and allow for effective participation in *cantón* or community affairs by converts. There is naturally some friction between *evangelistas, costumbristas* (as adherents to the traditional religion are sometimes called), and *catequistas* (participants in a more active form of Catholicism encouraged by priests) because there are no established mechanisms or institutions that allow for cooperation in matters of common interest. This can make it difficult to mobilize the *municipio,* the *pueblo,* or even individual *cantones* to deal with various impending problems.

CHAPTER TEN

Conclusions and Implications

Understanding Sacapulas: The Historical Perspective

Having gained some perspective on the historical experience of the Sacapultecos over the nearly five hundred years from before the Spanish conquest to the present, it is appropriate to return to questions raised in Chapter 1. How is Sacapulas to be understood? How can Sacapulas, with its organization of highly independent *cantones,* be classed, if at all, within the existing cultural typologies for Mesoamerica, based as they are on generalizations from ethnographic studies alone?

Seen historically, we would classify Sacapulas in different ways, depending on the period. Early in the colonial period (c. 1572), Sacapulas could have been seen as a dual *barrio* system. The two *barrios* or groups of *barrios*—the two *amaq'*, each of multiple *chinamitales*—saw to their own internal affairs, while formal political authority was divided between them. In the case of Sacapulas the division of political offices was achieved through a formal agreement, a successful compromise mediated by the Dominican friars. At this time, Sacapulas might also have been classified as a town-nucleus type of *municipio.* Presumably, the eight hundred to nine hundred people constituted too small a population to require settlements in addition to the *pueblo.*

Viewed late in the colonial period (late 1790s), Sacapulas would be seen to conform to a multiple *barrio* system. The old Lamakib *amaq'* had broken down, the component *parcialidades* of Santo Tomás and San Francisco now held their land separately, as did San Pedro. Presumably, daughter settlements had arisen in the *parcialidades'* territories as the increasing population began to exploit land far from the *pueblo.* Thus, before roads and motor transport, Sacapulas might have closely resembled a vacant-town type *municipio.* People from San Pedro, Santo Tomás, and San Francisco in particular lived near their agricultural plots, while some maintained houses in the *pueblo* for use on market days and when called upon to serve in the *cabildo* and *cofradías.*

With motor transport and increased *ladino* and immigrant Maya populations, an intermediate type of *municipio* emerged in the twentieth century. Roads passing through the outlying *cantones* and frequently scheduled buses and trucks simplified the trip to the *pueblo,* allowing people almost to commute to town as the need arose.

Today, Sacapulas seems an artificial collection of semiautonomous *cantones* precisely because of its origin and continuity of internal dynamics. Historically, Sacapulas was an artificial creation—a number of previously autonomous groups brought together by the Spaniards through their program of *congregación*. Many of the component units, the various *amaq'* and especially the *chinamitales,* survived. The survivors of remnant groups were incorporated socially into existing *chinamitales-parcialidades.* Though individual *parcialidades* ceased to exist, the *parcialidad* principle continued to organize the Sacapulas people as it had in the past. Even the Spaniards' attempts at directed change in the colonial period, aimed at eliminating the *parcialidad* principle, were successfully deflected, and newly introduced concepts such as *pueblo* and *ejido* were interpreted in terms of the preexisting Maya principles of *amaq'* and *chinamit.* The *chinamitales-parcialidades-cantones* have retained their utility and many of their functions as autonomous groups down through the centuries. Sacapulas today appears to be an artificial collection of *cantones* because that is what it has been since its creation.

Implications for Highland Maya Ethnology

What does this review of the historical experience of Sacapulas reveal about highland Maya cultural dynamics and reactions to Spanish domination? It is, of course, difficult and dangerous to generalize for the entire area from just one example. Indeed, one would expect variations in response to differing intensities of Spanish influence, with Maya groups closer to centers of Spanish population or areas of economic exploitation probably subject to more varied and intense pressures for change. Still, the experience of Sacapulas suggests a number of processes not normally associated with the highland Maya during this period.

The most striking finding is the extent of continuity in the *parcialidad* as the basic sociopolitical unit of the Sacapultecos from before the Spanish conquest to the late nineteenth century. It was only in the late 1880s that marked changes in the functions of the *parcialidad* occurred. These changes followed closely the implementation of new economic policies by the national government. As *fincas* were created there came the demand for seasonal labor. Laws were passed that forced the Indians to work on the *fincas* under unfavorable conditions. *Ladinos* also began settling in some numbers in Sacapulas itself and acquiring land under government programs intended to promote individual landholding. At the same time, immigrants from Santa María Chiquimula were colonizing the upland areas of the *municipio* and acquiring titles to that land as individuals, not as *parcialidades*.

Prior to the start of this modern period, however, little change seems to have occurred in the *parcialidad* principle. Had we more full descriptions of Sacapulas from previous centuries, the similarities among them would probably be overwhelming. Had famous travelers like John L. Stevens and Karl von Scherzer visited and written about Sacapulas in the mid-nineteenth century as they did about other parts of Guatemala, their accounts would probably have differed little from that of Tovilla in the early seventeenth century.

One might reasonably ask to what extent continuity in terms of a principle of social organization may be taken as an index of continuity in other aspects of culture. The nature of the documentary record makes it impossible to adequately address the question here. However, it should be noted that *parcialidades* were the targets for Spanish reform. That the *parcialidades* have persisted for so long must be taken as highly suggestive of continuity in other principles of Maya culture, though changes undoubtedly occurred.

The study of Sacapulas also suggests a historical context for ethnograhic studies of highland Maya peoples, at least those in Guatemala. Beginning as they do in the 1920s and 1930s all studies of the Maya by trained ethnographers (as opposed to the accounts of travelers and natural historians) were made long *after* the new pressures for change of the late nineteenth century came into play. Thus, all our ethnographies of the highland Maya of Guatemala document not only differential responses to the colonial experience due to time and place (the familiar acculturation theme), but also differential disruption due to more recent upheavals in national politics. Should this picture of continuity be accurate for the region as a whole, then the chance to study a traditional Maya way of life, stable for centuries, was missed by only a few decades.

The picture of continuity as represented by Sacapulas is at odds with the commonly held conceptions of the highland Maya peoples' cultural experience in general under Spanish colonial rule. The periodization tentatively proposed by Oliver La Farge must be considerably modified to fit Sacapulas. To review, La Farge (1940) proposed five periods. A Conquest Period extended from the Spaniards' first contact up to 1600, during which time native culture was "shattered." In Sacapulas in this period there occurred contact with the Spanish friars, town formation, population loss through disease, the imposition of tribute and *encomienda* obligations, and the native rulers' loss of sovereign status (to the extent they had ever enjoyed it). Religious conversion was carried out as was *congregación*. Far from seeing their culture shattered, however, we have noted that by the early 1570s the Sacapultecos had worked out an accommodation with Spanish *congregación* policy under which *parcialidades* were preserved and each *amaq'* retained a degree of political parity in the new *cabildo*. The native aristocracy initially filled the new offices, and its status as nobility was officially recognized.

Next in La Farge's scheme, the Colonial Indian Period lasted from 1600 until about 1720 and supposedly was characterized by the Indians' "wholesale absorption" of Spanish culture, while the remnants of Maya culture were destroyed, mutilated, or changed. After the Colonial Period there followed the First Transition Period, lasting until 1800, during which Spanish control weakened and suppressed Maya elements emerged, integrated into a new, syncretic pattern. The Recent Indian I Period lasted through 1880; it was a stable period ended only by the invasion of Spanish-American culture and the inception of the Machine Age.

In Sacapulas, this period of stabilized cultural adjustment seems to have lasted from the late sixteenth to the late nineteenth century. Spanish control in Sacapulas was never particularly strong, but, if anything, it was of greater importance in the later eighteenth century as population, tribute, and the tempo of litigation all increased. Even during this time, the attempts at directed change (such as the introduction of municipal *ejido*) failed. The centuries of stability were interrupted only in the late nineteenth century by colonization of the area by *ladinos* and Chiquimulas and by new national policies regarding land owning and labor.

Continuity in Sacapulas: Contributing Factors

As becomes evident from an examination of the documentary sources, the *chinamit-parcialidad* principle continued to organize the Sacapulas people socially and politically throughout the colonial period and much of the nineteenth century. The pressures for and perceived benefits of change were, by definition, not sufficient to induce the Sacapultecos to significantly alter their basic principle of organization. Unfortunately, it has been impossible to resurrect much of the Sacapultecos' view of their situation. The reasoning and motivations of individuals who initiated specific actions are largely lost to us. For the most part, it is the incomplete record of statements and actions in the stylized context of legal proceedings that has been preserved. Yet, above the level of individuals and personalities, it is possible to identify a number of factors that contributed to the continuity of the *parcialidad* principle.

Except for the San Pedro people, the members of the *parcialidades* forming Sacapulas were not resettled far from their preconquest homes. Rather, they remained in or near their traditional territories, where there were specific natural resources they had long known how to exploit efficiently. Their patterns of settlement were altered, but their immediate universe does not seem to have been changed and their ability to subsist was not impaired.

From the Sacapultecos' standpoint, the *parcialidad* principle must have been seen to be still useful in the new colonial situation. *Parcialidades* were crucial in the litigation process because these units could meet the costs of such action by pooling their members' resources through preexisting customs like *nut*. A few examples serve to illustrate this point. In 1601 the Ah Canil and Ah Toltecat *parcialidades* were together assessed 61 *tostones* for payment of costs connected with their litigation against San Andres Sajcabajá. This sum compares with 50 *tostones*, 2 *reales* paid by the entire *pueblo* of Sacapulas on the *tércio* of San Juan in 1638 as half of its tribute obligations for that year (A3.1 Leg. 2501 Exp. 36520). In 1794 the Santo Tomás and San Francisco *parcialidades* paid a total of 300 *tostones* for the first survey of their land in their long dispute (AI.80 Leg. 6040 Exp. 53305:19v). In 1797 the same two groups paid a total of 210 *tostones* as part of another survey connected with the case (AI.80 Leg. 6042 Exp. 53327:140, 152). During the same period, the entire *pueblo* owed 528 *tostones* per *tércio* (A3.16 Leg. 2152 Exp. 32279, year 1792). It is highly doubtful that an individual Sacapulteco could acquire such resources; only a group of people pooling their funds could afford a lengthy litigation. The very fact that *parcialidades* as units pursued and paid for litigation may have served to reinforce the concept of the *parcialidad* as the landholding entity, and may have delayed the breakup of corporate holdings into individual plots as permitted under Spanish law.

A key factor in accounting for *parcialidad* continuity is that Spaniards and Spanish policies were often working at cross-purposes with regard to the task of directed change, thus unintentionally helping maintain Sacapulteco social organization. We have seen how official Spanish policy called for the creation of single municipalities from multiple *parcialidades* and how, in an obvious contradiction, the Spanish administrators allowed the two *amaq'* groups, congregated to form Sacapulas, to set up what amounted to separate jurisdictions through the selection of their own *alcaldes* and *regidores*. Initially, even the introduction of a Peninsular model of town organization had little impact since the offices were at first controlled by the indigenous aristocracy of the *parcialidades*. While official Spanish policy was to form single *pueblos*, *parcialidades* quickly proved to be very handy units from an administrative standpoint. They could be used as subunits for purposes of tribute assessment. To this end, the Santa María Magdalena *parcialidad* continued to be listed on the tribute records long after its surviving members had been incorporated socially into the other Sacapulas groups. More important, the *parcialidades* could be used as units in making up *encomienda* grants, especially as the colonial period wore on and the number of Spanish applicants for such grants increased.

While the Spanish policy was to eliminate *parcialidades*, the legal right of the Indians to appeal any initiative, process, or ruling of the Spanish-run legal system effectively hamstrung official efforts to implement policy. The courts were also unable to perform their function of adjudication since any decision could be appealed. Settlements of land disputes could not be imposed and the *parcialidades* were allowed—actually forced—to arrive at mutually satisfactory compromises on their own, based on the *parcialidad* principle. In the course of lengthy disputes, some Spanish officials seem to have become conditioned to thinking in terms of landholding by *parcialidades*, even recommending to their superiors settlements based on the explicit recognition of that principle. On at least one occasion, the *Audiencia* abdicated its responsibility, effectively ordering the two parties to settle the dispute themselves and submit their agreement to the court for approval.

Finally, a factor whose importance cannot be overestimated: The Spaniards were not interested in acquiring the Sacapultecos' land. As we have seen, all the disputes over land were between Indians. Presumably, the relatively small amount of useful land around Sacapulas was not enough to be attractive to the Spaniards. Similarly, Sacapulas was far enough removed from major Spanish centers at Totonicapán and Chiantla to be inconvenient for Spanish settlement and exploitation. The importance of this distance is illustrated partly by the experience of Aguacatán, the *municipio* bordering Sacapulas to the west. To its west, Aguacatán was bordered by Chiantla and by 1607, at the latest, the Spaniards had begun purchasing Aguateco lands lying near that border (AI Leg. 5937 Exp. 59314). This encroachment continued through the seventeenth and into the early eighteenth century. In Sacapulas, competition for land among the *parcialidades* was keen enough. Had the Spaniards purchased tracts there as they had in Aguacatán, it is probable that a true crisis would have developed by the mid- to late 1700s as the Indian population peaked. As it happened, however, there was simply an increase in the intensity of land litigation, with the ultimate solutions being worked out by the Sacapultecos themselves.

Comparisons

Anecdotal evidence from Aguacatán aside, it is appropriate to briefly explore the extent to which evidence from Maya communities in other parts of the highlands validates the factors that have been proposed as contributing to the continuity of basic principles of social organization in Sacapulas. In the process we shall be returning, at least tangentially, to the topic raised in the Preface of the origin of the area's closed corporate communities. Unfortunately, there is very little comparative information in the literature. Ethnographers have usually taken a synchronic approach to Maya social organization, while the interests of ethnohistorians have tended more toward the reconstruction of the preconquest culture. In attempting to use the extant ethnographic literature, one is confounded by several other difficulties. First, as noted in Chapter 1, different terms are used for at least superficially similar units in different parts of the highland Maya area. It is hard to determine through ethnographic investigations alone whether a *barrio* was always the same as a *cantón* or *paraje*. The reverse is also true in that the same terms are sometimes used for different kinds of units.[1] Second, there is evidence that the terms themselves have changed in meaning or referent over time.[2] Third, we lack historical control over the events and processes that produced these variations in organization and terminology in the ethnographic record. Still, it may be worthwhile to sketch a comparison using the limited material available, if not as a definitive statement, at least to suggest areas for further research.

Our best choices for comparison are the Tzotzil-Maya communities of Zinacantán and Chamula, the histories of which have been touched upon by Wasserstrom (1983) in his general treatment of Chiapas. Along with Sacapulas, these communities seem to represent a gradient of change in social organization from the considerable continuity of preconquest principles to an almost prototypic closed corporate community. While we lack specific information on their preconquest organization and postconquest formation into towns, some type of *chinamit* organization must be assumed. The colonial period and the later experiences of these two communities are fairly well documented.

Of the three, Zinacantán alone suffered the effects of the Spaniards' encroachment on its lands very early in the colonial period. Wasserstrom notes that the community's position along the royal highway made its land attractive to Spaniards interested in commercial agriculture and stock raising beginning around 1540 (ibid., 90). Thus, from an early date, the Zinacantecos were forced to support themselves through work outside the community as bearers, muleteers, and peddlers, the men having to spend most of their time away from home (ibid., 91–92). As a result of land poverty and the exodus of men from the community, individual nuclear families (many of them headed by women) were the normal social units by the middle of the eighteenth century (ibid., 93). Social units (such as *parcialidades*) intermediate between the nuclear family and community levels were apparently absent, not being mentioned in either the historical or the ethnographic literature on Zinacantán. Instead, today we find small, descent-based kin units at the core of outlying settlements called *parajes* (Vogt 1969, 148). However, Wasserstrom is of the opinion that these kin groups developed in the nineteenth century as some innovative Zinacantecos began purchasing land, formerly held in common, as a defense against *ladino* encroachment. With individual ownership, only people who could claim relationship to a titleholder would have rights to occupy a plot within his holdings (Wasserstrom 1983, 141–42).[3] Not coincidentally, of the three, it is Zinacantán that most closely approximates a prototypic closed corporate community.

In contrast, during the colonial period, Chamula seems to have "escaped direct [Spanish] settlement and loss of territory" (ibid., 90). Serious loss of land to outsiders did not occur until the expropriations carried out during the first half of the nineteenth century (which also further impoverished Zinacantán) (ibid., 120). In both communities, land loss usually resulted in permanent migration to *ladino* ranches and *fincas*. Yet today, in contrast to Zinacantán, Chamula retains a system of *barrios* similar in some respects to the *cantones* of Sacapulas. Based on his observations in the 1940s, Ricardo Pozas ([1959] 1977) reports that there are three such *barrios* in Chamula, each constituting a basic social, political, and territorial division of the *municipio*. Local government is composed of representatives of all three *barrios*, each providing a specific number of functionaries in the community's political-religious hierarchy. An individual's obligations to his *barrio* include filling whatever religious or political post that is the group's responsibility and working on the lands of those *barrio* members who are filling such posts. The houses in the *pueblo* itself are grouped according to *barrio* membership. In Chamula there is even a degree of economic specialization among the *barrios*: one is composed basically of agriculturalists, in another people are small-scale merchants, in the third the people exploit forest products. Pozas characterizes Chamula as a confederation of *barrios,* even as a confederation of *pueblos,* because of the social distance and distinctiveness maintained by the three *cantón*-like groups despite their inclusion in the same *municipio* (Pozas [1959] 1977, 78–91; Vogt 1973). Significantly, the colonial chronicler Remesal briefly related that Chamula was originally formed by congregating three formerly distinct groups or "*pueblos*" (Remesal [1615–17] 1964–66, 2:178). Though sparse, the evidence strongly suggests that the *barrios* of Chamula are the descendants of late preconquest-early colonial *chinamitales-parcialidades.* Evidently, the fact that Chiapas communities were able to recover formerly alienated lands in the 1930s contributed to the endurance of *barrios* in Chamula, while in Zinacantán such units, to the extent they had ever existed, were already extinct and could not be revived.

As already noted, the Spaniards and other outsiders never had much desire for the land in Sacapulas. The community's remoteness and limited amount of useful land made it unattractive for economic exploitation during the colonial period. Its climate was unsuitable for the cultivation of cash crops, such as coffee, that were introduced in the later nineteenth century. Such commercial agriculture did develop to some extent in the Ixil communities to the north, where the soils and climate were favorable, but it had little discernible effect on Sacapulas.

Sacapultecos have long been forced to make or add to their living through activities outside the *municipio,* but in their case the impetus came from permanently limited natural resources and population pressure, not from the loss to the Spaniards of resources they had previously enjoyed. At the same time, Sacapulteco absence from the community does not generally seem to have been permanent. Salt production and trade are primarily dry-season activites, the latter requiring only visits to markets in other communities. In Sacapulas, such auxiliary economic activities are part of the traditional life, the way in which for centuries the people have dealt with the limited resources in their area.

To summarize the results of this limited comparison, we find, not surprisingly, that loss of land as the community's economic base to encroaching Spaniards/*ladinos* appears to have been a significant factor in determining the extent of continuity in traditional Maya units of social organization. Encroachment was encouraged when a community was near a Spanish or *ladino* center or along a major road, which made commercial agricultural enterprise possible. When such land loss resulted in permanent Indian out-migration, it is easy to imagine the changes that must have occurred in a place like Zinacantán. In such a fluid and insecure socioeconomic situation the maintenance of social units above the level of the nuclear family would have been difficult. While a similar situation developed in Chamula, it occurred much later and the adverse conditions did not last as long and, perhaps, were not as severe.

While economic factors have been shown to be of importance in social continuity, this does not suggest that other factors were irrelevant. Population and mortality were crucial as well, at least in Sacapulas. Some *parcialidades* ceased to exist when their populations became too small; the survivors were incorporated into other such units. Catastrophic population loss through disease (as appears to have occurred in other parts of the region) or through population dispersal (as in Zinacantán) would have made the maintenance of *parcialidades* very difficult. We do not know about the *congregaciónes* that formed the two Chiapas towns—the original diversity of the component groups, their sizes, or the distances from which they were brought. Similarly, the question of the utility of *parcialidad*-type groups vis-à-vis the complexities of Spanish colonial administration and later regimes in Chiapas cannot currently be addressed. Yet all of these appear to be factors in the continuity of social organization in the case of Sacapulas.

Viewed in this light, prototypic closed corporate communities lacking the intermediate level of *cantones* or *barrios* are perhaps best understood as the result of a process characterized by desperate responses to extreme pressures. Even in such cases, however, the similarities between the contemporary community and the preconquest-colonial *chinamit-parcialidad* are compelling. Perhaps more important, through the present study we begin to see that the processes through which these communities were formed must have been more complex than previously thought and were by no means universal. Presumably other communities in the region with *cantón* or *barrio* organization are the end result of similar processes of accommodation and continuity—parallel in some ways to the case of Sacapulas—but we are only beginning to identify the variations and specific conditions that produce them. We hope that the present study of the Sacapulteco experience constitutes a step in that direction.

Notes

CHAPTER 1

1. Sacapulas also lies at the heart of an area extensively studied by ethnographers and archaeologists. Smith traversed much of the region in his pioneering archaeological survey (Smith 1955). He returned, as have others, to the Ixil zone (Smith and Kidder 1951; Bequelin 1969). The modern Ixil have been the subjects of several ethnographic investigations (Lincoln 1942, 1946; Colby and Van den Berghe 1969; Colby and Colby 1981), as have the Aguatec (Brintnall 1979). The archaeology of the Sajcabajá-Canillá area has been exhaustively studied by the Misión Científica Franco Guatemalteca and the results of these studies are still being published (Ichon 1975). Farther to the south is the Quiché Basin, where Carmack and associates have conducted extensive archaeological and ethnohistorical investigations (Carmack 1977, 1981), and the well-known market town of Chichicastenango, which was the subject of Bunzel's ground-breaking ethnographic study (Bunzel 1952).

2. In rendering Maya terms *ax waab'* and *Kajawixel* in this chapter, we have followed the orthography used by DuBois in his study of Sacapultec (Dubois 1981).

CHAPTER 2

1. The material presented in this chapter appeared in a slightly different form in Hill (1980, 1984). In the earlier versions the concern was to establish continuity between the preconquest *chinamit-molab* units and contemporary closed corporate communities. However, as the present work demonstrates, the preconquest units, in some cases at least, endured down to the present in the form of *cantones*.

2. A Kekchí cognate term *molam* is contained as a fragment of a late seventeenth- or early eighteenth-century Spanish-Kekchí dictionary (Freeze 1975, 40). Its Spanish equivalent was given as *barrio* by the compiler. The presence of the *chinamit-molam* type unit in the isolated Kekchí area supports the contention that it was general among the highland Maya. It also raises interesting possibilities for the reconstruction of Classic lowland society along the same lines. In addition, Orellana has remarked upon the importance of the *chinamit* as an organizing principle among the Tzutujil Maya on the south side of Lake Atitlán, and has noted evidence of the continuity of *chinamitales* down through the early seventeenth century (Orellana 1984). Unfortunately, her study does not follow the Tzutujiles' experiences down to more recent times, so we cannot tell the fate of such social units for this Maya group. Finally, Calnek notes the presence of the term *chinamit* as a loan word in the Tzeltal and Tzotzil Maya languages of Chiapas, Mexico (Calnek 1962, 23). However, his sources did not provide enough information to allow a characterization of such units or an enumeration of their functions. Still, the presence of the term among the two Chiapas groups is further support for the

assertion that *chinamit-molab* were basic principles of late preconquest highland Maya social organization.

3. The significance of the general-specific distinction among sources has also been noted by Harvey for central Mexico in his review of land tenure principles in that area (Harvey 1983, 84–85).

4. For ease of reproduction, the original Parra characters, used to express the different stops present in Maya languages, have been changed to their standard equivalents. Otherwise, since the terms were taken from dictionaries compiled by Spaniards, Spanish orthography and pronunciation rules apply. The only exception is the letter "x" which, for Maya terms, has the value of "sh" in English. English translations of the longer Spanish quotations appear in brackets following the definitions; translations from Spanish to English were made by Hill.

5. The primary reliance on elite-status informants by Spanish friars in conducting their inquiries has been noted in Mexico. Olmos, Sahagun, and Torquemada all employed this technique (Franch 1973, 266; Nicholson 1973, 207; Wilkerson 1974, 64, 72–73). It is known that Las Casas used the work of Olmos in his *Apologétia Historia* (Wilkerson 1974, 75). Thus, while Olmos and Sahagun were Franciscans, it appears there was some exchange of ideas on how to conduct investigations into native culture. Probably more important was a Spanish cultural bias toward working with the elite segments.

6. Several ethnohistorians have attempted to deal with the *chinamit* or *molab* in anthropological terms. Miles, in her study of the Pokom, characterizes the *molab* as a clan, though the criteria for this classification are not explicitly stated (Miles 1957, 759–60). Miles also proposed a subclan or lineage principle. Her interpretation in this regard appears based on the Spaniards' use of the word *linaje* when referring to several Maya surnames (ibid., 758). As has been discussed, the word *linaje* does not indicate "lineage" in the anthropological sense of a descent group, but rather a line of descent. The operative principle seems to have emphasized the individual's place in a line of descent rather than his membership in a descent group. Additionally, these concerns probably were only of importance for the proportionally small group of rulers.

Similarly, Pedro Carrasco characterized the *chinamit* as an exogamous patrilineal clan (Carrasco 1964, 324). The definition of clan used by Carrasco was not stated. However, he also noted that the *chinamit* "también formaba el nucleo de de una subdivisión territorial o barrio bajo la autoridad de un jefe propio" (ibid., 324). Carrasco noted the important entry in the Varea dictionary defining *chinamit* as "linaje y gente debajo un apellido y de un cacique aunque recogen a cualquier que se quiera llegar a éste linaje y hermandad de gente" (Varea, in Carrasco 1964, 325). However, as Carrasco was more concerned with personal names and their transmission, he did not explore the apparent contradictions between the dictionary definitions and his proposed clanlike structure.

Concentrating on the political and cultural Quiché elite of Utatlán, Carmack has come to a different interpretation of the *chinamit*. Based on dictionary entries, he applies a model of feudal organization in which the members of a *chinamit* constitute the "estate" of a "chief" or lord (Carmack 1977, 11–12; 1981, 164–65). Based on a strict translation of *chinamit* as a "fenced in place" Carmack envisions it as an actual walled-in estate (ibid., 12–13). It is more likely the fenced-in place is used figuratively to denote the social insularity of *chinamit* groups. Such an interpretation is supported by the fact that, despite intensive archaeological surveys, no remains of any walled-in estates have come to light. From the point of view of the Utatlán ruling elite, such a lord-vassal relationship may indeed represent the interaction between *chinamit* and lord. However, it is not at all certain that all *chinamitales* were so directly under the control of such highly placed individuals. Based on the sources consulted, it appears that the "chief" of a *chinamit* could also be interpreted as a much less imposing and more familiar figure than the lords of Utatlán. Based on references in the nineteenth-century Tamub *título* mentioned in the text, Carmack goes on to suggest another, higher level of socio-territorial organization based on units referred to as *calpules* (Carmack 1977, 12–13; 1981, 165–66). This additional level is made necessary in Carmack's scheme because of his interpretation of *chinamit* as a walled-in area. As has been seen in the documents cited, *calpul* was simply used as a synonym for *chinamit*, much in the same way that *parcialidad* and *linaje* were used.

CHAPTER 4

1. Students of highland Maya archaeology will notice some discrepancies between the *chinamit* reconstructions presented here and the scheme offered by John Fox (1978, 69–91). These are not just differences of interpretation. Fox relied entirely on Smith for an understanding of the Sacapulas-area archaeology and visited only four of the sites. No additional surveys or excavations were conducted. Similarly, Fox appears (with the exceptions of published versions of the Título de los Señores de Sacapulas and the so-called Título Uchabajá) to have relied only on the major chronicles from the central Quiché area, which he seems to have used uncritically. Apparently, he examined none of the colonial documents relating specifically to Sacapulas in the course of his research.

2. A land survey of 1680 indicates that the other Postclassic site in the area (called Comitancillo) was originally inhabited by people who later formed the San Pablo *parcialidad* of San Pedro Jocoplias, the *municipio* adjacent to Sacapulas on the south. Representatives of Sacapulas were present during the survey and confirmed the boundary with the Jocopilas people. Again, we note the pattern of site placement near borders (AI Leg. 5958 Exp. 52210).

CHAPTER 5

1. The classic work on this subject is by Simpson (1966). More recent treatments include MacLeod (1973), Rodriguez (1977), and Sherman (1981).

2. More detailed information on the workings and abuses of the *repartimiento* system can be found in MacLeod (1973, 206–9, 257–59, 295–98).

CHAPTER 8

1. Hidalgo must have made some error in reading or recording the name of the *Presidente de la Audiencia* and the date when the *título* was granted. Alonso Criado de Castilla occupied the post, but only at a later time, from 1598 to 1611 (MacLeod 1973, 391).

CHAPTER 9

1. This is not to say that there are no documents pertaining to Sacapulas from the nineteenth century. Though there is a relative dearth of documents during the first half of the century, the pace of administration increases after 1880. Some of these documents have been cataloged in the AGCA. However, most are still un-catalogued and filed along with the other documents pertaining to the *Jefetura Política del Quiché*. Hill has examined all of the cataloged documents for this period and a very large sample of the uncataloged ones as well. Unfortunately, for the purposes of reconstructing the careers of the Sacapulas *parcialidades,* almost none of the documents are useful. For the most part, they record the pro forma responses of *ladino* officials to the orders and edicts of the national government, via the appointed *Jefe Político del Quiché*.

CHAPTER 10

1. For example, units termed *cantones* are important in the organization of Chichicastenango and San Miguel Totonicapán (Bunzel 1952; Carmack 1966). However, in neither case are the sizes and functions of these units similar to those of the Sacapulas *cantones.* Tedlock reports that early in the colonial period, Momostenango exhibited an organization similar to that of late sixteenth-century Sacapulas. At that time, Momostenango was divided into four *parcialidades,* each selecting its own *alcalade* and *regidor* (Tedlock 1982, 16). Today, these four divisions evidently endure as *barrios* or wards of the town center. In addition there now exist some fourteen *cantones* (ibid., 33). Unfortunately, Tedlock's summary description is not detailed enough to allow a structural comparison of the Momostecan *barrios* and *cantones* with those of Sacapulas, despite some outward similarities. Also, there currently exists little historical information concerning the groups forming Momostenango. Thus, we are unable to determine the precise historical relationship (if any) between the four early-colonial *parcialidades* and the fourteen contemporary *cantones.* We hope that Carmack's work on this topic will clarify matters.

2. In Totonicapán, the term *parcialidad* is used today to denote a localized group of related kin who occupy the same *cantón* (Carmack 1966, 51). Carmack assumes that use of the term *parcialidad* indicates continuity from early colonial times. However, as documented in the present study, the term *parcialidad* had a significantly different referent during the colonial period. In Chichicastenango, the terms *calpul* and *chinimtal* are still used. Today, however, they refer to positions held by individuals, not to groups. A *chinimtal* is a marriage spokesman, while a *calpul* is a witness of contracts (Bunzel 1952, 183). Again, the contemporary usage of terms is vastly different from their original usage.

3. The implications of this line of reasoning are significant. Several students of contemporary highland Maya social organization have assumed that the kin-based units described ethnographically represent survivals of preconquest organization (Vogt 1969, 591–92; Carmack 1966). To the contrary, the Wasserstrom work and the present study strongly suggest that such kin-based groups represent adaptations to the disorganization caused by commercial exploitation in the colonial period and nineteenth century.

Glossary

ALCALDE. Mayor and judge or justice of the peace of a town.

ALCALDE MAYOR. An appointed royal official charged with the administration of a district called an *alcaldía mayor*. His duties typically included tribute collection and, during the earlier part of the colonial period, adjudication of disputes. Later in the period, the adjudicative function declined and such officials served more as information gatherers for higher courts.

ALCALDÍA INDÍGENA. Since the late nineteenth century, the subordinate political organization of communities in charge of Indian affairs.

ALDEA. A small, rural settlement, usually dependent on a *pueblo*.

AMAQ'. A preconquest unit of political organization consisting of a group of confederated *chinamitales*. This was probably the highest level of political integration among the highland Maya of the period. The size of the confederation was dependent on the number of component *chinamitales*. (See Chapter 4.)

ÁMPARO. A colonial-period writ, technically similar to a restraining order, that protected the party to which it was granted from summary actions by another party. Requests for such protection were frequently made to the Spanish authorities by litigant Indian groups in their disputes with each other.

AUDIENCIA. Highest royal court of appeal; additionally, a governing body with limited legislative authority. Also, the area under its jurisdiction.

AUTO. A proclamation, order, or decree from an official legal or administrative entity.

AUXILIAR. Lower-level municipal officers, usually resident in rural *aldeas*.

AX WAAB'. The twelve-man council for elders that traditionally ran the affairs of a *parcialidad/cantón*. (See Chapter 1.)

BARRANCA. A ravine.

BARRIO. In Sacapulas, a wardlike division of the *pueblo*. Elsewhere it can also refer to a social unit similar to the *cantones* of Sacapulas. (See Chapter 1.)

CABALLERÍA. A unit of land equal to approximately 111 acres.

CABILDO. Town government; also, the building in which it is housed.

CACIQUE. An Arawak term used by the Spaniards to denote any leader among the Indians of the New World.

CAJA DE COMUNIDAD. The strongbox in which community funds were kept during the colonial period.

CALPUL. Hispanicized from the Nahuatl *calpulli, calpul* may refer to (1) a *chinamit*, or (2) an individual office in a community political-religious hierarchy.

CAÑAVERAL. A sugarcane grove.

CANÍCULA. The short dry period occurring toward the middle of the rainy season.

CANTÓN. In contemporary Sacapulas, a corporate social unit and division of the community and the direct descendant of the preconquest *chinamit* and colonial *parcialidad*. Elsewhere in Guatemala today the term also refers to small rural settlements that are also administrative subdivisions of a municipality. While outwardly similar in some respects to the *cantones* of Sacapulas, it is currently unclear whether such units in other communities are descendants of preconquest/colonial-period groups or simply the product of nineteenth-century national government actions. (See Chapters 1, 9, and 10.)

CASA DE COMUNIDAD. A house for the use of travelers that Indian communities were required to maintain during the colonial period.

CASERÍO. A rural settlement even smaller than an *aldea*.

CATEQUISTA. A catechist; someone instructed in the formal aspects of contemporary Catholicism.

CÉDULA. A royal order or decree.

CHINAMIT. The basic unit of preconquest highland Maya social organization above the level of kinship, similar to the Pokom *molab* and Mexican *calpulli*. All three were basically corporate, rather closed social groups, the members of which held land in common and recognized a number of primary rights and obligations vis-à-vis other members of the group. (See Chapter 2 for an extended discussion.)

COFRADÍA. Among Indian peoples of Mesoamerica, a type of religious sodality dedicated to the celebration of the days associated with a particular saint.

COMISIONADO. A minor royal official, detailed for a specific task.

CONGREGACIÓN. The Spanish program of concentrating the Indian population in *pueblos* of Spanish design.

COSTUMBRE. The traditional, institutionalized culture of an Indian community.

COSTUMBRISTA. One who follows or observes *costumbre*. In contemporary usage, a traditionalist Indian.

CUERDA. A unit of land corresponding to approximately one-fifth of an acre.

DEFENSOR. A Spanish lawyer or official of the colonial administration appointed to represent Indians before the *Audiencia*.

DOMINIO DIRECTO. Roughly equivalent to legal ownership of land during the colonial period.

EJIDO. In general, a community's common land. During the colonial period, such land was legally granted to the community by the Crown.

ENCOMENDERO. A grantee or recipient of an *encomienda* and its attendant income.

ENCOMIENDA. A royal grant of Indians to a Spaniard in recognition of the latter's service to the Crown. Originally including both labor and tribute rights, *encomienda* eventually focused on tribute.

ESTANCIA. An area used for grazing livestock.

EVANGELISTA. Name given to an adherent of any of the various evangelical Protestant sects active in Guatemala in this century.

FANEGA. A unit of dry measurement equal to approximately one and one-half bushels.

FISCAL. A royal official whose duties approximated those of an attorney general, but who also reviewed the legality of court rulings.

GOBERNADOR. An Indian official appointed by the Spaniards, responsible for tribute collection and the maintenance of order in his community.

HACIENDA. A large rural estate.

JEFE POLÍTICO. From the formation of the republic, a governor of a department.

JUEZ COMISARIO. A low-level Spanish official, commissioned to investigate a legal dispute at the local level.

JUEZ DE PAZ. Justice of the peace.

JUEZ PRIVATIVO. Highest Spanish official in the administrative department of the *Audiencia* concerned with matters relating to land.

KAJAWIXEL. In Sacapulas, the top position in a *cofradía*.

LADINO. A Guatemalan who identifies with the dominant national culture.

MAESTRE DE CAMPO. Literally, a field marshal, though this term evidently was applied to much lower ranking officers than the army commanders to whom it was applied in western Europe.

MANDAMIENTO. An order or writ.

MANTA. A length of woven cotton cloth.

MASEGUALES. A term borrowed by the Spaniards from Nahuatl. Used in colonial Guatemala to denote non-noble or common Indians.

MESTIZO. A person of mixed Spanish-Indian descent.

MILPA. An Indian cornfield.

MOJÓN. A boundary marker.

MUNICIPIO. In modern Guatemala, the basic administrative unit consisting of a town and its hinterland.

OCOTE. An extremely resinous form of pine, the wood of which is still widely used in highland Guatemala for kindling and torches.

OFICIO. Literally, office; term used by Maya people to refer to their traditional community-defined economic pursuits.

PARAJE. In Mexico, a dispersed rural settlement, sometimes equated with a *cantón*.

PARCIALIDAD. In colonial Guatemala, a division of a community's population. In Sacapulas, these units were direct descendants of the area's preconquest *chinamitales*.

PATAN. Literally, burden; term used to denote one's obligations in life and one's role in the universe. In Sacapulas, the concept still underwrites the participation of individuals in community affairs, especially in the *alcaldía* and *cofradía* organizations. (See Chapter 1.)

PESO. During the colonial period, a silver coin equal to eight *reales* or two *tostones*.

PRECARIA POSESIÓN. During the colonial period, limited, revocable rights of ownership to a piece of land.

PRINCIPAL. A leading Indian elder.

PROCURADOR. Legal counsel in the colonial period.

PUEBLO. A town; the basic unit of colonial administration; today, the seat of a *municipio*.

REAL. A silver coin equal to one-eighth *peso*.

REGIDOR. A member of the municipal council or *cabildo* of a community.

REPARTIMIENTO. During the colonial period this term could refer to a forced labor draft (through the seventeenth century) or the forced sale of goods to the Indians (eighteenth century).

RESERVADO. During the colonial period, an individual exempted from paying tribute because of age or service in the town government.

SALINAS. Salt deposits.

SECRETARIO DE CÁMARA. Chief secretary of the *Audiencia*. Among his other duties, he might review legal decisions or opinions rendered by other royal officials.

SÍNDICO. A position in the municipal government of Indian communities, ideally a legal adviser.

SUBDELEGADO. A lower-level royal official who could temporarily be assigned to a wide range of duties depending on the needs of a judge or *alcalde mayor*.

TÉQUIO. Obligatory service to the colonial government to which the Indians were subject. This frequently took the form of work as porters and messengers for royal officials.

TÉRCIO. Literally and originally, a third part of a community's yearly tribute obligations. By the seventeenth century, the term was applied to the twice-a-year occasions on which tribute was collected.

TIERRAS REALENGAS. Land belonging to the Crown.

TÍTULO. Literally, title; term used by Indians to denote their traditional histories and any other documents that they felt gave them rights to land. In Spanish legal parlance, the term denoted a royal title only.

TOSTÓN. A silver coin equivalent to four *reales* or one-half *peso*.

TRIBUTARIO ENTERO. Literally, a full tributary; the basic unit by which the Spaniards determined an Indian community's tribute obligations.

VARA. A unit of linear measurement of approximately thirty-three inches. Also, the staff of authority carried by Indian municipal officials.

VECINO. A citizen.

VISITA. In the colonial period, the term could refer to an inspection tour by royal officials or to the periodic arrival of a priest to a community in his care.

VISTA DE OJOS. An on-site inspection tour carried out by a royal official in cases involving land disputes.

Bibliography

ARCHIVAL DOCUMENTS

Chapter 3

*Archivo General de
Centro America (AGCA)*

AI	Leg. 5942 Exp. 51995
A3.2	Leg. 825 Exp. 15207
A3.16	Leg. 1601 Exp. 26391
A3.16	Leg. 2074 Exp. 31570
A3.16	Leg. 2025 Exp. 36584
A3.16	Leg. 2075 Exp. 31588
A3.16	Leg. 2504 Exp. 36576
A3.16	Leg. 502 Exp. 10284
A3.2	Leg. 707 Exp. 13120
AI	Leg. 5978 Exp. 52517
AI.80	Leg. 6042 Exp. 53327
AI	Leg. 5979 Exp. 52518
AI	Leg. 6097 Exp. 55507
AI.80	Leg. 6040 Exp. 53305
AI	Leg. 6037 Exp. 5305
B84.3	Leg.1134 Exp. 26011
Imp. 1933:435	

Archivo General de Indias (AGI)

AGI Guatemala 948
AGI Guatemala 128
AGI Guatemala 529

Chapter 4

AGCA

AI.80	Leg. 6040 Exp. 53305
AI.80	Leg. 6042 Exp. 53327

Chapter 5

AGCA

AI	Leg. 5979 Exp. 52536
AI	Leg. 5942 Exp. 51995

Chapter 6

AGCA

AI	Leg. 5936 Exp. 51914
AI	Leg. 5978 Exp. 52518
AI.45	Leg. 2924 Exp. 27326

Chapter 7

AGCA

AI.80	Leg. 6025 Exp. 53126
AI	Leg. 6021 Exp. 53083
AI.45	Leg. 2906 Exp. 26938
AI	Leg. 6037 Exp. 53257

Chapter 8

AGCA

AI	Leg. 6040 Exp. 53303
AI	Leg. 6021 Exp. 53084
AI.80	Leg. 6040 Exp. 53305
AI.80	Leg. 6042 Exp. 53327

Chapter 9

AGCA

1890A Doc. 22 Jefetura Político del
Quiché (JPQ)

AI	Leg. 6024 Exp. 53119

Chapter 10

AGCA

A3.1	Leg. 2501 Exp. 36520
AI.80	Leg. 6040 Exp. 53305
AI.80	Leg. 6042 Exp. 53327
A3.16	Leg. 2152 Exp. 32279
AI	Leg. 5937 Exp. 59314

OTHER SOURCES

Barnett, Homer G. 1953. *Innovation: The basis of cultural change*. New York: McGraw-Hill.

Bequelin, Pierre. 1969. *Archeologie de la region de Nebaj*. Paris: Institut D'Ethnologie.

Berdan, Frances F. 1982. *The Aztecs of Mexico: An imperial society*. New York: Holt, Rinehart, and Winston.

Borah, Woodrow. 1982. The Spanish and Indian Law: New Spain. In *The Inca and Aztec states, 1400–1800*, ed. G. A. Coller, R. I. Rosaldo, and J. D. Worth. New York: Academic Press.

Brintall, Douglas E. 1979. *Revolt against the dead: The modernization of a Mayan community in the highlands of Guatemala*. New York: Gordon and Breach.

Bunzel, Ruth. 1952. *Chichicastenango*. American Ethnological Society pub. no. 22. New York: J. J. Augustin.

Calepino grande Castellano y Quiché. N.d. Newberry Library, Chicago. Manuscript.

Calnek, Edward E. 1962. Highland Chiapas before the Spanish conquest. Ph.D. diss., University of Chicago, Chicago.

Cancian, Frank. 1967. Political and religious organization. In *Handbook of Middle American Indians*, ed. Robert Wauchope. 6:282–98. Austin: University of Texas Press.

Carmack, Robert M. 1966. La perpetuación del clan patrilineal en Totonicapán. *Antropología e historia de Guatemala* 18 (no. 2): 43–60.

———. 1973. *Quichean civilization*. Berkeley: University of California Press.

———. 1977. Ethnohistory of the central Quiché: The community of Utatlán. In *Archaeology and ethnohistory of the central Quiché*, ed. Dwight T. Wallace and Robert M. Carmack. Institute for Mesoamerican Studies Publ. no. 1: 1–19. Albany: State University of New York.

———. 1981. *The Quiché Mayas of Utatlán*. Norman: University of Oklahoma Press.

Carrasco, Pedro. 1963. La exogamía según un documento Cakchiquel. *Tlalocan* 6 (no. 3):193–96.

———. 1964. Los nombres de personas en la Guatemala antigua. *Estudios de Cultura Maya* 4:323–34.

———. 1971. Social organization of ancient Mexico. In *Handbook of Middle American Indians*, ed. Robert Wauchope. 10:349–75. Austin: University of Texas Press.

Chance, John K., and William B. Taylor. 1985. Cofradías and cargos: An historical perspective on the Mesoamerican civil-religious hierarchy. *American Ethnologist* 12 (no. 1): 1–26.

Cobarruvias, Sebastián. [1610] 1977. *Tesoro de la lengua Castellana o Española*. Madrid: Ediciones Turner.

Colby, Benjamin N., and Pierre van den Berghe. 1969. *Ixil Country*. Berkeley: University of California Press.

Colby, Benjamin N., and Lore M. Colby. 1981. *The daykeeper: The life and discourse of an Ixil diviner*. Cambridge: Harvard University Press.

Collins, Anne C. 1980. Colonial Jacaltenango, Guatemala: The formation of a corporate community. Ph.D. diss., Tulane University, New Orleans.

Cortés y Larraz, Pedro. [1770] 1958. *Descripción geográfico-moral de la diocesis de*

Goathemala. 2 vols. Biblioteca "Goathemala," vol. 22. Guatemala: Sociedad de Geografía e Historia.

Coto, Tomás. [c. 1690]. *Vocabulario de la lengua Cakchiquel y Guatemalteca*. American Philosophical Society Library, Philadelphia. Manuscript.

Diccionario Geográfico de Guatemala. *See* Dirección General de Cartografía de Guatemala 1961.

Dirección General de Cartografía de Guatemala. 1961. *Diccionario geográfico de Guatemala*. 2 vols. Guatemala.

Dirección General de Estadística de Guatemala. 1975. *VIII censo de la población*. Guatemala.

Dubois, John W. 1981. The Sacapultec language. Ph.D. diss., University of California, Berkeley.

Edmonson, Munro S. 1971. *The Book of counsel: The Popol Vuh of the Quiché Maya of Guatemala*. Middle American Research Institute Publ. no. 35. New Orleans: Tulane University.

Farriss, Nancy M. 1984. *Maya society under colonial rule*. Princeton: Princeton University Press.

Fox, John W. 1978. *Quiché conquest*. Albuquerque: University of New Mexico Press.

Franch, Jose Alcina. 1973. Juan de Torquemada, 1564–1624. In *Guide to ethnohistorical sources: Part two. Handbook of Middle American Indians*, ed. Howard F. Cline. 13:256–75. Austin: University of Texas Press.

Freeze, Ray A. 1975. *A fragment of an early Kekchí vocabulary*. University of Missouri Monographs in Anthropology, no. 2. Columbia, Missouri: Museum of Anthropology.

Fuentes y Guzmán, Francisco Antonio de. [1690] 1932–33. *Recordación Flórida*. 3 vols. Biblioteca "Goathemala," Vol. 11. Guatemala: Sociedad de Geografía y Historia.

Gage, Thomas. [1648] 1929. *A new survey of the West Indies, 1648: The English American*. New York: R. M. McBride and Co.

Gibson, C. 1964. *The Aztecs under Spanish rule*. Stanford: Stanford University Press.

Hallowell, A. Irving. 1945. Sociopsychological aspects of acculturation. In *The science of man in the world crisis*, ed. R. Linton. New York: Columbia University Press.

Harvey, H. R. 1983. Aspects of land tenure in ancient Mexico. In *Explorations in ethnohistory*, ed. H. R. Harvey and H. J. Prem. Albuquerque: University of New Mexico Press.

Hill, Robert M., II. N.d. Informe de las investegaciones realizadas en el municipio de Sacapulas, Dpto. de El Quiché, Guatemala. Mimeo.

———. 1980. Closed corporate community and the late postclassic highland Maya: A case study in cultural continuity. Ph.D. diss., University of Pennsylvania, Philadelphia.

———. 1984. Chinamit and molab: Late postclassic highland Maya precursors of closed corporate community. *Estudios de Cultura Maya* 15:301–27.

Hunt, Eva, and June Nash. 1967. Local and territorial units. In *Handbook of Middle American Indians*, ed. Robert Wauchope. 6: 253–82. Austin: University of Texas Press.

Ichon, Alain. 1975. *Organización de un centro Quiché protohistórico: Pueblo Viejo Chichaj*. Traveau de la Mission Scientifique Francaise au Guatemala. RCP294. Guatemala.

———. 1979. *Rescate arqueológico en la cuenea del Río Chixoy: 1. Informe preliminar*. Misión Científica Franco-Guatemalteca. CNRS-RCP 500. Guatemala: Editorial Piedra Santa.

Ichon, A., M. F. Fauvet-Berthelot, and R. M. Hill II., 1980. *Archeologie de sauvetage dan la vallee du Rio Chixoy: 2. Cauinal*. Guatemala: Editorial Piedra Santa.

Jones, Chester L. 1942. Indian labor in Guatemala. In *Hispanic American essays: A memorial to James A. Robertson*, ed. A. Curtis Wilgus. Chapel Hill: University of North Carolina Press.

King, Arden F. 1974. *Coban and the Verapaz: History and cultural process in northern Guatemala*. Middle American Research Institute Publ. no. 37. New Orleans: Tulane University.

Kroeber, A. L. 1957. *Ethnographic interpretations 1–6*. University of California Publications in American Archaeology and Ethnology no. 47. Berkeley, California.

La Farge, Oliver. 1940. Maya ethnology: The sequence of cultures. In *The Maya and their neighbors,* ed. C. L. Hay, S. K. Lothrop, and H. L. Shapiro. Pp. 281–91. New York: D. Appleton-Century.

Las Casas, Bartolomé de. [c. 1550] 1909. *Apologética historia de las Indias*. Nueva Biblioteca de Autores Españoles, vol. 13. Madrid: M. Serrano y Sanz.

Lincoln, J. Steward. 1942. *The Maya calendar of the Ixil of Guatemala*. Contributions to American Anthropology and History no. 38. Washington, D.C.: Carnegie Institution of Washington.

———. 1946. An ethnological study of the Ixil Indians of the Guatemala highlands. Middle American Cultural Anthropology, no. 1. University of Chicago, Chicago. Microfilm.

Lovell, W. George, 1983. Settlement change in Spanish America: The dynamics of congregación in the Cuchumatán highlands of Guatemala, 1541–1821. *Canadian Geographer* 27 (no. 2): 163–74.

MacBryde, Felix W. 1934. *Sololá: A Guatemalan town and Cakchiquel market center*. Middle American Research Institute Publ. no. 5. Pp. 45–152. New Orleans: Tulane University.

———. 1947. *Cultural and historical geography of southwest Guatemala*. Institute of Social Anthropology Publ. no. 4. Washington, D.C.: Smithsonian Institution.

MacLeod, Murdo. 1973. *Spanish Central America: A socioeconomic history, 1520–1720*. Berkeley: University of California Press.

McCreery, David. 1983. Debt servitude in rural Guatemala, 1876–1936. *Hispanic American Historical Review* 63 (no. 4): 735–59.

Miles, S. W. 1957. The sixteenth-century Pokom-Maya: A documentary analysis of social structure and archaeological setting. *Transactions of the American Philosophical Society* 47: 731–81.

Nash, Manning. 1958. *Machine-age Maya: The industrialization of a Guatemalan community*. Memoir 87. American Anthropological Association, Menasha, Wisconsin.

Nicholson, H. B. 1973. Sahagun's 'Primeros Memoriales,' Tepepulco. In *Guide to ethnohistorical sources: Part two. Handbook of Middle American Indians,* ed. Howard F. Cline. 13:207–18. Austin: University of Texas Press.

Offner, Jerome A. 1983. *Law and politics in Aztec Texcoco.* New York: Cambridge University Press.

O'Flaherty, E. 1979. Institutionalization of the Catholic Church in the Americas: The case of colonial Guatemala, 1524–1563. Ph.D. diss., University of Pennsylvania, Philadelphia.

Orellana, Sandra. 1984. *The Tzutujil Mayas: Continuity and change, 1250–1630.* Norman: University of Oklahoma Press.

Pozas, Ricardo. [1959] 1977. *Chamula: Un pueblo indio en los altos de Chiapas.* Mexico D.F.: Instituto Nacional Indigenista.

Recinos, Adrian. 1957. *Crónicas indígenas de Guatemala.* Guatemala: Editorial Universitaria.

Reina, Ruben E. 1966. *The law of the saints.* Indianapolis: Bobbs-Merrill.

———. 1973. *Paraná: Social boundaries in an Argentine city.* Latin American Monographs 31. Austin: University of Texas Press.

Reina, Ruben E., and Robert M. Hill II. 1978. *The traditional pottery of Guatemala.* Austin: University of Texas Press.

Reina, Ruben E., and John Monaghan. 1981. Ways of the Maya: Salt production in Sacapulas, Guatemala. *Expedition* 23 (no.3): 13–33.

Remesal, Antonio de. [1615–17] 1964–66. *Historia general de las Indias occidentales y particular de la gobernación de Chiapa y Guatemala.* 2 vols. Biblioteca de Autores Españoles, vols. 175 and 189. Madrid: Ediciones Atlas.

República de Guatemala. 1921. *Censo de la población de Guatemala.* 2 vols. Guatemala: Ministerio de Fomento.

Rodriguez, Salvador. 1977. *Encomienda y conquista: Los inicios de la colonización en Guatemala.* Publicaciones del Seminario de Anthropología Americana, vol. 14. Sevilla: Universidad de Sevilla.

Saenz, Carmelo de Santa María. 1964. *Estudio preliminar: fray Antonio de Remesal, O.P., y su obra.* Biblioteca de Autores Españoles, vol. 175. Madrid: Ediciones Atlas.

Schultze-Jena, Leonhard. 1933. *Leben, Glauben und Sprache der Quiché von Guatemala.* Indiana, vol. 1. Jena: Gustav Fischer.

Sherman, William L. 1981. *Forced native labor in sixteenth-century Central America.* Lincoln: University of Nebraska Press.

Simpson, Lesley B. 1966. *The encomienda in New Spain.* Berkeley: University of California Press.

Smith, A. L., and A. V. Kidder. 1951. *Excavations at Nebaj, Guatemala.* Carnegie Institution of Washington Publ. no. 594. Washington, D.C.

Smith, Augustus L. 1955. *Archaeological reconnaissance in central Guatemala.* Carnegie Institution of Washington Publ. no. 608. Washington, D.C.

Solano y Perez Lila, F. de. 1974. *Los Mayas del siglo XVIII.* Madrid: Ediciones Cultura Hispanica.

Tax, Sol. 1937. The municipios of the midwestern highlands of Guatemala. *American Anthropologist* 39: 423–44.

Tax, Sol, and Robert Hinshaw. 1969. The Maya of the midwestern highlands. In

Ethnology: Part one. Handbook of Middle American Indians, ed. Robert Wauchope. 7:69–132. Austin: University of Texas Press.

Tedlock, Barbara. 1982. *Time and the highland Maya*. Albuquerque: University of New Mexico Press.

Tirado, J. F. [1787]. *Vocabulario de lengua Kiché (1787)*. University Museum Library, University of Pennsylvania, Philadelphia. Photocopy.

Torquemada, Juan de. [1615] 1975. *Monarquía Indiana*. 3 vols. Mexico D.F.: Editorial Porrua.

Tovilla, Martin Alfonso. [1635] 1960. *Relación histórica descriptiva de las provincias de la Verapaz y de la del Manché*. Guatemala: Editorial Universitaria.

Varea, Francisco. [1699]. *Calepino en lengua Cakchiquel*. American Philosophical Society Library, Philadelphia. Manuscript.

Vázquez, Francisco. [1714–17] 1937–44. *Crónica de la provinca del Santísimo Nombre de Jesus de Guatemala de la Orden de Nuestra Seráfico Padre San Francisco*. 4 vols. Biblioteca "Goathemala," vols. 14–17. Guatemala: Sociedad de Geografía e Historia.

Viana, Francisco, Lucas Gallego, and Guillermo Cadena. [1574] 1955. Relación de la provincia de la Verapaz hecha por los religiosos de Santo Domingo de Cobán. *Anales de la Sociedad de Geografía e Historia de Guatemala* 28:18–31.

Vico, Domingo de. N.d. *Vocabulario de la lengua Cakchiquel y Quiché*. Newberry Library, Chicago. Photocopy.

Villacañas, Benito de. [c. 1692]. *Arte y vocabulario de la lengua Cakchiquel*. University Museum Library, University of Pennsylvania, Philadelphia. Microfilm.

Villacorta, J. Antonio. 1934. *Memorial Tecpán-Atitlán (Anales de los Cakchiqueles)*. Guatemala: Tipografía Nacional.

———. 1942. *Historia de la capitanía general de Guatemala*. Guatemala: Tipografía Nacional.

Vogt, Evon Z. 1969. *Zinacantan: A Maya community in the highlands of Chiapas*. Cambridge: Harvard University Press, Belknap Press.

———. 1973. Gods and politics in Zinacantan and Chamula. *Ethnology* 2 (no. 2):99–113.

Wagley, Charles. 1941. *Economics of a Guatemalan village*. Memoir 58. Menasha, Wisconsin: American Anthropological Association.

———. 1947. *The social and religious life of a Guatemalan village*. Memoir 71. Menasha, Wisconsin: American Anthropological Association.

Wallace, Anthony F. C. 1970. *Culture and personality*. 2d ed. New York: Random House.

———. 1972. Paradigmatic processes in culture change. *American Anthropologist* 74: 467–78.

Wasserstrom, Robert. 1983. *Class and society in central Chiapas*. Berkeley: University of California Press.

Wauchope, Robert. 1948. *Excavations at Zacualpa, Guatemala*. Middle American Research Institute Publ. no. 14. New Orleans: Tulane University.

Wilkerson, S. J. K. 1974. The ethnographic works of Andres de Olmos, precursor and contemporary of Sahagun. In *Sixteenth-century Mexico*, ed. Munro S. Edmonson. Albuquerque: University of New Mexico Press.

Wolf, Eric R. 1955. Types of Latin American peasantry: A preliminary discussion. *American Anthropologist* 57: 452–71.

———. 1957. Closed corporate peasant communities in Mesoamerica and central Java. *Southwestern Journal of Anthropology* 13 (no. 1):1–18.

———. 1986. The vicissitudes of the closed corporate peasant community. *American Ethnologist* 13 (no. 2): 325–29.

Ximenez, Francisco. [c. 1729], 1929–31. *Historia de la provincia de San Vicente de Chiapa y Guatemala*. Biblioteca "Goathemala," vols. 1–3. Guatemala: Sociedad de Geografía y Historia.

Zuñiga, Dionysius. [c. 1610]. *Diccionario Pocomchí-Castellano y Castellano-Pocomchí de San Cristóbal Cahcoh*. University Museum Library, University of Pennsylvania, Philadelphia.

Index

Abolorio, 31
Acculturation, xix, III, 127, 130, 131, 149
Acul, 82
Aguacatán, 1, 56, 65, 82, 92–101, 115, 152, 153
Aguirre, Francisco Xavier de, 122–24, 126, 129
Ah Canil, 47, 49, 55, 68, 70, 73, 85, 88, 91, 151
Ah Toltecat, 47, 49, 53, 55, 68, 70, 73, 85, 88, 91, 151
Alcalde Mayor, 27, 38, 43–44, 59, 96, 99, 107, 110, 111, 112, 113, 114, 118, 119, 122, 123, 124, 125, 126
Alcaldes, 14, 16, 17, 33, 48, 59–60, 76, 84, 86–89, 97, 116, 134, 137, 151
Alcaldía Indígena, 15–17, 21, 22, 139, 142
Aldeas, 8, 9, 10, 11, 22, 65, 143
Alonso, Juan de, 26
Alvarado, Pedro de, 76, 77, 81
Amaq', 47, 58, 61, 74–75, 83, 85, 89, 100, 115, 132, 147–48, 150, 151
Angulo, Pedro de, 78
Annals of the Cakchiquels, 29, 47, 75
Apellido, 31–32
Arias, Gaspar, 76
Audiencia, 25, 26, 28, 37, 43–44, 83, 103, 108, 110, 111, 112, 113, 122, 152
Auxiliares, 14, 15, 16
Ax waab', 13, 15, 16, 18, 22, 134, 138–39, 157n
Ayuntamiento, 85

Bacín, 58
Baijoon, 93
Balamihá, 82
Barnett, Homer, xix
Barrios, 8, 9, 10, 11, 18–22, 109, 137–39, 147, 153, 154, 157n, 160n
Barroeta Manuel, 104–11, 113, 114, 116, 119
Berdan, Frances, 41
Berendt, Karl H., 27
Betánzos, Pedro, 25, 81–82
Borah, Woodrow, 44

Cabildo, 85
Cacao, 34–35, 84, 88, 128
Cacique, 29, 32–33, 47–48, 78–81, 85
Caja de comunidad, 86, 87
Cakchiquel-Maya, 6, 25, 27, 74, 78, 80

Calpules, 30, 32, 36, 37, 38, 42, 58–60, 92, 109, 110, 116–18, 120, 122, 127, 134–36, 159n
Calpullec, 42
Calpulli, xiv, xvii, 30, 41–42, 127
Cáncer, Luís, 78, 80
Canillá, 73
Cantones, 8, 9, 10, 12–23, 24, 41, 42, 46, 49, 137–46, 147, 160n
Cárdenas, Rodrigo de, 119
Carmack, Robert M., xv, 26, 74, 90, 158–59n, 160n
Carrasco, Pedro, 41, 158n
Caserío, 8, 9, 11, 22
Casta, 31
Castellanos, Francisco de, 77
Castilla, Alonso Oviedo de, 119, 159n
Cauinal, 78
Cavek, 74
Chajul, 1, 77, 78
Chalchitán, 56, 82, 92–101, 115
Chamula, 153–55
Chiantla, 99, 152
Chiapas, 81, 157n
Chibulbux, 123
Chichicastenango, 28, 76–77, 160n
Chimul, 73
Chinamit, xiv, xviii, xix, 24–42, 43, 46, 49, 61, 62, 63–75, 102, 114, 144, 147–48, 153, 157–59n
Chiquimulas, 3, 7, 12
Chuchun (Papsaca), 63, 68, 70
Chuicajbab, 130
Chulubalya, 71
Chutinamit, 67, 70, 73
Chutixtiox, 63, 67, 68, 73
Closed corporate community, xvi, 8, 153, 156
Coatecas, 47, 48, 55, 62, 68, 72, 73, 85, 88, 119
Cobán, 80, 81, 136
Cofradías, 15, 17–18, 20–22, 34, 59, 90, 94, 98, 100, 138, 144, 146, 147
Collins, Anne C., 85, 90
Comisionado, 43, 113, 124, 126
Comitancillo, 159n
Congregación, 34, 38, 99, 101, 148, 150, 156; Spanish policy of, 83–85; in Sacapulas, 85–89
Corpus Christi, 21, 139

Cortés y Larraz, Pedro, 57
Corzo de Rivera, Joséph Manuel, 51
Costumbre, xvi
Coto, Tomás, 26, 35, 128
Cotzal, 1, 77, 78
Cuchumatanes Mountains, 1, 90
Culture, defined, xviii
Cunén, 49, 51, 57, 59, 60, 77, 82, 94–95

Defensor (procurador), 97, 110
Dictionaries, use of, 25; described, 25–27
Dominican Order, 78, 81, 82, 83, 86, 88
DuBois, John, 3, 6

Ejido, 102–7, 109–14, 118, 126, 130, 150
El Quiché (department), 1, 6
Encomienda, 28, 55, 84, 149, 152
Endogamy, 34, 38–40, 62
Exogamy, 34, 38–39

Fiscal, 44, 109, 110, 111, 112, 122
Fox, John, 159n
Franciscan Order, 81, 82
Fuentes y Guzmán, Francisco Antonio de, 27, 28, 35, 56, 76–78

Gage, Thomas, 29, 36
Galvéz, Mariano, 26
Geraldino, Francisco, 110, 116, 118, 119
Gibson, Charles, xiii, 90
Gobernador, 48, 59, 119, 130

Hallowell, A. I., xix
Henríquez, Andrés, 59
Henríquez, Pedro, 116–18, 126, 127, 130
Hidalgo, Domingo, 118–26, 129, 159n
Huehuetenango, department of, 65, 73, 82, 92, 96, 101; town of, 94, 97, 98, 136, 137
Huil, 82
Hunt, Eva, 9
Hurtado, Juan, 111, 113

Ilon, 82
Ixil-Maya, 77, 81
Iximché, 74
Ixpapal, 68, 73, 88, 117
Iztapanecas, 47, 48, 58, 62, 88

Jacaltenango, 85, 90
Jefe Político, 134–35, 160n
Juarros, Domingo, 57
Juez Comisario (comisionado), 93, 94, 95
Juez de paz, 14, 137, 141

Juez Privativo, 43–44, 92, 95, 96, 97, 98, 99, 100, 107, 109, 111, 118, 122, 123, 124, 125

Kajawixel, 18, 157n
Kekchí-Maya, 25, 157n
Kroeber, A. L., xix

Ladinos, 2, 3, 11, 14, 15, 19, 42, 57, 133, 134, 136, 137–38, 141, 148, 150, 154, 155, 160n
Ladrada, Rodrigo de, 78, 81
La Farge, Oliver, 148–50
Lake Atitlán, 6, 23, 74, 157n
Lamakib, 47, 82, 85, 115, 132, 147
La Montaña, 144
Land, ownership by *calpulli,* 41–42, 127; ownership by *cantón,* 13–14, 143; ownership by individuals, 13–14, 127–32; ownership by *parcialidad,* 64–73, 88, 112–14, 115–18, 130–32; quality of, 5, 64, 68–69, sales, 14, 102–3, 115, 117, 118, 123–25, 126–29; surveys, 45, 68, 94–95, 97, 99, 103–6, 119–20, 123, 124–25
Lara, Francisco Orozco Manrique de, 92
Lardízaval y Llosa, Manuel, 97–98
Las Casas, Bartolomé de, 28, 29, 39–40, 78–81, 158n
Legal procedures, 43–46
Letona, Nicolás Ortiz de, 111–12
Linage, 31, 39, 158n
Lineage, 30–32, 158n

MacLeod, Murdo, 50, 55, 84
Maestre de Campo, 92
Maldonado, Francisco, 27, 40
Mandamiento, 133
Marroquín, Francisco, 81
Maseguales, 118
Medios Tributarios, 51
Méndez, Gonzalo, 81–82
Miles, S. W., 27, 158n
Mixco, 36
Mixcolajá, 91
Mojones, 45, 64–65, 92–94, 95, 104, 109, 116, 117, 119
Molab, xiv, xviii, 31, 33–38, 40–42, 158n
Momostenango, 160n
Mora, Thomás, 96–97
Municipio, 1–4, 8–12, 65, 142–46, 147, 152, 155

Nash, June, 9
Nebaj, 1, 77, 78, 81, 96, 97–98, 136
Nuestra Madre y Señora de los Mercedes (*cofradía*), 98

Nuestra Señora de la Encarnación (*cofradía*), 94
Nut, 34–35, 84, 151

Oficio, 9, 37–38, 41
O'Flaherty, Edward, 25
Olmos, Pedro de, 76

Paché, 144
Pacot, 65, 67, 73
Papsaca (Chuchun), 68, 70, 73
Paraje, 9, 10, 153
Parcialidades, xiv, xviii, xix, 30–32, 34, 37–38, 43–62, 64, 82, 83, 84, 87–89, 90–100, 102–14, 115–32, 133–36, 143, 144, 147–48, 160n
Parentela, 31
Parra, Francisco de la, 25, 82, 158n
Parraxtut, 144
Patan, 15, 16, 18
Patzagel, 68, 73, 117
Patzam, 144
Pichiquil, 92–100
Pokom-Maya, 25, 30, 33, 35, 36, 158n
Pokomám-Maya, 25, 30, 36
Pokomchí-Maya, 25, 30
Popol Vuh, 28, 29, 47, 74, 75, 76, 77
Population, importance of, 46; loss, 48–51; method for estimating, 51–54; estimates, 54–58; mentioned, 91, 98, 101, 115, 116, 120, 123, 127, 138, 145, 152, 156
Pozas, Ricardo, 154–55
Precaria posesión, 125, 126
Principales, 60, 87, 97, 108, 109, 116, 118, 127, 128
Procuradores, 43–46, 92, 96, 98–99, 112

Quetzaltenango, 82
Quiché-Maya, 1, 3, 25, 74–75, 76, 80, 158n

Rabinal, 28, 29, 78, 80–81
Ramírez, Antonio, 119, 130
Rancho de Teja, 144
Redfield, Robert, xiii, xiv
Regidores, 14, 15, 16, 33, 60, 85, 86–89, 151
Reina, Ruben E., xv, xviii, xxi
Relaciones, 27–28
Remesal, Antonio de, 29, 78–81, 86, 155
Repartimiento, 84, 133, 159n
Reservados, 51, 52–57
Río Blanco, 1, 5, 49, 65, 73, 95, 98, 120, 123, 125; Aldea, 138–42
Río Chixoy, 1, 37

Río Negro, 1, 5, 26, 65, 66, 68, 70, 73, 77, 78, 102, 113, 117, 120, 122, 123, 125, 126

Sacatepéquez, 27
Salinas, 73, 99, 102, 104, 105, 107, 108, 109, 110, 111, 113, 114, 115
Salt, xv, 5, 20, 22, 38, 55, 75, 155
San Andrés Sajcabajá, 1, 13, 73, 81, 88, 91, 100, 151
San Bartolomé Jocotenango, 1, 142
San Cristóbal Cahcoh, 37
San Francisco, *cantón,* 12, 18, 21, 137, 141; *cofradía* of, 18, 21, 92, 139; *parcialidad,* 49, 51, 52, 53, 61, 65, 68, 82, 105, 106, 110, 115–26, 129–31, 147, 151
San Pablo (*parcialidad*), 159n
San Pedro (Beabac), *cantón,* 12, 21, 134–35, 137; *cofradía,* 21; *parcialidad,* 49, 62, 65, 71, 102–14, 118, 126, 129, 134–35, 144, 147, 151
San Pedro Jocopilas, 159n
San Sebastián, *cantón,* 12, 13, 14, 19–20, 138, 140–43; *cofradía* of, 21; *parcialidad,* 49, 58, 61, 65, 68, 70, 100, 102–14, 118, 126, 129
Santa Cruz del Quiché, 1, 83, 90, 97–98, 136, 137
Santa María Chiquimula, 1, 58, 143–44, 148
Santa María Magdalena, 48, 49, 53, 58–61, 62, 66, 94–95, 145, 152
Santiago, *cantón,* 12, 13, 14, 19–20, 138, 140–43; *cofradía* of, 21; *parcialidad,* 49, 58, 61, 65, 68, 70, 100, 102–14, 118, 126
Santísimo Sacramento (*cofradía*), 92
Santo Domingo, 2, 21, 87; *cofradía,* 18, 21, 92, 94, 95, 139
Santo Tomás, *barrio,* 20; *cantón,* 12, 20, 21, 137–43; *cofradía,* 20; *parcialidad,* 49, 51–53, 61, 65, 82, 92, 95–96, 98, 100–101, 105–6, 115–26, 129–31, 147, 151
Scherzer, Karl von, 149
Secretario de Cámara, 111, 112, 113
Síndico, 14
Sitaltecas, 47, 48, 55, 58, 62, 85, 87, 88
Smith, A. L., 63, 67
Solano, Felix, 26
Sololá, 6
Stevens, John L., 149
Subdelegado, 43, 103–6, 108, 116, 118, 123

Tax, Sol, 9, 22
Tedlock, Barbara, 160n
Tenam, 65
Tierra Colorada, 144
Tirado, Fermín José, 26

Título de los Señores del Sacapulas, 105, 159n
Título Tamub, 42, 159n
Títulos, 92, 93, 103, 108–9, 116, 117, 119–20, 146
Torquemada, Juan de, 82, 158n
Totonicapán, 103, 152, 160n
Tovilla, Martín Alfonso, 27, 38, 75
Tributario entero, 51, 52, 53–57
Tuhal (ha), Maya name for Sacapulas, 13; *Amaq',* 47, 75, 86, 100
Turbalya, 102
Tzololá (Sololá), 74
Tzotzil-Maya, 153, 157n
Tzutujil-Maya, 74, 157n

Uchabajá, 47, 48, 58, 61, 62, 71, 75, 85, 88
Uspantán, 51, 57, 76–78
Utatlán, 74, 75, 76, 77, 158–59n

Varea, Francisco, 26
Vázquez, Francisco, 29, 82, 86
Vega, Juan Martínez de la, 92
Vega, Valentín Laso de la, 93
Verapaz, 5, 28, 29, 38, 55, 77, 78

Viana, Francisco de, 27
Vico, Domingo de, 26
Villa Urrutía, Jácobo de, 124, 125
Villacañas, Benito de, 26–27

Wallace, Anthony, xviii, xix
Wasserstrom, Robert, 153, 160n
Wolf, Eric R., xvi, xvii, 8, 9

Xecatloj, 70, 73
Xechiley, 130
Xecu, 123
Xetzagel, 68, 73, 117
Ximenez, Francisco, 28, 68, 82
Xolchun, 63, 65, 73, 82, 96, 98, 101
Xolcoxoy, 63, 67–68
Xolpacol, 63, 65, 68, 73
Xoltinamit, 66, 67, 73

Zacualpanecas, 47, 48, 65, 67, 68, 73, 85, 88, 119
Zerón, Francisco, 26
Zinacantán, 153–55
Zuñiga, Dionysius, 27, 35, 37

University of Pennsylvania Press

ETHNOHISTORY SERIES

Edited by
Anthony F. C. Wallace and Lee V. Cassanelli

Lee V. Cassanelli. *The Shaping of Somali Society: Reconstructing the History of a Pastoral People, 1600–1900.* 1982

Lawrence J. Taylor. *Dutchmen on the Bay: The Ethnohistory of a Contractual Community.* 1983

Derek Nurse and Thomas Spear. *The Swahili: Reconstructing the History and Language of an African Society, 800–1500.* 1985

James McCann. *From Poverty to Famine in Northeast Ethiopia: A Rural History, 1900–1935.* 1986

Christopher Boehm. *Blood Revenge: The Enactment and Management of Conflict in Montenegro and Other Tribal Societies.* 1987

Robert M. Hill II and John Monaghan. *Continuities in Highland Maya Social Organization: Ethnohistory in Sacapulas, Guatemala.* 1987